MW00328236

JOURNEY THRU THE UNKNOWN...

BY MURRAY LANGSTON
A.K.A. THE UNKNOWN COMIC

Jourrney Thru the Unknown…

© 2013 Murray Langston

For information, address:

BearManor Media
P. O. Box 71426
Albany, GA 31708

bearmanormedia.com

Book design and layout by Valerie Thompson

Published in the USA by BearManor Media

ISBN—1-59393-879-9
978-1-59393-879-6

TABLE OF CONTENTS

*Dedicated to my mom and dad,
my girls Myah and Mary,
and my siblings, Annette, Suzanne,
Ronnie, and Gary.*

ACKNOWLEDGMENTS

So many thanks To Chris Bearde, who seemed to always be there for me. To Chuck Barris, for being smart enough to use me. To my five best friends: Ted, Freeman, Pat, Jimmy—who have gone—and Kent, who is still here with me.

JUNE 27, 1944

THE HIGHLIGHTS AND LOWLIGHTS OF EACH YEAR OF MY LIFE.

The Headline of the *New York Times* on June 27, 1944, read... CHERBOURG FALLS TO AMERICAN TROOPS; RUSSIANS CAPTURE VITEBSK AND ZHLOBIN... The end of the Second World War was nearing.

The other surprising news on that same day, at least to me, was that I was born in Dartmouth, Nova Scotia, a small town in Canada. I was actually so surprised that I couldn't speak for a year and a half. Because my parents were extremely poor, to celebrate my birth, the best my dad could do was hand out cigarette butts. When my father first saw me, he gave me a funny look... and I've had it ever since. My parents named me Murray, which I'm grateful for because to this day that's what everyone calls me.

Years later, I remember wanting to know the exact time of my birth so a friend could more thoroughly research my horoscope. I called my mom, and the best she could offer was that I was born sometime between midnight and two in the morning. She further informed me that I wasn't born in a hospital but in a manger—I mean a small bungalow where my parents lived at the time. My father's birthday was the day before mine, and a party celebrating it was being held, so I was born amidst an abundant amount of drinking going on.

According to Mom, the doctor who showed up to deliver me was a bit of a drinker himself, and he immediately joined in the festivities. He became inebriated to the point where he forgot to write down on the paperwork the exact time of my birth, so it was never recorded. I've often wondered whether being born in the midst of a party could be the reason for the positive, fun attitude that has defined me throughout most of my life.

I was my parent's second child; my older brother Ronald was born less than a year before, on July 3, which meant that for six days every year we were the same age. Not that that means anything.

What does mean something is that during that first year, I was not breast fed because my mom had been convinced that formula was better for babies than breast milk. When years later she informed me of this, it would forever account for my lack of trust in the world of big business. Like the foundation of a building, a child's foundation is also very important for its longevity and powdered formula would be akin to using wood instead of concrete for support.

I do however miss that first year of having my diapers changed, my private areas slathered with warm soap and water and my butt washed and powdered, but I'm told if I hang in there long enough, nurses will be doing all that again for me. Yippee!

Other than that, I don't remember much of that first year, except that it was very hard to find work. Looking back, although we were very poor and had little material wealth, I was loved by my mom and dad, and for that I was one lucky baby.

My pretty mom at age nineteen.

My handsome dad in the Navy, at age twenty.

1945

This was the year I attempted walking, and I would get confused when the adults around me laughed whenever I fell on my face. I also found it frustrating trying to understand what everyone around me was talking about—especially my mom and dad.

I did later learn that Dad met Mom when he was twenty and she was nineteen. He barely spoke a word of French, and Mom, a pretty French-Canadian girl, barely spoke a word of English; nevertheless, they fell in love. They couldn't talk much but obviously understood "body language," so, without much discussion, they had five kids in rapid succession. Mom eventually learned English, though she always had a slight accent, but Dad never learned French, except for the kissing part. I'm pretty sure Mom's first English phrase must've been something like, "Get off me."

I also learned Dad had a troubled and violent relationship with his father and left home at the age of twelve or thirteen. Mom was raised mostly in an orphanage because her parents couldn't afford to raise all their fourteen children.

Another interesting tidbit is that I have no recollection of having ever met any of my grandparents, neither on Mom's nor on Dad's side of the family. Apparently, they all passed on in their fifties, but somehow a couple of my great-grandparents lived to be over a hundred. I've often wondered in which group's longevity footsteps I would follow, especially with my lousy foundation.

Toward the end of 1945, in fact on New Year's Eve—probably during another drunken soiree at our tiny home—my sister Annette was born. I was a lucky baby to have a sister, and along with my brother we probably learned to make rudimentary toys out of beer bottles and silly party hats. Though I was only two, I learned that my parents were rather strict and didn't want me to date girls until I was at least six.

My mom and dad. A beautiful couple.

1946

In April of this year, my parents moved from Dartmouth to Bathurst, New Brunswick, where Mom was raised. Almost all of her numerous relatives lived there.

Here's a little more on Dad: During the Second World War, serving in the Canadian Navy, he was attacked by one of his own comrades, who went berserk and began stabbing him in the leg with a knife. He forever walked with a limp after that, and in later years he always seemed more comfortable at those cheaper restaurants where they only served food with utensils made of plastic.

Though I was still fairly immature at the age of two, nothing really out of the ordinary happened, except perhaps playing with newly discovered body parts. All these decades later, nothing much has changed, except for the parts being new.

Dad on a home leave from the Navy.

1947

Because of my dad's loveless and troubled upbringing, he became known in his hometown as a bad boy. In Bathurst, many of my mom's older relatives considered themselves devout in their religious beliefs and frowned on my dad's reputation.

Nevertheless, my dad loved my mom, and so she gave birth to another sister they named Suzanne. With little work available in Bathurst and a family of four to feed, they decided to move to a larger city, hoping for better opportunities. So it was off to Toronto, Ontario, for a better future and the Canadian dream: similar to the American dream, but with mittens.

My dad, with an injured knee from the incident he encountered in the military, was still able to secure a job with a railroad company, guiding trains as they entered the station. With four kids, my dad still didn't want my mom working, even though she was a seamstress and known to be a whiz on a sewing machine. She could keep anyone in stitches.

Me on the right with my brother Ron and my two sisters Annette and Suzanne.

1948

In Toronto, we lived on a street called Jarvis, which at that time was part of a neighborhood known for prostitutes and drunks. Where I lived, being told you might get to marry the girl next door was not necessarily considered a good thing.

This was also an area where black families lived, and at around the age of four, those were the kids with whom I became friends. I believe this might have something to do with why I've never felt prejudiced. How could I? They were my friends growing up at an age where our personalities and much of our thought processes are formed. I think everyone knows that hatred is taught, and hating black people was not a part of my limited early street education.

I learned through my sister Annette that I was a stubborn child. She once related to me how at the age of four, I was standing in our small front yard urinating when my dad saw me and yelled for me to stop. But for some reason, which only a four-year-old would comprehend, I continued. According to my sister, my siblings all watched nervously, knowing I was about to get the beating of my life. Thank goodness my life was only starting. I was dragged into the house and had the crap beaten out of me, which thinking back, might have prevented me from also crapping in the front yard. Interesting to note is that I still like urinating in my front yard: but from my second-story window.

Mom and Dad with us four kids. One more to go.

1949

I was five when my mom gave birth to a fifth child, and another boy, Gary, was born. Saddled with four brothers and sisters and being poor, little did I know then that I would never sleep alone again— at least not until I got married. I was at the age where I continued to play with toys because I still hadn't figured out what girls were all about yet.

As luck would have it—most of it bad—my father was again involved in an accident. In the station where he worked, a train that was set to hook up with another, accidently crushed my dad's other knee. Now both his legs were injured and he had to give up that job, which required him to be on his feet most of the time. Needless to say this scenario made it more difficult for him to find other work, which resulted in my mom finding a job. From that day on, she became the breadwinner, but it would be stale bread because in those days, like today, seamstresses were paid minimum wage at best.

My father was extremely frustrated at this second injury. He felt anger at the doctors who he felt were incompetent when they botched his surgery, which resulted in him having to spend many months on crutches. It was around that time that he developed a tremendous fear of the medical profession. Consequently in the future, he preferred to try to mend his own injuries rather than be subjected to another doctor's knife.

I often wondered how my mom managed to raise five kids while dealing with a somewhat crippled husband who always tried but rarely succeeded. Luck was seldom a friend of my dad's.

My mom once told me that she never thought raising five kids in those days was that difficult. She said we all seemed to instinctively know how to take care of ourselves, which might have accounted for my independent spirit.

To this day, I believe the greatest gift a parent can give a child is helping them learn to be an independent thinker. In my case, my parents didn't plan it that way, but I do believe it led to all five of us kids rarely working for anyone but more or less always doing our own thing. To this day, I'd rather do my own thing than do someone else's thing. Because when you do someone else's thing, their thing gets done and you're left with an undone thing. Not a good thing.

1950

I do not ever recall being hugged or told "I love you" by either of my parents. It was something that just did not occur in our family. The reason we seldom experienced physical or verbal love became obvious to me when I learned more about my parents. My dad was raised by a violent father who beat him, and he ran away from home at an early age after his dad broke a shovel over his back. My dad's uncaring father never said "I love you" to him, so my dad never learned to say "I love you" to us either.

My mom was raised in an orphanage where she too was never shown physical or verbal love, especially by the strict nuns of that era. When I thought about how my parents were raised, I could never blame them for their lack of the ability to show us they loved us. Love, like hatred, is also taught. How could they show emotions of that sort when they never experienced them? Unfortunately, Dr. Phil just wasn't around back then to explain it to them.

My parents' inability to express love had an emotional effect on most of my siblings to some degree, but I don't think it had a major impact on me. However, it might have had a distinct influence on my wanting to get into show business, which provided me with not just one but a multitude of people showing me that they loved me.

I don't believe I ever felt unloved, because I knew that what my parents were going through to feed me, take care of me, and somehow keep a roof over my head; that was their way of showing me that they loved me. To this day, I prefer to have someone show me that they love me rather than tell me—though getting both methods of affection is the best.

That's me on the left with my two brothers Ronnie and Gary.

1951

In Toronto, we moved from Jarvis Street to Gladstone Avenue, which was a better neighborhood. I was in school, leading the typical life of a small boy who didn't have a clue about what he wanted for his future.

I do remember having a beautiful woman for a teacher who had the odd name Miss Duck. I was seriously infatuated with her, so one day I brought her an apple and she gave me a big kiss. The next day I brought her a watermelon. Okay, that didn't really happen, but I do recall my interest in girls growing in more ways than one. In fact, I remember several instances where I tried to play doctor with my sisters friends, especially when I realized I had a built in thermometer.

Besides learning new things about myself, I also recall a boy with Down syndrome, who was a few years older than me, and who lived across the street from us. I remember initially feeling fear when he would approach me, but that changed as I got to know him, and although he was barely able to talk, we often played together in his front yard. I'll never forget how he cried when we moved and I had to say goodbye. I cried too.

My brother and I with our Aunt Lucienne.

1952

My parents decided Toronto was not giving them the opportunities they had sought. My mother had two brothers who lived in Montreal, so they decided that would be our next move. With five kids and little money, we moved into a tiny cabin several miles outside Montreal in an area known as Riviere-des-Praries.

The cabin was so small and so old that we had an outhouse in back for toilet activities. The harsh winters made it almost unbearable, trekking through the cold winter snow to go poop, but that's what we did. We made poopsicles.

One other thing I recall from this period of my young life is how we five kids learned to play the game Monopoly to occupy ourselves. We played it all the time. If we couldn't be rich in real life, we could at least pretend.

Another ugly memory of that place, was an animal clinic located directly behind us where dogs were put to sleep on a regular basis. Well they weren't exactly put to sleep; in those days, dogs were destroyed by being shot in the head. As curious kids we would sneak close enough to peek over the fence where we saw dog carcasses piled on top of each other. One look was enough for me.

The cabin we lived in, or rather existed in, was tiny, and my brothers and sisters and I slept cramped together in makeshift bunk beds against a wall opposite of where our parents slept. Late at night, I would often awake hearing my dad attempt to make love to my mom, who seemed to always plead with him to leave her alone.

Thankfully, I was still fairly ignorant about sex, and most of the time I thought they were just playing around. Sex in those days was simply something kids had no clue about. That was probably a good thing, though I began to notice that my thing was beginning to feel good the more I felt it.

Family picture of Mom, Dad, and us five kids—I'm the cute boy on the left.

1953

Despite two injured legs, my dad was able to find a job working in a printing factory inside the city of Montreal, which enabled us to gleefully leave the dreary and isolated country life we had grown to dislike. We moved into an apartment complex closer to the outskirts of the city, and although we still lacked in many essentials like new clothes, shoes, and decent medical and dental care, life for us was beginning to improve.

As is often mentioned, when you're poor you just assume everyone lives the same way, so in many ways we never really knew how badly off we were. But poor we were. On Christmas Eve, my dad would wait until the lots selling Christmas trees had closed, then sneak by and grab one. He'd then set it up in our living room and we would all decorate it, and then be sent to sleep to wait for Santa to arrive.

In the morning, we mostly received pictures of presents. Actually, if we received a gift it was a belt or a piece of clothing, rarely anything resembling a toy. My distaste for Christmas and the festivities associated with it would gradually worsen, as my request to Santa and my parents every single year for a bicycle was fruitless—I never got that bike. During those years, hearing of the gifts my friends had showered upon them while I received next to nothing, gave me reason to think that Christmas sucked. I was nine years old and logic was beginning to form in my little brain, which doubted the existence of some fat guy in a beard landing on our house with reindeer shitting on our roof.

Me with my younger brother Gary and our dog, which is no longer with us.

1954

We moved again, into a small duplex closer to the center of Montreal on Saint Andre Street, where there was even more activity and life. My main memory of that dwelling was that we lived across the street from a place that trained professional wrestlers.

My parents got to know some of the wrestlers who would hang outside, and though we all became acquainted, I never thought much of it. I instinctively knew that if I was going to get into a wrestling match, I wanted it to be with a girl. The thought of rolling around on a stretch of canvas hugging and holding another sweaty guy had little to no appeal for me. My mom, however, remained a wrestling fan for the rest of her life, always seeking out and watching matches on television.

The area we lived in was still considered a poor area, and my parents were determined to find a better place. The only way they could accomplish this was if my mom found a better job to increase their income. So she did that, and she was hired as an upholsterer in a factory. They were thrilled to get my mom since her abilities on a sewing machine were mesmerizing and would only improve over the years.

1955

With Mom's increased income, we finally moved to a nicer area and larger house. Life was beginning to look better for all of us, except for my father. As luck would have it—and luck would not have it with my dad—he was involved in another accident. The printing company he worked for had huge circular presses which printed out many items including doilies used in restaurants and the wrapping for loaves of bread. Apparently, while feeding material into it, my dad's hand got pulled into one of the presses while they were rolling, sucking his arm into it up to his shoulder.

With all the strength he could muster, he pulled his arm out, but not before the large presses crushed most of it. In the process, most of the fingernails on his hand were yanked out. Once again against his will, he was taken to a hospital, but just long enough to repair the injuries. The frustration he must have felt at his horrible luck had to be unimaginable.

Two crippled legs, and a crippled arm was bad enough, but soon after rheumatoid arthritis began to invade all of his injured joints to the point where he was in constant pain making it almost impossible for him to work a full-time job. But my dad was not one to be pitied and he always searched for work, any kind of job that would make him feel vital and needed.

Eventually he found part-time work in a machine shop, helping out in the shipping department, while my mom began working extra hours.

Having been raised in an orphanage by nuns, my mom made us go to church every Sunday. We were given a dime to put into the collection plate, but I soon learned how to fake putting it in so I could keep the dime to buy candy later. Not sure why, but I did not enjoy the church-going experience at all. I especially grew to dislike those days after school when my mom gathered us in the living room to say prayers. Often in the midst of saying the rosary, I would look out the window and see my friends playing outside and think this prayer thing was no fun and a huge waste of time. I would actually pray to not have to say prayers.

Though also raised Catholic, my dad was not much of a believer in religion. This afforded us kids the opportunity to see both sides, unlike most kids who were brainwashed by two parents into believing the way they did. I'm sure my dual image of religion had a major impact on how I think today.

During this period, television was a favorite pastime. We were fortunate to have color television but only two colors: black and white. My favorite shows were *Superman, Roy Rogers,* and *Leave it to Beaver,* but I was especially fixated on a new era of comedy shows from Red Skelton and Jackie Gleason to Milton Berle and Lucille Ball.

Our family always gathered around our tiny television set to enjoy them along with *The Ed Sullivan Show*, where I saw comedians like George Carlin, John Byner, and Bill Dana. I didn't always laugh at the comics, but I absolutely loved watching my parents laughing at them. It made me happy to see them happy.

1956

Once again we moved, to an even more desirable house on a block where two of my uncles lived. My dad's part-time income along with my mom's salary were not enough to take care of the bills, so they took in two boarders who paid rent. They lived in one of the three bedrooms, causing an even more crowded situation for us five kids.

Every day, my mom would get up early to make breakfast for the boarders and then go to work, returning when it was dark. In those days, we rarely saw my mom except in the evenings. My dad would do his best to raise extra money by roaming the back alleys of our neighborhood searching through trashcans for artifacts or small furniture he could fix and sell. Often he would take me along to help him rummage through the garbage, which probably explains why I've always loved garage sales.

Our new house had a basement where we kids could go to get away, though much of it was occupied with a large furnace and a huge storage bin loaded with black coal. On those cold winter days and nights, we kids would have to take turns making trips to the basement to shovel coal into the furnace. I do feel relatively older when I think back to those days and how we had trucks delivering huge chunks of ice for the icebox in our kitchen.

My friend's dad owned a shop a block from us where he built coffins. One day when I was hanging out with him, I noticed a coffin lying in the trash area. When I asked about it, he told me it was mismeasured and was going to be dismantled and thrown away. I jokingly mentioned I'd love to have it in my bedroom and was surprised when after a brief chat with his dad, I was told I could take it. My friend and I carried it through the alley to my house where I put it in my room, which I shared with my two brothers. Interestingly, my parents showed little reaction to my keeping a coffin next to my bed. I would often sleep in it and awake with my arms folded in front of me on my chest, which is still how I sometimes wake up.

As was expected of any young Catholic kid, I became an altar boy and joined the choir. I have to admit there were some social aspects which I appreciated. At one point, observing how the priests had it pretty good, living in a large house and having their needs met with people cooking and cleaning after them, I momentarily thought this might be a life I could enjoy. But thankfully, it was only momentary. I think what finally turned me off was realizing I'd have to continually be saying those friggin' prayers.

Because we were considered underprivileged, every Christmas, the church dropped off boxes of food for us. Most of our gifts were still limited to clothing. Except every Christmas one of our uncles handed each of us kids five dollars, which later increased to ten dollars. This was the one gift we eagerly looked forward to every year.

One of my friends confided in me that he shoplifted in department stores to get gifts for himself and his family. One day I joined him and became quite proficient, shoplifting presents for my parents and siblings. Shoplifting may have its drawbacks, but it sure saves you money.

When questioned by my parents where I got the money for those gifts, I lied and told them one of the priests gave it to me for helping him count the money out of the collection plates.

Having been an altar boy for a couple of years, I knew all the priests intimately, though not that intimately. I've often joked that the reason I left the Catholic church was because I found out the priests were molesting my friends but not me, which made me feel very insecure. Why wasn't I good enough for them?

Though I never had any physical experiences with a priest, I did have an uncle who occasionally molested me. He was the uncle who lived next door to us and gave us money every Christmas. The first time he touched me was when he let me sit in the driver's seat of a new car he had just purchased. He didn't let me drive but let me turn on the engine and pretend to drive while he reached over and fondled me.

He only attempted to fondle me when he got drunk and I always resisted until he handed me money which would convince me to give in. In a sense, I guess at the age of twelve, I was somewhat of a male prostitute. Thankfully, the fondling never went beyond his touching me inappropriately.

I have often thought about that early molestation and why I don't believe it had any serious effect on my sexuality or mental outlook. I've always been heterosexual and believed that the reasons people were gay had little to do with being molested. But I could be wrong.

I was molested perhaps eight to ten times. Years later, when I mentioned it to my sister Annette, I was surprised when she told me that several of our male cousins had also been molested by that same uncle.

In the 1950s, homosexuality was deep in the closet as was my uncle. I can't help but think that if that kind of sexual abuse were discovered today, he would be spending many years in prison. Unbelievably, he later married and is still with the same woman today. Over the years I have seen him at various family functions and awkwardly joked with him, but those sexual incidences were never mentioned. I've always wondered if he ceased molesting boys back then or if he continued with others throughout his married life.

Despite that rude intrusion into my sexuality, girls were a constant curiosity to me, especially whenever I experienced an erection. Needless to say, I knew little about sex, but I instinctively knew girls had something to do with it. We had no Internet or porn to inform, so I had no idea how we multiplied. I remember going to church and finding little pamphlets that were supposed to explain sex, the extent of which was how birds procreated. In my family, sex was never mentioned, so asking your parents about the birds and the bees was not going to happen.

I was very confused when the priests told us that sex was dirty and that if we engaged in it before marriage we could go to hell. Then one day, I saw two dogs going at it and I thought they didn't seem to be concerned about what the priest thought, so why should I? Sex was simply another aspect of religion which made little to no sense to me.

As I approached my teen years, the music scene was changing dramatically. My friends and I began to appreciate a new music form called rock 'n roll. The popular songs on the radio suddenly went from "How Much is That Doggie in the Window," by Patti Page, to "Rock Around the Clock," by Bill Haley. Rock 'n roll exploded with legends like Elvis Presley, Little Richard, and Bobby Darin, whose song "Splish Splash" was the first record I bought.

Some friends from school formed a club with a name that would not have been acceptable years later, "The Spades". When I heard that there were girls who were also part of the club I asked if I could join and they agreed. We would meet at the home of one of our richer friends where he had a nicely renovated basement. In the club, I had developed a crush on a pretty girl named Sandra.

What I didn't know about joining "The Spades," was that there was an induction associated with becoming a member. In the absurd initiation, new male members had their pants pulled down, whereupon shoe polish and toothpaste would be applied to their pubic hair.

The girls were kept in a rear section of the basement when the boys suddenly surprised me, grabbed me, and threw me to the ground while at the same time pulling my pants off. To their amazement, it was discovered that I had not yet developed any pubic hair. The result was that all the kids laughed hysterically at me. When they shouted out, "He's got no pubic hair!" I could hear the girls in the background also laughing, especially Sandra.

In my mind, it was catastrophic, as I yanked my pants back up, ran from the basement, and cried my eyes out all the way home thinking my world had come to an end. Why didn't I have pubic hair? My only conclusion was because I was not breast-fed as a baby. I had no proof, but I blamed that fucking baby formula for my lack of pubic hair and never went back to that club again. Sandra ended up marrying the rich kid who had the basement anyway. From that time on, a spade was never to be a lucky suit for me. I preferred a heart.

That's me on the right with my brother. Altar boys at my aunt's wedding.

1957

It was a hot summer night and I was engaged in massaging my dad's feet for thirty minutes. My dad's injuries, compounded with rheumatoid arthritis, were causing him almost constant pain. On a daily basis, each of us kids had to take turns massaging his feet. I hated it. Even today, the thought of massaging someone's feet strikes fear and loathing in my fingers.

To be fair, in return for a foot massage, my dad would give us a nickel or a dime to buy candy or a soda. Unfortunately, my dad's legs had reached the point where he could not bend them any longer and he was forced to use a cane or crutches to get around. Fortunately for us kids, when he would get angry with us he couldn't chase us, but he could throw things and that he did. Many times he would thrust his cane toward us like a missile when we took off running. I can't count the number of times his cane came into contact with my back at a high speed.

By that time, I knew that fictitious jerk Santa wasn't going to bring me a bike and my parents couldn't afford to buy me one, so I got a job delivering newspapers. I was determined to raise enough cash to finally buy myself a bicycle.

In the summer, having a paper route was almost fun, but that enjoyment quickly faded during those harsh winter months in Montreal. I still vividly recall getting up at five in the morning in pitch-black darkness and going to our freezing porch where the newspapers were bundled and covered in snow. I dragged them into our small hallway entrance where I sat and folded each and every paper so that they were easy to throw. There were mornings when I was so tired and groggy that each folded paper began to look like my dad's foot. They were then placed into a large bag that I carried around my neck as I walked from house to house pitching them on the porches of the houses on my delivery route.

After months, I had finally saved enough money to buy a bike and though it was a used bike, it was mine. It took a while to learn how to ride it, having never had the opportunity, but once I did, it was thrilling to no longer have to walk to each house to deliver papers or collect my newspaper money.

Now I glided along the sidewalk and I'll never forget my first weekend collecting. After having the bike a week, while I was inside an apartment building, it was stolen. I was devastated and remember again crying nonstop all the way home. What a crybaby I was. I never did get another bike.

At thirteen, I developed a crush on another girl, named Carol Doyle. It was frustrating because my older brother Ronnie also liked her and everyone considered him cuter. So did Carol, and they wound up dating. For some reason any girl I had a crush on had no interest in me. The only girls who seemed to like me in those days were overweight, and I was not a fan of sitting around chewing the fat.

Another person I developed a huge crush on—though not romantically—who became a major influence in my life, was Jerry Lewis. As a young boy growing up in Montreal, Jerry Lewis was practically a god to me. Dean Martin and Jerry Lewis were suddenly ubiquitous, becoming major film stars, television stars, nightclub sensations, and recording artists. I saw every movie they made, saw every television appearance, bought their comic books, bought their lunch boxes, and bought their records.

I loved every one of their films from *Sad Sack* or *In The Army* to films featuring Jerry Lewis without Dean Martin—after their break-up—such as *Scared Stiff* or *The Delicate Delinquent*. When I watched their movies, I travelled into a different world that made me laugh and feel good about myself. I knew, sitting in that theatre, a lonely figure, transfixed by their comedy, that was what I had to do with my life: make people feel good by laughing at me. I don't know exactly why and probably never will.

The thought of ever actually meeting Jerry Lewis was something so remote that it wasn't worth thinking about. I was not sure how

I was going to do what they do, but in the back of my young brain the wheels were set in motion to somehow, someday, figure it out.

Living so far from Hollywood, it was going to be a major challenge for me to get involved in show business. They say life is a series of coincidences and my first was about to take place. I was on my way to see a movie called *I Was a Teenage Werewolf* that starred a young newcomer, Michael Landon; I didn't know that at the theater along with the film was a live stage show featuring "Frankenstein" in person.

An ambulance was parked in front of the theater along with a huge billboard describing a lavish stage spectacle that would scare everyone out of their wits. It also touted that audiences would be entertained with magic, hypnotism, and comedy. Comedy? Now I really wanted to see the show.

Unfortunately, because of the stage show they were charging extra, and I didn't have enough money to get in. Disappointed, I began walking away when I was suddenly approached by a man who asked if I wanted to see the show for free. When I asked how, he said that if I would participate in the show, I could not only see it for free but would be paid five dollars. "Participate in what way?" I asked. He explained that the owner and host of the show, Wyman Baker, hypnotized people from the audience—but he didn't know how to hypnotize, so he needed stooges to pretend they were under his hypnotic spell.

Though I had, for the most part, been a rather shy and introverted kid, I immediately felt this was something I could do. Without hesitation, I agreed, whereupon the man escorted me through a backstage door and took me to a dressing room to meet Mr. Baker.

Several beautiful young girls who were dressing for the show, one of them his wife, surrounded Wyman Baker, a magnetic personality who I guessed to be in his forties. He explained that besides pretending to be hypnotized, he needed my assistance in performing a magic trick, and I was fitted with a circular tube placed around my waist under my shirt.

I was then sent to sit in the crowded theater and when Wyman called for people to come on stage, I was to make sure that I was among the first ones to make it. The show started and once on stage for the first time, it seemed natural to me. Wyman pretended to hypnotize me and I faked it to the best of my ability. As I sat, supposedly transfixed, he told me I was watching a movie, which was no problem for me. He then told me it was a funny movie and I began to laugh loudly. Suddenly, I heard the audience laugh. This was the first time I heard an audience laugh at me or with me, and I found it exhilarating.

Wyman continued, telling me I was then watching a scary movie. I immediately screamed and jumped on my seat pretending I was terrified. Again, the audience broke into laughter. To me this was a giant step forward in finding out if I had what it took to be in show business, and as far as I was concerned, I did.

Next, Wyman took a large sword, stood me up, and gingerly placed it against the center of my shirt. He carefully slid it into the tube and began pushing it slowly. From the audience it looked as though the sword was going right through me and they gasped. It was great.

After the show, Wyman thanked me, telling me he had used kids in every town he visited and had never found someone like me who was a natural on stage. He then asked if I would like to earn more money repeating my performance in the remainder of the shows that week. I jumped at the opportunity, but told him I would have to run home and let my mom know what was going on.

I knew my parents, who were not overly protective, would allow me to pursue this fledgling career, and they did. So now I was officially in show business, at least until the end of the week. In each show, I got better at perfecting my reactions to Wyman, getting bigger laughs from the audience, and I loved every minute of it.

At the week's end, Wyman told me the show would be moving to another theater on the other side of the city and asked if I could continue with them. When he said that he would have me picked up and dropped off at my home for each show, again my mom agreed.

I wasn't one of the three stooges, but I was a stooge and a good one, and for several weeks throughout the summer, I was part of show business. When the tour of Montreal was over, Wyman told me that before they headed back to Hollywood, they had a few more shows, all one-nighters, at various theaters in a few towns several miles outside Montreal. Would my parents allow me to go? The problem was that school had just begun and I would have to take part of the first week off.

I begged my mom, who told me that before she would allow me to go I had to invite Wyman Baker to dinner at our house and she would make a decision after meeting him. Wyman agreed, and at dinner he told my mom how important I was to the show, that I would be paid more money, and that they would take excellent care of me. Even though I was going to have to take five days off from school, my mom agreed, which was great because I didn't have to kill her.

Prior to going on the road, Wyman sent two of his gorgeous girls in a limousine to pick me up at school. I was so happy and felt very special when my buddies gathered around me as the limo approached. The girls exited and then kissed me on the cheeks as they dragged me inside the limo with them. As we drove off, my school chums stood there watching with their mouths hanging open—for probably a long time.

When the tour was over, it was almost unbearable thinking my show business career had careened to a screeching halt. I cried at our final goodbye as Wyman tried to console me, telling me that the tour in Montreal was so successful, they would return again the following summer. I hoped it was true and couldn't wait for school to be over again. That experience convinced me that without a doubt, show business was definitely something I wanted to pursue. I knew someday I was going to have to move to Hollywood.

My dad, then unable to work a regular job, took a home electronics course, believing he could make money repairing small appliances such as toasters, radios, etc. One day, he called me into the basement where he was studying and suggested that I learn alongside him. He tried to warn me of the perils of show business and suggested this would give me a trade to fall back on. I told him I honestly had no interest in anything to do with repairing anything, and that I wanted to be in show business one way or the other. He smiled and advised that I should go for "the other" rather than "one way" because the other might have more than one way, then agreed that if I didn't have a desire for repairing things, I wouldn't be any good at it anyway. I loved my dad.

My dad with his little corner fix-it shop in our basement.

1958

Rock 'n roll was becoming more important to me. Elvis was the biggest thing in music, while Fabian, Frankie Avalon, and Pat Boone were also gaining fame. But my favorites were the Everly Brothers; I had every one of their songs memorized.

It's almost like déjà vu that today, a fifteen-year-old Canadian singing sensation named Justin Bieber is a worldwide phenomenon, while in my day another fifteen-year-old Canadian singing talent took over the music scene and had girls screaming everywhere he performed. His name was Paul Anka.

Likewise, today's generation has Britney Spears, who became a music star at fifteen, while my generation had a tiny bombshell of a singer named Brenda Lee, who also at the age of fifteen burst onto the music scene with one hit after another. I fell in love with Brenda Lee, frequently dreaming about marrying her and living happily ever after. Brenda Lee's performance in Montreal was the first live concert I ever attended, and sitting five rows from the stage, I saw her wink and was absolutely positive it was aimed directly at me. After the show, along with a throng of other kids, I ran to the side entrance, thinking I might get to see her, but alas, she was whisked away through another exit and our marriage was not to be.

I loved music, and after listening to my favorite Montreal disc jockey, Dave Boxer, I thought perhaps radio might be another way for me to get into show business. So with the little money I had saved from working with Wyman Baker, I purchased a small tape recorder.

In my room I taped myself, pretending I was a disc jockey and playing songs in between commercials that I read from newspapers.

I had a large radio that didn't work, but I kept it, hoping my dad would one day fix it. Often, when someone came into my room, I would place the tape recorder inside the old radio, push play and was surprised how many people thought they were listening to a real radio program.

I eventually reached Dave Boxer on the phone, and when I told him I had a desire to be a deejay, he invited me to the station to sit in the booth while he ran his radio show. It was inspiring and awesome.

But what was really awesome was when summer arrived and Wyman Baker's stage show returned to Montreal for a month. I was again invited to be a part of the show that had a shorter run because they were going to travel across Canada. I desperately wanted to go with them, but my parents and Wyman agreed that having just turned fourteen, I was just too young to miss that much school.

When they left, I told Wyman I would someday, somehow get to Hollywood, and he replied that if I ever made it there, he would help me get into the business. When they left, I felt abandoned by this new world I had grown to love. I was now severely bitten by that showbiz bug.

After they left, I found a part-time job cutting metal in a machine shop. It was hard work, and one day, as I was showing off how fast I could cut the pieces of metal, two of my fingers were almost chopped completely off.

My boss was gone, and the only other person working with me was another teenager who went into shock at the sight of all the blood pouring from my fingers. As I wrapped a rag around my hand in an effort to stop the flow of blood, I asked him to call my father on the phone. Upon hearing what happened, my dad told me he would send a taxi to the shop and to wait outside until it arrived to take me to a hospital.

Back in the 1950s, child labor laws were not what they are today. In fact, there was no law at that time prohibiting a kid from quitting school and going to work. A few years later, a law did come into effect preventing children from leaving school until the age of sixteen.

I was still fourteen, which was probably a great age for a first time sexual experience. Most of my friends had already lost their virginity, at least they said they had and I became determined that it was my turn. In my mind, since the odds of losing my virginity to Brenda Lee were now highly unlikely, any girl would do.

Luckily, Carol Doyle, who I had previously had a crush on, was no longer interested in my brother, especially since he decided to move to a religious college to possibly become a priest.

I asked Carol to go to a movie with me and was excited when she agreed. Once we sat next to each other in the theater, I had no clue and neither did I care about the movie being shown. All I cared about was wanting to know what a boob felt like. Even as a baby, because I wasn't breast fed, I had never touched one, and this was my moment. Ten minutes into the film, I ever so slowly slid my arm around her shoulder and as I lightly massaged it, my penis became erect immediately. After about another ten minutes, I slowly and methodically moved my hand down her side grazing her breast, well really her bra. It was fantastic. I was so close to feeling a real titty. It seemed like forever, but after about another ten minutes, as I attempted to slide my finger under her bra, I was shocked when she suddenly took my hand and placed it firmly on her boob. I began to caress it and within seconds, I experienced an orgasm in my pants. Nothing more was to take place that day.

Our next sexual encounter occurred in the darkness of my basement when no one was around. Carol and I were laid out on an old sofa and she moaned and squealed as we made out. I knew I was finally going to get laid and I was so horny, my penis was about to rip through my pants. I struggled to open my fly as she spread her legs revealing she had no panties on. As I continued trying to release my penis with one hand, I placed my other hand on her vagina, which was sopping wet. I wondered if this was the way it was supposed to be. I wasn't sure what was supposed to happen or what exactly I was supposed to do and she didn't seem to offer any help either, just lying back with her eyes closed, moaning. Yet somehow I was finally able to release my penis and place it between her legs somewhere on or around her vagina. And then I thrust forward... only once... and that was it... an immediate orgasm and it was over. To this day, I doubt whether I actually succeeded in entering her. Nevertheless, as far as I was concerned, I lost my virginity. At least, that's what I told the guys.

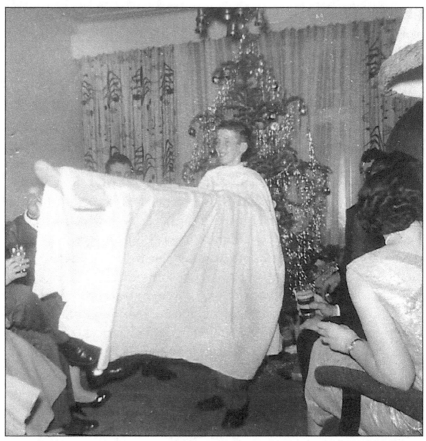

That's me attempting my own magic trick at home for my family.

1959

The first major celebrity I ever encountered was film star Mickey Rooney. I had heard from a friend that he was eating dinner with a group of people at an Italian restaurant not far from my home in Montreal. It was a cold, snowy wintry evening, but I rushed to the place, stood outside peering through the window and there was Mickey Rooney. Even though he was from my parent's generation, I had seen so many of his films that in my mind he was a legendary movie star.

At one time, he had been the most famous film actor in the world and now there he was, only feet from me. I stood motionless outside the window, watching him eat and wondered if he would talk to me. I wasn't interested in an autograph. It's odd that I have never asked a celebrity for an autograph. I think it's because I always wanted to feel I was an equal and asking someone for an autograph made them special and me less than them... and I wanted to be special too. I wanted to be one of them.

I waited until they were finished, and as they prepared to exit the restaurant, I quickly grabbed the door and held it open. As he walked by, I smiled and said, "Hi, Mr. Rooney," convinced he would stop and chat with me for a minute. Perhaps he'd give me some advice on how to get into show business. But that didn't happen. Talking loudly to the group he was with, he strutted past me without a hint of acknowledgment and into a waiting car. I thought Mickey Rooney was rude. He could have at least given me a tip for holding the door open.

About a month later, sexy blonde starlet Jayne Mansfield was the second celebrity I would actually meet. It was outside a television station, only blocks from our house. I recall her being very friendly to the crowd of fans who showed up to meet and greet her. She chatted with the small group, myself included, and introduced me to her daughter, Jayne Marie Mansfield, who was about the same age I was. Miss Mansfield signed autographs and took the time to say hello to everyone. I knew then that if I ever became famous, I would treat my fans the same way.

I wondered if the most famous person in the world to me, Jerry Lewis, was nice to his fans. Hopefully, one day I would find out. I wasn't sure how this kid, who lived thousands of miles from Hollywood, would be able to accomplish this goal, but I knew at some point I would have to begin my journey.

I was in my ninth and final year of school, and I don't recall much except spending lots of time in theaters watching films, which would transport me away from the boring day-to-day existence I felt I was living.

And that was the year I decided to start smoking. It seemed most of my friends along with many movie stars including Jerry Lewis smoked, and it made you look cool. That is until you were hooked up to a lung machine. But back then there was absolutely NO information whatsoever that smoking could be injurious to your health. Though most of my buddies became chain smokers who lit up immediately upon waking up, I kept my habit under a pack a day. Winston was my choice—and not surprisingly, I became addicted to them.

When summer arrived, my parents decided it was time to leave Montreal and move back to my mom's hometown of Bathurst, New Brunswick, some 500 miles away. They felt they could do better financially by living in a small city, and they discovered that because of my dad's injury while in the Navy, he could get a military pension if he was living in the place where he enlisted.

When they first told me of their plans, I was shocked and upset; having spent years in a large city, the idea of moving to a remote town where I had no friends was not appealing to me in the slightest. And Bathurst was further from Hollywood, where I planned to eventually move to, even though at this stage of my life I felt the moon would be easier to get to.

I informed my parents that I did not want to move with them and if I were forced, I would most likely run away. To my surprise, they seemed to understand, and they told me that if I could find a job and a place to stay, they would consider it.

The Canadian National Railway Company was looking for young boys aged sixteen and over to help deliver packages in the express department. I lied about my age, was hired immediately, and had a job. A place to stay was just as easy. My best friend at the time was Mike Jones who lived with his alcoholic mother, and we were both able to convince her and my parents to let me move in with them. My parents, though nervous about leaving me, knew that they had little choice, even though I was only fifteen about to turn sixteen. I was always fiercely independent and instead of being fearful, I looked forward to a new direction in my life.

My older brother Ron, considered the brains in the family, was already living in a college run by religious brothers: a sect of the Catholic church. I don't know why he chose a religious college to further his education. We never talked about it then and that same absence of conversation between us continues to this day. Not sure why, but even though we never became very close—in fact we became more distant as the years passed—as with the rest of my family, I love him too.

The sight of my parents leaving has played itself over in my mind many times. It was in the back alley of our house where my dad's small open bed truck was loaded with everything they could put into it, including my two sisters and younger brother. My mom was crying as I tried to explain that being on my own was an adventure I was looking forward to. My dad shook my hand and told me that though they were moving into another house in another city, it would always be my home and would be there for me if I ever needed it.

There was no hugging but there was love. I felt it then and have felt it ever since. As I watched the truck slowly pull away, waving at them waving back, there had to have been a measurable amount of angst roaming somewhere in my brain. Maybe not. I'm pretty sure I was not bright enough to consider that I might be facing some pretty hard times now that I was on my own. I didn't know it then, but I would not see my family again for five years. Years later, my sister Susan informed me that my mother cried all the way to Bathurst.

Staying with Mike's alcoholic mother did not last long, and after two months, I decided I needed my own place. Another friend of mine, Warren Chan, who worked in his father's Chinese restaurant, also wanted to be on his own. With my salary of a dollar an hour delivering packages, we were somehow able to afford a small apartment owned by a friend of Warren's dad.

Our apartment became a place to party for many of our friends, many of whom would spend the night when they had a fight with their parents. Though there was plenty of beer drinking, I drank very little. I just didn't understand why my friends would sometimes get so wasted they didn't know where they were. I liked knowing where I was, and I knew where I was going... to Hollywood. The only questions remained, when and how?

My buddy Warren Chan and I shared my first apartment.

1960

My favorite song was "The Wanderer" by Dion. I sang it all the time while delivering parcels for the express company, envisioning myself wandering across the border to the U.S.

I worked with a guy named Tom who was in his twenties, though I thought he was much older because he was married. At the train station, we would load up the truck with packages of all sizes, then he would drive to the appropriate addresses, and I would physically carry them to their destination while he waited for me.

What I remember most about Tom is easy to recall, because he was literally a Peeping Tom. He didn't reveal his perversion to me until he was sure I wouldn't say anything to anybody. He was proud of his kinky appetite for voyeurism, showing off how he accomplished his warped task. I have to admit that at the time I didn't think it was that perverted, considering most of the women seemed completely aware of him.

At specific times, he would drive down a street, park the truck, take out binoculars, and look into an apartment window. Then he would hand me the binoculars to take a look. I was shocked, but pleasantly shocked, to see a woman in her bathroom completely naked, getting ready to take a shower. I asked Tom, "Doesn't she know people can see her with her window open and the shades up?" His reply was, "Oh, she knows I'm looking all right. That's what turns her on."

He drove to another area, up an alley, and parked again. He obviously had these episodes timed because within seconds of his looking upwards, a woman came out on a patio to hang out some clothes. Again, he pointed up her dress and to my amazement, curiosity and a bit of excitement, she was wearing a dress, but it was obvious from our vantage point, she had no underwear. I eyeballed her until my eyelids were sore. Again Tom told me that she was completely aware that he was checking her out.

Tom and I worked for probably six months, when one day I showed up for work and was told he had been fired. Apparently a complaint had been lodged against Tom and it turned out it wasn't the first. I was asked a multitude of questions related to peeping Tom's activities and when I admitted I was witness to some of his nasty deeds, I was also let go. To some degree it was all worth it. Hell, I was only making a dollar an hour.

1961

I was out of work, and my roommate Warren was growing weary of my not having enough money to pay the rent, so he moved back with his parents, which resulted in my getting booted out of our apartment. I resorted to spending nights with anyone who would have me. In the meantime, I searched for any kind of work I could find. At a golf course, I chased after balls. I picked apples in the country. I spent nights working part-time in a restaurant mopping and cleaning the place after it closed. But these part-time jobs earned me barely enough to feed me.

I was grateful that some of my buddies who had partied with us in our apartment, let me stay with them for a day or two, but unfortunately they weren't the right kind of friends.

In those days, most people had their milk delivered to their homes and left change in empty bottles on their front porches to pay for it. My buddies showed me how they would get up early in the morning, sneak up to the houses, and steal the money from the bottles. Regrettably, I joined them in some of their pilfering.

What happened next I'm not proud of, but I feel I have to talk about it if only to give insight into how one's life can easily swing into the wrong direction because of life's pressure, peer pressure, and the lack of pressure from the criminal justice system.

With no money left and no place to live, my buddies revealed to me that for extra cash they would engage in breaking into and robbing apartments. They seemed to always have money in their pockets and when they described how easy it was, my first reaction was an absolute no.

What changed my mind was when they explained to me that if I got caught, nothing would happen. In those days, anyone under eighteen who had a first offense for breaking and entering was merely given a slap on the hand and no jail time.

I don't know why I didn't consider the victims, but I figured I would try it a couple of times and if I got caught, I wouldn't do it again. There seemed to be no risk. We all convinced ourselves we were starving and had little choice. I had a choice. I could have gone to my home in Bathurst, but I was fiercely reluctant to let my parents know I was already a failure. The sad fact is, I'm absolutely positive if I had thought that I would be subject to jail time if caught on my first offense, I would never have allowed myself to become a part of this young hoodlum gang.

So, for the next few weeks, I took part in a limited number of burglaries. Being kids, we only looked for cash or small, expensive-looking items such as watches, jewelry, or radios which could be sold. For a while, I had money again, but inside I knew what I was doing was seriously wrong. What I didn't think about was that at any one of these apartments, once inside, someone could have been sitting there with a gun or rifle and blown our heads off. Which was exactly what happened to one of my cronies a couple of years later.

Luckily, the end of my crime spree came shortly after it began, when we broke into an apartment and upon opening a closet we saw police uniforms hanging. I freaked out, especially when the guys I was with discovered two handguns inside one of the drawers. They laughed and stuffed the guns into their pockets. I knew right then that this was way over my head and not for me. All I could think of was if I continued I would end up in prison and never make it to Hollywood.

I also thought about how my mom would be devastated if she found out I turned into a thief after she allowed me to be on my own at such a young age. My mom and dad did not raise me this way. My parents instilled in me a sense of right and wrong, not necessarily by words but by their deeds. They struggled through so many obstacles to make a living, and they would never steal from anyone no matter how desperate they had become. I felt I was stealing honor and respect from my parents. For the next several years, the guilt of what I had done lingered in my brain and ate away at my subconscious.

The next day, following the cop's apartment robbery, I ran as fast as I could to the local Canadian Armed Forces Recruitment Center to enlist in the Army. I was paranoid all through the recruiting process thinking that the police might have discovered I was one of the thieves who broke into that cop's apartment and might show up at any minute to arrest me. I knew I had to get as far away as possible from that gang. Joining the army seemed the quickest way. I didn't understand Karma then, but I later learned to understand and believe in it. When you do bad things to others, the odds of bad things happening to you increase a hundredfold. I sure hoped I wouldn't get killed once I was in the Army.

Once I was signed, I was sent to Ottawa, the Capital of Canada, to military grounds outside the city. I was put in an outfit called the Canadian Guards, a British section of the military since we were still aligned with England. I lasted less than a year in the army, getting discharged against my will because of my fallen arches. My feet, flat as pancakes, could not handle the twenty-mile hikes with fifty-pound backpacks attached to me, and the doctors gave orders to the Army to let me go.

On my own again, I was nervous about returning to my old neighborhood, not wanting to run into any members of the gang who I heard were still engaged in criminal behavior. After about a week of sleeping in cars and bathtubs of friends, I knew I had to make a choice. Either go to my parent's home in Bathurst or make my way to Hollywood. How was I going to accomplish this? I had just turned eighteen and after having tasted military life, I decided I was going to cross the border and join the United States Navy. Hollywood, here I come.

In uniform in the Canadian Army.

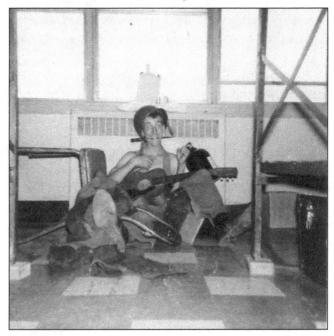

Taking a goofy picture in the Army.

1962

I hopped a bus from Montreal to Plattsburgh, New York, and upon arriving, I searched for the U.S. Navy recruitment center. Now call me an idiot, call me ignorant, or call me both, but I had no knowledge of a little skirmish the U.S. was having with a country known as Vietnam.

I was also not aware that at that time, hundreds of Americans were crossing the border into Canada to escape having to serve in the military. Watching news on television was something I assumed only adults did, so I had no clue about worldwide events.

Looking back, I now understand why the enlisting officer chuckled once I signed the paperwork. I later discovered that the enlisting officers were paid a bonus of fifty dollars for any non-U.S. citizens they could get to enlist.

The next step was passing a physical, and I feared getting rejected for my flat feet. My nerves were on edge when I was asked to remove my shoes and socks. When the doctor approached me, I somehow forced my arches upward, leaning outward on the sides of my feet long enough to fool him. I thankfully passed the inspection and was then officially sworn into the U.S. Navy. I would have preferred signing a two-year contract which would have allowed me to get to Hollywood earlier but the minimum number of years required was three. I signed, and the next several years of my life were about to become a new adventure. I sure hoped I wouldn't get killed along the way.

I, along with several Americans, was loaded onto a plane which was my first experience flying. As we flew over the countryside, I had a window seat overlooking the propellers. I remember being frightened, fascinated, and excited at the same time. We were flown to Chicago for basic training, which in those days was no picnic. Today, volunteers are treated with much more respect and dignity than during the draft era when recruits were treated atrociously.

Once at the base, we spent three months learning how to march, shoot, kill, and other things you wouldn't need outside the military. We were gathered, separated, pushed, and shoved into various barracks where we were often deprived of much needed sleep for innocuous infractions.

They asked if anyone had previous military experience and I was excited to be able to tell them that I had been in the Canadian Army. Because of that experience, I was selected to be in charge of one of the groups of new recruits. I felt proud and a bit cocky that I was put into a position of leadership. My duties included making sure that my group showed up on time at various designated places.

One time that didn't happen, because I couldn't get one of the recruits up on time, which resulted in my group being two minutes late. I knew I couldn't squeal on the guy who'd slept in because it wasn't my nature and besides, he was huge. He would have probably kicked my ass, so when asked why we were late, I blamed it on my watch not working properly.

I was immediately told to give them fifty. When I asked, "Fifty what?" I was told at full volume to fall to the ground and give them fifty push-ups. I was a very skinny kid with arms to match and I knew this wasn't going to be easy.

After perhaps ten strained push-ups, my arms felt like they were going to collapse, and I told them I didn't think I could continue, which was followed by more ear-piercing screaming to shut up and resume the push-ups. As I continued with number eleven, my commander, along with the recruits, joined in counting down the remaining push-ups. I spent the next several days unable to lift my arms, which hung like two large limp slabs of meat.

Another unpleasant incident occurred around the same time. It was a major infraction to be caught with cigarettes, and I was positive I had thrown mine away. But at a bedding inspection, one of the recruits whose bunk was obviously close to mine, in order to protect himself, managed to sneak his full pack under my pillow.

When it was discovered, they had me remove every cigarette from the package and place each and every one of them in my mouth. I was then handed a match and ordered to light all of them. As the smoke engulfed my entire face, they placed a small garbage can over my head. I heard laughter but it was not the kind of laughter I had been yearning to hear.

Being in the Navy, it's important to know how to swim, but like most Canadians, swimming was not something I had learned. The manner in which the Navy taught swimming back then would certainly not be accepted or approved in today's military. They gathered us around a large pool and asked if anyone didn't know how to swim.

About five of us raised our hands and we were escorted to the side of the pool. We were then told to form a line and I thought we were going to be given special treatment: it wasn't special, it was downright terrifying. From behind and without warning, all five of us were shoved into the pool and ordered to swim.

I struggled to stay above the water, pushing my arms and legs every which way, aiming myself toward the edge of the pool in an attempt to grab onto the side. My attempts were futile when long poles were then used to push us away from the sides, forcing us to desperately figure out how to swim on our own. I have to say, as cruel as it might seem, I did learn to swim almost immediately. Later, I also had to clean the crap out of my trunks.

When I finally graduated from basic training, I felt a vast sense of accomplishment standing in formation at the ceremonies as the National Anthem was played. As we left the base for the final time and saw the new recruits marching in, I was so grateful my time was done, especially knowing what was in store for them.

Next, I was bussed to a naval base in Philadelphia and told I would be serving aboard an aircraft carrier. It was number CV-38, the U.S.S. Shangri-La. As I approached the entrance, I couldn't believe how large the ship was and wondered what kind of assignment I would be given.

I was met by an officer who asked what kind of work I was interested in, and not having any idea, I replied it didn't matter. As far as I was concerned, after the three months of the crap I had just gone through, anything they gave me to do would be acceptable. I was told they needed new recruits in the radar division. I had no clue what radar was or what it would involve, but I agreed and was quickly assigned to that department. I'm sure no matter where they would have asked me to work, I would have agreed. I just had to kill time before heading to Hollywood and was hoping my remaining two years and nine months in the Navy would zip on by.

I worked in CIC, which stood for Combat Information Center. I thought it was going to be an interesting job, though I worried having only completed the ninth grade, I might not be up to the task. Once we were at sea, I was immersed in a completely different world and I knew this life would be better than what I might have faced had I stayed in Montreal.

In the radar room, we were referred to as "Scope Dopes", with our faces glued to the tiny screens we were fixated on. Our job was to always be on the lookout for blips on the radar screen which might indicate other ships, aircraft, or simply debris in the water. Once anything was identified, that information was passed on to the officers in charge so they could investigate further.

Within a month, our ship was relocated to Jacksonville, Florida, which I appreciated immensely: heading for sunshine and beaches, far from the cold, freezing weather I had grown to dislike. We were told we would spend a few months in this port preparing the ship, before heading out on a six-month Mediterranean deployment. Not too shabby.

The year was 1962, and on one of my days off, I journeyed into the city for some sightseeing and was shocked and bewildered when I strolled into a bus station to take a leak. When I approached the men's room an attendant told me that I was going into the wrong toilet. "What? Was I about to enter the ladies room?" I asked. I was sternly informed the toilet I was about to use was for blacks only and that the white men's room was located on the other side.

I had witnessed minor racism back in Montreal, but nothing to this degree. It's almost unbelievable and to this country's credit that years later, in my lifetime, a black President would be elected. No one in that bus station would have ever believed it.

As months passed, I slowly became acclimated to life in the Navy and on occasion would even enjoy it. My job was relatively easy and my quarters, though crowded with about thirty in our section, was bearable. We slept in cots, which were set up in threes: top, bottom, and middle. I was given the middle, which was okay with me because it was easy to get in and out.

During basic training, I learned the U.S. was in a conflict with Vietnam, which was worrisome enough until I heard other talk that President Kennedy was about to lead the country into what was to become known as the Cuban Missile Crisis. Our plans for a cruise overseas were abruptly cancelled, and instead, the Shangri-La and its crew, including myself, were sent to Cuba as part of a blockade. My brain was suddenly infested with negative thoughts, mostly involving being blown to bits, and all I could think of was I was never going to make it to Hollywood. Fortunately, the threat did not last long, but we were nevertheless ordered to stay in Cuba, where the U.S. owned a military base.

After weeks at sea, we were finally allowed time for ourselves. They loaded us onto boats that took us to our Cuban military base for some recreational time. The threat had passed and Hollywood was still on. The chance of a war between Russia and the U.S. had subsided, but I was nonetheless about to embark on another minor, though still threatening, adventure. Three of my shipmates talked me into going fishing with them, a first time experience for me.

We applied for and received a small fishing boat and were told to be careful because the waters off the coast of Cuba were infested with hammerhead sharks and barracudas. We were given a walkie-talkie to communicate with the shore if any trouble arose and were told not to venture too far from the shore. The Cubans were constantly patrolling the area and we didn't want to end up in Cuban waters.

The four of us, loaded down with fishing gear, left about noon and were told to return by five, before dark. I never really liked the thought of fishing that much. It wasn't the actual fishing but the drowning of those poor little worms that bothered me. Nevertheless, I was eager to experience it for the first time, though the thought of being in water too far from shore also concerned me. Though we were wearing life vests, my swimming abilities had not progressed to the point where I was fully confident in the water.

After about half an hour of cruising about, we settled down and turned off the motor. The guys showed me how to place the bait on my hook and we cast our lines. We didn't have to wait long. I was the first to get a bite. Everyone helped as we began reeling in the fish, which turned out to be a rather small hammerhead shark. I was amazed at how it had a head shaped like a hammer. Go figure. Because I was a novice, I quickly handed my reel to one of the other guys who yanked it hard and as he did, the shark managed to free itself, swimming away and we all chuckled.

Within minutes, another guy got a bite. He fought with the fish that was larger than the shark, much larger. When he yanked it into the boat, it was ferocious, thumping and jumping every which way and at the same time snapping at us with its teeth. It was a barracuda, which I later discovered had several sets of teeth.

As it flailed about, one of the guys fell into the water then grabbed onto the boat. I held on to him as the other guys jumped around trying to avoid getting bitten by the barracuda until finally, one of them pulled out a knife and cut the line. As I was peeing in my pants, another guy grabbed one of the oars and hit the barracuda over and over, finally driving it over the side.

We gathered our wits and equipment, chuckling slightly, but not for long because when we tried to start the motor, it wouldn't turn over. Over and over we tried but to no avail. The news got worse when we discovered the walkie-talkie given to us for an emergency had been in the pants pocket of the guy who fell in the water. It was soaked and refused to work. We felt we had no choice but to take turns paddling back to shore with the two oars given to us for emergency. But the more we paddled the more distant the shoreline appeared. The tide was pushing us further out to sea.

Hours later and as darkness began to set, we began to worry about Cubans patrolling the area coming after us. A lot of time had passed and it was almost five: the time we were supposed to report back. I hoped when they realized we hadn't showed up, they would send someone to search for us.

The lights on shore were getting dimmer and dimmer. Then we saw two bright lights off in the distance heading in our direction. We cheered, fairly confident they sent a boat to find us. The two lights grew brighter as we waved and shouted, even though we knew they couldn't possibly see or hear us.

One guy had a cigarette lighter and tried flicking it on, but the wind was picking up, repeatedly blowing it out. We were desperate for them to see us, but how were they going to find us in this huge expanse of water? Fortunately it seemed luck was with us. The lights were now dead ahead and aimed directly toward us. We were also comforted, hearing the sound of the roaring engines on the boat.

"Wait!" one of the guys shouted, looking ahead, "That's not a boat. It's a seaplane and it's about to take off. But first it's going to crash into this boat and smash us all to pieces!" All four of us began yelling and screaming as the one guy kept flicking his lighter trying desperately to get a small flame.

As the plane got closer, we all knew we were going to have to jump into the barracuda-infested waters or get killed by the plane's impact. What choice did we have? We prepared to jump.

Then, at the last second, without warning, the seaplane veered sharply away from us going into a half-circle. We all breathed a sigh of relief, when it continued into a full circle and to our dismay began heading back directly toward us again. And again we all prepared to jump, but this time we heard the engines cut off as it slowed down and positioned its lights directly on us. They spotted us.

They radioed in our position and we waited until a larger boat arrived. We all jumped into the boat and had some explaining to do, but as they say, "all's well that ends well." I decided if I ever went out on such a fishing adventure again, I would definitely bring along a roll of toilet paper.

My home for three and a half years: on board the aircraft carrier *The USS Shangri-La.*

1963

A new year began, and we were finally off on our first Med cruise where along the way we would play war games with other ships. It was a six- to eight-week voyage and I couldn't wait. This kid from Canada was actually going to Europe for the first time, to visit places like Italy, France, and Spain.

Our ship stopped at many of the Mediterranean ports including Cannes in France, Palermo in Sicily, Athens in Greece, and Istanbul in Turkey. In Italy, we spent a lot of time in cities like Genoa and especially Naples, which for a few years became my home away from home because of the time spent there.

For the most part, I had a blast with my fellow sailors, but it was in Genoa where I got falling down drunk for the one and only time in my life. I was mainly a beer drinker and didn't care much for hard liquor. On this occasion, I think my buddies were intent on getting me plastered. We were in a bar and they ordered several shots of tequila, something I had never tried. I didn't want to feel like a party-pooper, so I joined in the festivities. There wasn't much of a taste except for the twist of lime and salt I was told to lick off the back of my hand, and I really didn't think I was getting drunk as I downed one, or possibly five, too many.

Next thing I knew, we were in a cab headed back to our ship, and I was heaving while the other guys were singing loudly so the driver wouldn't hear me throwing up in his back seat. I was then dragged to the shore boat, which took us back to our ship, and then taken to my barracks where I was left to die.

The last thing I recalled was waking up with my head inside the toilet bowl and as my eyes slowly opened, I understood why people who were close to death reported seeing a "white light." What they failed to say was that the white was porcelain.

To this day, that is the only time I have ever been drunk to the point where I had absolutely no control over myself or any clue where I was or who I was. I'm convinced the reason I refused to ever get drunk again is because I like to be in control of myself. Though I'm not sure where that kind of thinking stemmed from, I'm forever grateful.

From that point on, I learned how to pretend I was drunk, which my experience acting with Wyman Baker's stage show taught me how to do. For years, when I was amongst friends who drank, I would take small sips of booze and act drunk, fooling everyone.

Besides drinking excessively, prostitutes, ubiquitous in every port, also never appealed to me. Knowing they were in it for the money was a complete turn off. When we were in Nice, France, I told one of my buddies that I had never been with a prostitute, and he told me that if you know what you're doing it can be fun and I should at least try it once, so I agreed. Next, he told me that before going on shore I should masturbate or I would most likely orgasm right away because that's what the prostitutes are trained to get you to do.

I followed his suggestion and afterward we made our way to the nearest known bar where horny sailors and willing ladies were plentiful. My buddy—a tall, strapping, good-looking guy—and I—a not very attractive, skinny runt—entered the bar and looked over the multitude of money-hungry girls.

Picking two, we strolled next to them, grinning in their direction and waited for them to make their move. They smiled and winked at us, giggling and whispering in French to each other. Having been raised in Montreal, I still had a fair grasp of the language and strained to listen to what they were saying. The words were a bit hurtful as one girl said to the other in French, "I owe you ...so this time you take the cute one and I'll take the ugly one," pointing at me.

I quickly responded back in French.... "Wait a minute. How come he gets the cute girl and I get the ugly one?" pointing at the girl who had slighted me.

She couldn't believe I spoke French and laughed, trying to apologize, but I was too embarrassed to continue any further and left. I'm not sure if that incident was the reason, but to this day, I have never paid a prostitute for sex.

After my first Med cruise, we headed back to Jacksonville, only to be met with a hurricane. You'd think on something the size of an aircraft carrier you wouldn't feel much turbulence, but you'd be wrong. We were thrown around significantly, making it difficult to sleep or eat. I couldn't wait to get back to shore, but learned that during hurricanes, aircraft carriers were not allowed to approach land. Large ships would get severely battered against the dock, damaging both.

I soon discovered that, as a novice when riding out hurricanes, my duties were more than sitting in front of a scope. I was ordered to go to the bow of the ship and position myself inside one the catwalks, which were small spaces outside and beneath the flight deck.

Because radar was not very effective during severe weather, it was my job to spend hours outside in the blistering storm as a lookout with a walkie-talkie to communicate with the inside. I was to continually look through binoculars for debris, oil slicks, lights, or anything that would indicate that another vessel was headed in our direction.

I remember the first time I walked onto the carrier deck toward the catwalk: an enormous gust of wind suddenly knocked me down. I rolled toward the side of the ship, thinking I might be thrown overboard.

As the gusting wind tossed me toward the side of the ship, to prevent from being swept overboard, I desperately clawed at the deck with my fingers, trying to grab onto anything. Luckily, most of the ship is surrounded by catwalks below the flight deck and I fell onto one of them. Not really hurt, but shaken up, I slowly crawled the rest of the way to my position at the bow. I didn't enjoy this experience and decided I would one day study and get upgraded to seaman-first-class in the radar division. Petty officers weren't subjected to that menial job.

Each year we were permitted two weeks vacation, and I looked forward to returning to Montreal to relate my Navy experiences to my friends. Back at the same bars I had previously hung out at, my first impression was that most of my friends had not grown very much, and I don't mean physically. They were all doing the exact same thing every day, then spending nights getting drunk and talking hockey and girls. I also discovered that one of the guys with whom I had burglarized, had been shot and killed in an exchange with the cops. Another guy was sent to prison for other crimes he committed. I'm often baffled at what an idiot I was and how stupid I had been for getting so close to that life.

My first vacation was interrupted when one night at a bar, after a few drinks, I began to feel a searing pain in my side. The agonizing pain grew more intense causing me to pass out and my friends rushed me to a hospital. I had experienced an appendicitis attack and was wheeled into surgery. Three days later, my vacation ended and I was back on board my ship minus a small part of my anatomy.

One day I was suddenly awakened from a sound sleep by the sound of GQ (General Quarters). A loud ringing sound warned us to immediately rush to our previously assigned areas on the ship and prepare for battle.

I ran to my position and waited for the Captain to tell us what to do next. Within minutes, we heard over the ship's intercom, "This is your Captain speaking. We have been placed on high alert. President Kennedy has been assassinated," his voice choked as he continued, "Our President is dead." Throughout the cavernous innards of the ship you could hear echoes of men crying as they expressed their grief. The next day, the entire ship was called on board the flight deck for a moment of silence and a period of mourning. It was one of those days you know you will never forget.

I'm working in Radar, if that's what you call what I'm doing.

Visiting Europe on one of the Med cruises.

Enjoying the French Riviera in color.

1964

A t the ripe old age of twenty, I had never driven a car. So one of my buddies, who was about to be discharged, offered to sell me his 1956 baby blue Mercury convertible for a hundred dollars. He sold it for that low amount because the transmission had no reverse, but he was willing to teach me how to drive, so I bought it. Eventually, I got used to always making sure I would only park in places where I wouldn't have to back out, just like he taught me. I remember feeling sorry for rich kids who could never know the joy of buying their first car without reverse for a hundred dollars.

After more than a year in the Navy, I decided it was time to improve myself. Having only reached the ninth grade, I wanted to see if I was smart enough to pass the GED high school test, which the Navy offered for free. I was amazed at how easy it was and I quickly became a high school graduate.

One of the reasons I couldn't wait to get out of the military was that there were too many Petty Officers in charge who attained their rank through time spent and not because they were intelligent. They were called "Lifers" because they found military life more secure than civilian life. It was frustrating sensing you were smarter than some of those who were always telling you what to do. Consequently, I decided it was time for me to move up in rank and become a Petty Officer.

There were several others in the Radar division who also wanted a promotion, and we were all given books to study. For weeks, I studied my ass off, and after taking the tests we all anxiously awaited the results. I was shocked when the results came in and I was told I was the only one in my division who passed the test. I was more than thrilled thinking that I was now going to be a Petty Officer, and instead of always taking orders, I would be giving them.

But my happiness was short lived. About a week later, I was told by my Commanding Officer that beginning immediately I was not allowed to work any longer in CIC as a radar man. He continued, informing me that when I took the Petty Officer test they discovered there was a mistake when I was put into the radar division. Most radar information was considered secret material and you needed to be a U.S. citizen in order to work with classified information. And I was a Canadian citizen.

He further informed me that I needed a background clearance before I could be given my promotion, and because it would cost the Navy thousands of dollars to undergo such an investigation, they required that I increase my enlistment period from three to four years.

I thought about it, and my initial feelings were no! I had already begun counting the days to when I would be discharged so that I could make my way to Hollywood. The thought of adding another 365 days seemed out of the question. In the meantime, they told me I would be reassigned to a division where my job was to clean toilets.

This really infuriated me. I had studied so hard to advance in rank and now here I was cleaning toilets under a new Petty Officer who was one of the most ignorant men I had yet met in the Navy. Obviously he was in charge of latrine duty because he was so full of shit. After weeks cleaning toilets, our ship pulled into Philadelphia for an overhaul, and I decided I was going to go back to Montreal and not return. I was going to go AWOL. Absent Without Leave. I had had enough.

Looking in my life's rear view mirror, I really wasn't mature enough to weigh all the facts properly, so my decision was made without much thought. After departing the ship for what was supposed to be a weekend, I boarded a bus and left for Montreal. I was only home a week before I realized I had made a huge mistake. I did not want to be a part of the same old, same old existence my buddies were living. Now that I had experienced a little taste of change, I wanted more. But I had brought to an end any chance of ever getting to Hollywood and being permitted to stay there legally.

From now on, I would never be allowed to enter the United States again because I would be considered a deserter, and I could be jailed if caught. This was some serious shit.

So serious that I decided I had to go back, regardless of the consequences. I left Montreal on a bus headed for Plattsburgh, New York, and returned to the same recruiting office where I had enlisted. After I told them I was AWOL, they radioed the Shangri-La, which informed them that my ship was at sea for two weeks and that I was to be detained until it returned to Philadelphia.

Not far from the recruiting center was an Air Force base, which was equipped with a military jail. I was sent there to spend the two weeks and was impressed with the facilities, which included a recreation room with TV, laundry facilities, even an outdoor lounging area with horseshoes. We had good food, a nice bed, and the airmen in charge were relatively pleasant. It was nothing like the jail on our ship, which was run by a small group of Marines who treated prisoners with rather unpleasant hostility.

Within days of returning to my ship, I was ordered to report to Captain's Mast—a courtroom setting where the Captain would decide my punishment for going AWOL. I was certain I was going to spend time in our jail, which I dreaded.

I nervously explained how I had studied hard, passing the test to become a Petty Officer, then was suddenly deprived of my rank and forced to clean toilets. I further explained that it was all through no fault of my own, and had someone checked on my citizen status before placing me in the radar division, none of this would have happened.

The captain appeared sympathetic and agreed it was not my fault, but also stated that going AWOL was not a solution either. I explained how I tried to talk to anyone/everyone on any and every level, but no one seemed to understand my plight. To my surprise, the Captain understood, and his decision was that my time spent in the Air Force jail was enough punishment for my having gone AWOL. He then offered me either an immediate discharge where I could return to Canada, or I could select any other job on the ship as long as it wasn't classified.

Shortly after I first boarded the Shangri-La, I discovered there was a small radio and television station on-board. It mainly ran old movies to the various video monitors located around the ship and broadcast news in the evening. I remembered wishing I had asked for that division when I boarded in the first place because I would almost be in show business, but then I had no knowledge of its existence.

So I told the Captain that I would be more than happy to finish the two years I still had left if I could work in that division known as "Special Services." He agreed, and I was immediately transferred to this new job and thought to myself that I was one lucky guy.

Only three people worked in Special Services: an officer in charge, one other seaman, and myself. Since as a kid I had acquired some experience in my bedroom as a disc jockey, I convinced my superior officer to allow me to broadcast my own radio show.

With a crew of almost 2,000, I hoped my listening audience would eventually reach a couple of hundred. I called my show, "Murray's Musical Murray-go-round of Music" and began having the time of my life. It was "Good Morning Vietnam" long before the movie.

My commanding officer was impressed, and he had me read the news on camera which was broadcast every night. Besides the news, I would also comment on the various birthdays and anniversaries of the crew. I soon became a minor celebrity, and often crew members would seek me out, thanking me for mentioning them.

My other duties included dressing up as Santa Claus at Christmas and being helicoptered aboard the ship with loads of presents for underprivileged kids. At the same time, I began to learn how to play drums and teamed with two other shipmates to form a band, and we played at various functions, events, and dances.

An awesome event occurred for me when Bob Hope came on board for his Christmas show while we were playing war games overseas. My duties were to insure Mr. Hope and his entourage were given anything they needed from our department to aid in the presentation of their show, and I was thrilled at the prospect of actually meeting more famous people.

I couldn't believe it when I found myself in the same room with one of the biggest stars in the world: Bob Hope. We exchanged a few words while he was having makeup applied, and I told him I hoped to one day become an actor. I had never given any thought to performing stand-up comedy. That seemed way beyond my capabilities.

However, Bob Hope was the first to implant that possibility in my mind, telling me, "Actors are a dime a dozen. Comedians can always become actors, but actors can rarely become comedians." He continued. "Who knows? Maybe one day, we'll get a chance to work together." "Yeah, right," I thought. Getting Mr. Hope coffee was going to be the extent of our ever working together.

In the show, I recall the biggest laugh Bob Hope received was when he sang a quick verse of "I'm forever blowing Bubbles," followed by actor Jerry Colonna prancing onstage yelling in a prissy manner, "Hi, everyone. I'm Bubbles." The audience reacted hysterically at such risqué humor, which you would never see on television.

This was the '60s, and one of the sexy starlets Bob Hope had traveling with him was Tuesday Weld. She and Sandra Dee were two actresses I had fallen in love with when watching them in movies, and now one of them was standing in the same room with me.

I was ecstatic when I asked Tuesday if I could take a picture with her and she agreed. I remember trembling as my arms circled her waist and she held on to me. I would have loved to have asked her to marry me right there, but I was too shy, so Dudley Moore got to marry her years later. She probably would have had a better time with me. I rarely drank.

I sent the picture to my parents living in Bathurst, and a few weeks later, I received their local newspaper where our picture was on the front page with a headline reading, "Local Boy Welds Friendship with Tuesday." It was pretty cool.

I was due for another two-week vacation, and at the age of twenty, I decided it was time to visit my parents. It had been five years since I last saw them, and I missed them. It was a long train ride to Bathurst from Philadelphia, but it was worth it. My family and I rarely showed emotions, but my mom would often sneak away and cry on the sly. She was obviously proud of me, taking me around to visit our many relatives, showing me off in my Navy uniform, and bragging about my working with Bob Hope.

My parents were still living on the edge of poverty, but my mom had scraped up enough money to open a small fabric store, finally enjoying her freedom from working for others. My dad was as cheerful as could be considering his health continued to deteriorate, due mostly to the arthritis. He continued repairing small appliances for added income, and in his spare time became a voracious reader. He became the local philosopher, willing to engage anyone at any time in conversation about anything and everything. He loved to discuss his views, whether it be aliens from outer space, which he believed in, to religion, which he didn't particularly believe in.

My parents were an odd pairing. My dad the atheist, who constantly questioned religion and my mom, the devout Catholic, rarely missing a Sunday mass. Seeing how proud they were of me, I knew I wanted to make them even prouder, which made me more determined to make it to Hollywood and become well known in show business. When I left, I knew I loved my mom and dad, and more importantly I knew that they loved me.

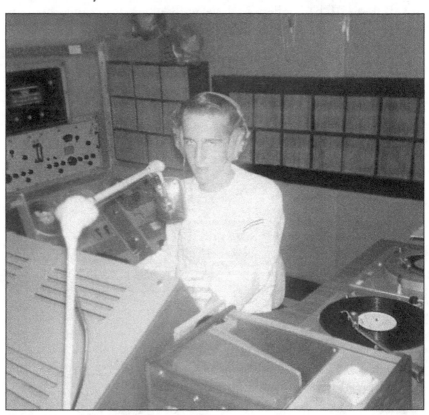

I'm lovin' my new job in Special Services.

Madcap Disc Jockey Keeps Crew Smiling

A write up about my antics as a disc jockey.

USS SHANGRI-LA—A Canadian-born U.S. Navy man has caused the crew of this attack aircraft carrier to perk up its collective ears for the past several months with his antics as a number one disc jockey on the ship's radio station. Murray Langston, seaman, hails from Montreal. He hosts a daily two-hour rock and roll show known as "Murray's Murray-Go-Round of Music" and, in a different vein, an

grew up in," he recalled. "Before I left the show I was hooked. I can't imagine myself working in any other field than show business when I leave the Navy."

* * *

LANGSTON entered the Canadian Army when he was 17 and left it six months later after developing a case of fallen arches.

Three months later he was marching again—this time at the Naval Training Center in Great Lakes, Ill.

"I was walking along a street in Albany, New York," he said, "when I noticed a recruiting poster in a post office. It hit me at the right time. I walked in and signed on for four years.

"I joined the Navy," he explained, "because I wanted to work in the U.S., and a military term was the way with the least red tape. Also, I wanted to visit the French Riviera. I did that during Shangri-La's last Mediterranean cruise."

That's skinny me playing Santa Claus.

REHEARSING for his radio stint aboard the carrier Shangri-La, Madcap Murray Langston is under a bit of restraint—in this case, a strait jacket.

early morning breakfast show. In addition Langston writes scripts, programs and helps operate Shangri-La's closed circuit television system.

The 20-year-old Canadian has made his rock and roll show the most popular program aired by the seagoing radio station by blending a mixture of rapid chatter, special sound effects and top music. His actions are so unpredictable and entertaining that the ship has at times, had the television station televise Murray's radio program.

* * *

LANGSTON fills the few idle moments which may crop up during his show with plugs for the "Madcap Murray Fan Club" which he started among the 3000 men aboard.

"It's growing by leaps and bounds," he quipped. "We've had a president and vice-president for two months, and we'll probably get some members any day now." The advertised entrance fee is $500.

Langston's interest in the entertainment field began long before he assumed his broadcasting duties. Before entering the Navy he worked with an American road show then touring Canada.

"Those people lived in a different world entirely from the one I

And A Good Time

Santa (Murray Langston) stopped in Shangri-La on December 20th to visit crippled children from Jacksonville.

Bob Hope and Tuesday Weld performing.

The Sexy Tuesday Weld and the even sexier Me.

1965

January arrived, and I was excited that it was my final year in the Navy. I began my countdown book, where you list the number of days you have left and cross one off every morning. Anyone who was not a lifer had a book with their days numbered. I was also aware that the time I spent AWOL, along with my two weeks in jail would be added to my time, which made my discharge date November 8. I had 320 days left, and then I was off to Hollywood. I couldn't wait, but unfortunately I had to.

By then, I had adapted well to being in the Navy. It's unbelievable how you eventually get used to thirty other guys screaming, yelling, and laughing while you try to get three or four hours sleep. We all had different shifts, so there were rarely times when someone wasn't getting up, or going out, or coming in and waking you up. Waiting in line was a constant irritation: from chow lines to pay lines to going ashore lines to shower lines, it was never-ending. It often felt like half your life in the Navy was spent waiting in line. That was also the year I would turn twenty-one and finally be allowed to legally drink. It really didn't make sense to me that if you were under twenty-one you could put your life on the line for a country that wouldn't allow you to drink. I had arrived at the conclusion that logical thinking was not a priority in the military.

We had just completed our third Med cruise and were again sent to Philadelphia for several months of overhaul. Because the three members in our band were now all over twenty-one, we decided to find a gig in order to make some extra money and meet girls. We landed a job at a small bar on the corner of Broad and Snyder, called The Dolphin.

At that time, go-go dancers were very popular, and two young girls were hired to dance on the bar to our songs. I developed a crush on one of the dancers named Roseann, and after several weeks I asked if she'd like to go out for a bite after work and she said yes.

At the restaurant, I discovered she had recently separated from her husband and had a small child with a severe case of Down syndrome, which she said was the reason for their break-up. He was unable to deal with a severely handicapped baby, so she moved in with her mother. I joked, "Why don't you take a break from your mom and spend the night with me at a hotel?" I was pleasantly taken aback when she replied "Okay," and off to a hotel we went, where in a very short time we got to know each other intimately. Unfortunately, our first evening together did not turn out to be a great night for me.

We were both sleeping, when suddenly we were awakened by the sound of a woman screaming outside our room. I jumped up and opened the door to see what all the commotion was about. In the hallway, I saw a man dragging a shrieking woman by her hair.

I've never considered myself heroic or macho and the thought of involving myself in this situation was not appealing, but I felt I had to intervene. I threw on my pants, headed toward the couple and asked the guy to leave the girl alone.

I didn't notice he had a lead pipe in his hand and without warning he whacked me over the top of my head. The sudden blow knocked me to the ground, and Roseann, who was watching the commotion, came running out of the room. Blood began pouring out of a gash on my head and, to my surprise, the girl I was trying to help, pointed at me and began to laugh.

It turned out the woman I was trying to help was a drunken prostitute and the guy, a hotel employee, was told to remove her from the premises. Apparently, when he saw me approach, he thought I was her pimp coming after him. When he realized I was not a threat, he apologized profusely and an ambulance was called. I was rushed to the hospital where they sewed me up with several stitches and informed me I had a mild to medium concussion.

Afterward, Roseann took me to her mom's house and put me to bed in her room where I immediately fell asleep. When I awoke some twenty-four hours later, I thought I had only slept a couple of hours and was not aware that I was an entire day late reporting back to my ship. When it was discovered I was missing, many of the crew went searching for me at all the possible hangouts but to no avail.

When I showed up on the gangplank twenty-four hours later with a bandaged head, I was surprised to see the confused looks on everyone. However, once I explained to my commanding officer what had happened, and the facts of my story were verified, no punishment was handed out.

Years after that incident, I thought back and realized I probably could have filed a lawsuit against that hotel and walked away with a lot of money. Unfortunately, I did not know Gloria Allred at the time. But I was still happy. I had less than thirty days remaining in the Navy and, at the age of twenty-one, I had found my first real girlfriend—and, for the first time, I was actively engaged in sex on a regular basis.

But that happiness came to an unexpected end when, out of the blue, the Captain came over the ship's speakers with a notice bringing me to tears. The Captain announced, "Because of the continuing war in Vietnam and the necessity for more troops in all areas of the military, everyone from this day on will have their terms of service extended four months."

At first I was confused, hoping I hadn't heard what I had just heard but it turned out I did hear what I had heard, which was that from that day on, we were *all* extended for four more months of duty. I looked at my now tear-stained notebook with twenty-eight days left, and I woefully had to add another 120 days, bringing the total time left to 148 more fucking days before I would be discharged. I was severely urinated off, I mean really pissed off. I had been so ready to get back to civilian life where I could do what I wanted to do, when I wanted to do it, and where I wanted to do it with no questions asked. And now I couldn't do it for another 148 more days. Was I ever going to make it to Hollywood?

My new girlfriend Roseann and I.

Me on the drums.

1966

Free at last... Free at last... I'm finally fucking free at last. March 8, 1966, and I was honorably discharged. I had saved a little over $1,000 but figured I would need more than that before heading off to Hollywood.

The other two band members, Lou and Ray were getting discharged at about the same time, so they convinced me to stick around for a few months to try to make money as a band. Ray had a friend named Don who played keyboards, so now with Ray on guitar, Lou on bass, and me on drums, we became known as The Bounty Hunters. Even though we were rock 'n rollers, we donned western wear and, seeking a gimmick, all dyed our hair grey. It was quite a sight.

My girlfriend Roseann also became a part of our band, as a go-go dancer, and we began performing around the Philadelphia area. We then moved on to New York, playing little clubs and bowling alleys, anywhere we could find a gig. At first, Roseann and I stayed in the basement of Ray's parents' home, but eventually we found ourselves a little room in Yonkers, New York.

We were not very good songwriters so we mainly played cover songs of hits. I sang two songs, both designed to garner laughs, which I loved. The first was "Do You Wanna Dance" by the Beach Boys, which I sang in a high-pitched falsetto voice, grimacing all through the song. The other was "La Bamba," where I would crucify the lyrics, screaming out unrecognizable words. The audience loved my songs and I loved hearing their laughter.

I never gave much thought to ESP or the supernatural, but I had an experience that sure made me ponder its existence. As previously mentioned, my girlfriend Roseann's baby was afflicted with a severe case of Down syndrome and was so physically deformed that he was permanently hospitalized.

We were about to go on the road for a month, and because much of our trip consisted of one-nighters, she was worried that if anything happened to her baby, the hospital would not be able to reach her. I told Roseann to simply tell her mother that we would call in once a day while we were gone.

A couple of weeks into our trip, Roseann and I were soundly sleeping in a motel room when suddenly, at about two a.m., she woke up screaming. Sweating profusely, she described a horrible nightmare where her baby had fallen out of its crib and smashed the entire right side of its head. She said it felt so real and in her dream, her baby had died and its head had turned a ghastly purple.

I tried to calm her down, telling her that the first thing in the morning we would call her mother who would know if anything happened because the hospital would surely have called her. We went back to sleep and as planned, when we awoke, we immediately searched for a phone booth so Roseann could call her mom.

When Roseann's mother heard her voice, she immediately screamed out, "Thank God you called. Something terrible has happened." When I saw Roseann's reaction to her mother, I had to hold her up, preparing her for the worst. Her mom continued, "About two in the morning, while your ex-husband was riding his motorcycle, he was hit by a bus which ran over his head, killing him instantly."

Wow! How did this horrific incident manifest itself through a dream? Was it spiritual? Was it a result of electrical energy that exists between us somehow being transmitted to Roseann's brain as she slept? My belief is there could be some sort of electrical link, especially between those close to us, which was triggered at the instant her husband was killed, waking her at the exact same time. Roseann rushed back for the funeral, and she later told me that when she saw his body, his head was purple, just like their baby in her dream.

Only a couple of months had passed since I was discharged from the Navy, and I was growing weary of the band, especially believing we weren't destined for any kind of stardom. Coincidentally, our lead singer Lou was notified that he had inherited a substantial amount of money and property following a death in his family, and he felt he needed to move back to his home in New Orleans. Though the other guys wanted to look for another lead singer, I told them to also find another drummer because I felt it was time for me to head to Hollywood.

I made a deal with Roseann that she should go back to Philadelphia to live with her mom while I flew to Los Angeles. Once I had a job, any kind of job, I would send for her, so off she went, and then it was time to prepare for my big move.

I had amassed a small fortune of almost $2,000, which I took out of the bank and went to a club where our band hung out, to say good-bye to everyone. At some point during my farewell, I foolishly mentioned that I had money on me, all in one hundred dollar bills. I was definitely not a brainiac.

As I left, walking the short distance to a friend's house where I was staying, I felt the point of a gun placed against my back and heard two gruff voices ordering me not to turn around or I was a dead man. Interesting to note that I instantly felt diarrhea churning in my bowels.

I was frozen in fear as they ransacked my pockets, emptying them of my money. They ordered me to get on my knees, I quickly obliged, and then crack; I felt a blow to the top of my head causing me to fall face down on the ground as they took off running.

I didn't go unconscious, but felt a trickle of blood running from the top of my head down the front of my face. It was not a lot of blood, so after I felt sure the robbers were gone, I slowly crawled back into the club and told the owners what happened. They called the police, who showed up and took a report, but I knew the odds of recovering my money were not good. They asked if I wanted to be taken to a hospital, but the cut on my head did not appear severe, so I declined and went back to my friend's house, where I placed my face into my hands and cried.

The more I reflected on the horrible event which had taken place, the more I believed that getting robbed was my karmic payback for the burglaries I took part in as a teen. The more I thought about it, the more I accepted it without feeling anger, though I hoped the guys who robbed me would one day feel the enlightenment of their karmic payback too.

So I had no money, except for a small new television set, which I was going to let our guitar player have for nothing, but, feeling sorry for me, he gave me a hundred dollars. I called Roseann, and though she had very little money, she was able to wire me another hundred dollars. With $200 to my name, I was not going to waste another minute. I was heading to Hollywood one way or the other, though it looked like it was going to be the other. Instead of a plane, I would be taking a bus. Regardless of the bumps in the road, along with the bumps on my head and a financial setback, nothing was going to stop me from getting to Hollywood this time.

My band, "The Bounty Hunters."

The band in a Beatles pose.

An ad in the paper for the Bounty Hunters.

Here we are, playing in a bowling alley.

Roseann and I with my hair dyed grey, a gimmick we used for a short time.

1967

The bus fare from New York to Hollywood was ninety dollars, which would leave me $110 to live on for who knew how long. I certainly didn't. At long last, after being in the U.S. for almost four years, I boarded a bus and began the final leg of my journey to Hollywood.

The trip took over four days, most of it sitting, with several stops a day at various points to eat and/or stretch out. I found the bus ride to be fun and exciting, for about twenty minutes, before I knew this adventure was going to be neither fun nor exciting. On day four, I finally arrived with aches in places I did not know existed. My back was so looking forward to a bed, any bed, to finally stretch out, finally lie down, finally.

The Hollywood I envisioned with sunshine, beaches, and movie stars everywhere was not to be on this day. The bus pulled into the terminal in downtown Los Angeles late at night and amidst pouring rain. This was not the Hollywood I had dreamed about for so long. It was dark and dreary as I walked out of the bus station, suitcase in hand, wondering where I would find a place to sleep. There was an element of the downtrodden roaming about everywhere, and I became nervous about being robbed again. With a little more than a hundred dollars to my name, I thought perhaps this would be a good time to change my name. "Trump" would have been good.

As I searched for lodging, I stumbled upon a rooming house that charged ten dollars a night or fifty dollars a week. I paid for a week, and after a grateful night of broken sleep, thanks to drunks loudly arguing, hacking, and coughing throughout the nifty resort, I awoke the following morning realizing I was hungry. That's when I decided

I needed to find a market to stock up on food with my remaining dollars.

Having a limited budget, I purchased several packages of baloney and just as many loaves of bread, thinking it would keep me fed for at least a week until I found a job. The only significant experience I gained from the Navy was working on the radio, so I located a station and sadly discovered that I needed a broadcast license and only U.S. citizens could apply for it.

I was aware that being a veteran I could become a U.S. citizen immediately, but the immediately was more like six months. I couldn't wait, and I only had one week to find a regular job before I ran out of baloney sandwiches and money to keep my room.

I roamed throughout downtown Los Angeles looking for "help wanted" signs. I noticed all the high-rise office buildings and figured there must be some kind of job I could do among these thousands of offices. I filed applications at every company that would let me, but with no luck. Then, on my third day, I applied at the Occidental Insurance Company whereupon reviewing my military status, they hired me to begin work immediately. My luck had changed. I was one lucky guy.

It only paid eighty dollars a week, but I was happy. My job description was "runner," which consisted of transporting boxes of IBM cards, paper, and other assorted office materials from the basement to the computer room on the seventh floor.

In those days, computers were still very much in their infancy. Business information and figures were typed onto small rectangular cards, which were processed through a large computer, the results then printed on sheets of paper.

I was impressed with the various pieces of computer-related equipment used, and in my spare time, I would watch the skilled operators working these alien machines, wondering if I could ever learn how to operate them. I knew that I would have to teach myself if I wanted to get a promotion and a raise in pay. I did not want to be a runner for the rest of my life—or even until I got into show business.

My job was relatively easy, and after a month, I asked the employment department if they were hiring women. They told me they had openings for keypunch operators, whose job was to type information onto IBM cards before they were placed into the computers. And even better, they were willing to train anyone who wanted to learn.

So after a month, I was able to send for Roseann who flew out to join me. Occidental hired her, and with our two incomes we were able to afford a relatively quaint apartment in the center of Hollywood. The only drawback was that we had to take a bus to work every day. I still recall sitting at the bus stop every morning, watching car after car pass by me, thinking every person driving by was more successful than I was.

Roseann and I quickly settled into our new lives. We had money for rent and enjoyed nice dinners, but after a few months I began to feel frustrated knowing that at some point I would have to make my move toward show business. Looking through newspapers, I saw an ad inviting aspiring actors to audition for a new agency that promised to guarantee exposure to top casting directors. This excited me.

I showed up at their office in the center of Hollywood, and after signing in, they gave me a short script to memorize. When I performed the scene, they seemed very excited at my performance, congratulating me and telling me I had a natural acting talent, which they seldom saw on a first reading. I couldn't believe my ears, but deep down I suspected they were right.

They told me that with their expertise in casting, they would have me working as an actor within a month. According to them, I was a star in the making and they would be the ones to get my career off the ground.

But first they needed pictures. Of course they did. You can't get into show business without pictures. They asked me to return the following day for a picture taking session and to bring $200 for the photographer and developing costs. I couldn't wait. I was excited beyond belief, and when I explained what happened to Roseann, she was happy for me.

After my pictures were taken, I was told they'd be ready in a week and for me to get ready to become a working actor. A week went by and to my surprise I didn't hear from them. Not to worry, they're a huge agency and probably really busy. Another week and I still hadn't heard from them so I decided to call, only to discover their phone was disconnected. Bewildered, I immediately raced to their office and was shocked to discover it was completely empty and had been vacated, with no forwarding address anywhere.

It didn't take long for me to realize that I, along with many other saps, had been victimized by a Hollywood scam. Thinking back, I would bet that the camera used to take our pictures had no film in it. I was upset, angry, and determined I would never get conned again. I wondered if this swindle was another residual effect of my karmic payback.

In other news, I was saddened when I heard that Jayne Mansfield died in a horrible car accident. I had fond memories of her being such a nice lady when I met her. I felt sad for her daughter.

Back at work, I watched attentively, asked questions, and in a short time learned how to operate the several machines linked with the computer. Again, luck was at hand when a strike occurred because many of the unionized operators were unhappy with their salaries. When management failed to give in to their demands, they took a leave from work to force a decision. Noticing that the supervisors were in a desperate situation, I told them I knew how to operate the machines. When they saw how proficient I was, they immediately promoted me from runner to full-fledged computer operator, and my salary was more than doubled.

I soon saved enough money to buy my second used car. I had sold my first car to a Navy buddy for fifty dollars. I know the best time to buy a used car is when it's new, but I still couldn't afford it, so I purchased a Ford Falcon, which I called my Falcon Ford. It was six years old and I paid a whopping $400, but it had low mileage and reverse. I paid cash, and to this day I have never purchased a car requiring monthly payments. I never saw the economic sense.

Having a good paying job did not deter my desire to get into show business. One day, I bought the showbiz magazine "Variety" and read an ad in which comedy acting classes were being offered by Ernest G. Glucksman, who produced a couple of Jerry Lewis's films, including *The Ladies Man* and *The Errand Boy*.

Not wanting to get scammed again, I researched and found that Glucksman was legit. Knowing that someone who worked with Jerry Lewis would teach me comedy acting was all the reason I needed to sign up. In his class, I met a fellow actor named Dennis

Dalrymple, who wanted to be a stand-up comic. Performing stand-up comedy was still something I refused to consider. I was sure telling jokes in front of an audience was not within my scope of abilities. I was too insecure and felt if I attempted it the audience would surely laugh at me rather than with me.

After about a month, Dennis and I both quit, having arrived at the conclusion that though Mr. Glucksman was legit and seemed like a nice guy, his glory days were over. We believed we weren't learning much and the main reason he offered these classes was because he needed the money.

I was making a nice living working downtown Los Angeles at Occidental, but I wanted to be closer to Hollywood, so I came up with an idea. Now that I had experience with computers, perhaps I could get a job at a place where movie stars were everywhere, like Universal Studios. So I applied for a job at Universal in their computer division and, to my surprise, I was hired. Wow! Now, I was really getting closer to show business.

1968

Now that I was working at Universal Studios, Roseann also wanted to quit her job downtown. It would hurt us financially, but I agreed, and we moved into a small bungalow-type house in North Hollywood that was walking distance to Universal.

We were running low on money when I saw a relatively clean sofa with little wear put out on the street by a neighbor. It was in better condition than the one we had, so I attempted to move it by myself, when an older gentleman who lived down the street offered to help. His name was Joe Battaglia.

We chatted and he bragged about his young son named Rudy who, at the age of eight, was already a successful entertainer and actor. He had recently appeared in the movie, *Ship of Fools*, with some big stars: Vivien Leigh, Jose Ferrer, and Lee Marvin. I was impressed, especially when he told me he taught his son how to impersonate famous people beginning at the age of two and that he had appeared on *The Merv Griffin Show*. There was no doubt that Joe was determined to make Rudy a major star.

When I told him I was also interested in getting into movies, he offered to help guide me. However, over the course of several months watching him with Rudy, it didn't take long to realize that Joe was forcing his son into show business, more to please himself than his son.

It became obvious that Joe lived, breathed, dreamed, and loved show business almost more than life itself. But it appeared it was more of an addiction that a love. I doubt that Joe ever uttered more than two sentences that were not related to movies or television. The more I observed, the sadder I felt for Rudy, realizing that show business was more important to Joe than his own family, including his son. I'm convinced Joe had an important impact on the way I made future decisions about my life in show business. I loved the thought of making it, but I made up my mind back then that if I didn't, I was going to be happy anyway.

The computer offices where I worked at Universal were located beneath the commissary, just feet below where all the celebrities ate. It was exciting to wander around the studio and see so many film stars walking past me. My boss seemed pleased with my abilities and told me he wanted to train me to become a computer programmer, which would earn me more money.

My job, at that time, was computing the money made on films shown overseas and calculating the taxes paid on those monies earned. Using IBM cards, I had to compile the information and feed it into a massive—by today's standards—computer, which would process all those numbers and print them out.

I was not really working in show business, but I was at least right there on the fringe of it. One of the benefits was if I heard that someone famous was shooting a film on the lot, I could sneak onto the set during a break or on my lunch hour. Because it was frowned upon for office employees to wander onto a set, I learned the secret was to never act like a fan or ask for an autograph because that would be a sure way of getting fired.

The first major star I encountered on the Universal lot was John Wayne, who seemed so much larger than life. He was filming an action movie called *Hellfighters*, and I just had to figure a way to see this iconic legend in person. I also learned that while on a set, you should always act like you belonged there. I accomplished this by holding a prop, like a broom or mop, anything that would imply I was one of the crew.

So when I walked into the studio where John Wayne was filming, everything seemed normal. The crew was busy readying for a scene as I looked around for a prop. Not seeing any, I strolled over to the craft services area and began to clean up around the coffee machine, adjusting the donuts as I scanned the set.

From where I stood, I could see they were about to shoot a scene, but this large, older bald guy eating a donut was standing directly in front of me. I kept trying to look around him to see if I could spot John Wayne, but he shuffled back and forth in front of me, talking to himself. I began to suspect that he might have also sneaked onto the set to get some free donuts.

As I moved closer toward the guy to peek around him, a woman approached, holding a toupee in her hands. She looked up at the old guy and said, "They're ready for your scene, Mr. Wayne." The old guy took the toupee and placed it on the top of his head as the woman stretched up on her toes, brushing his hair into place. Needless to say, I was stunned, witnessing this transformation of an old bald guy into... John Wayne.

The woman handed him a mirror to check out his appearance and somehow, not being able to juggle the donut and mirror at the same time, he dropped them both on the floor. I rushed over, picked them up, and handed the mirror back to him. I couldn't believe the sight of this giant screen legend before my eyes. "Thanks, kid," he said, in his unmistakable John Wayne voice.

I realized he wasn't talking to himself as I had previously thought. He was going over his lines for the scene he was about to shoot. "You're welcome," I said, as I continued holding his half eaten donut. "Let me get you another donut, Mr. Wayne," I offered. "Nah, no more for me," he replied, "Time to get to work. But thanks for offering." He extended his arm to shake and my hand felt like a baby's as it slid into what felt like an enormous catcher's mitt. He had massive hands.

Later that night, as Roseann and I watched TV, we both stared at the half eaten donut, which sat on a plate on our coffee table, with a note attached: "John Wayne ate this." Not sure what happened to it, but I can't help but feel that if we had eBay back then, I could have made a few bucks off that donut.

Of all the times I sneaked onto a set, and there were many, my most memorable was when Elvis was shooting a film with Mary Tyler Moore called *Change of Habit*. Again, I acted like I was part of the crew, always moving around pretending I was working. During the filming, I snuck into the studio several times and my main impression of Elvis was how thoughtful and polite he was to everyone, always uttering please or thank you.

One time, I grabbed a broom and began sweeping the set as I edged closer to Elvis. I was taken aback when he saw me and asked me to hand him the broom, which I did. He said "Thank ya' very much," then pretending it was a guitar, he began strumming it and singing a song. I probably could have made some good money for that broom on eBay too. Most of the time, Elvis had his own guitar at hand, and standing in the background, I would often join in, singing along under my breath, pretending I was also in the movie.

While at Universal, I got to see countless film and TV actors, but aside from a few legends, most did not interest me. One legend, an undeniably gorgeous woman who I bumped into as she walked out of the washroom in the commissary, was Natalie Wood. I'd always heard the expression "take my breath away," but never paid much attention to it until that day. My breath seriously stopped when she said, "Excuse me." When I looked into her eyes, her strikingly gorgeous face almost blinded me, and to this day, she is probably the most stunningly beautiful person I have ever seen. Of course, I could have been looking at my own reflection in her eyes.

1969

After about a year at Universal, I knew I was a competent computer operator but I found the work boring, and deep down I wasn't happy. Even deeper down, though I was earning a nice salary, I knew it wasn't about money either. I had concluded that I would rather make $10,000 a year and be happy, than make $10,000,000 and be unhappy. Inside me there was an unfulfilled passion to do something in entertainment. The problem was I still didn't know which area of entertainment to tackle or how to go about pursuing it.

Then one night, Roseann and I were at a friend's apartment watching the number one rated show on television called *Laugh-In*, starring Rowan and Martin. It was a huge hit, and on the show was a segment called "The Discovery of the Week," where they would introduce a new act, which was always a little ridiculous. That night it featured a slightly plump, not very attractive, long-haired, weird looking singer named Tiny Tim. He sang the song "Tiptoe Through the Tulips" in a high-pitched, prickly voice, and for some reason, he became an overnight sensation. Within months, this unknown character was headlining in Las Vegas.

Watching Tiny Tim's career evolve, I thought if he could make it by appearing on *Laugh-In*, then perhaps I might have a chance. My previous experience as a drummer and disc jockey wouldn't help, but in the computer room, I would often try to make my buddy's chuckle by doing ridiculous impressions, most of them not very funny.

One impression was of a fork, which was oddly funny because I was very thin—weighing less than 125 pounds. I would simply stand erect with my hands flat against my sides, and then place my arms in the air mimicking a fork. Truly a lame attempt at humor, but I thought it might be ridiculous enough to get me on *Laugh-In*.

I was still extremely naive regarding correct protocol in show business. I didn't know that you were supposed to go through an agent in order to connect with producers of a show. You were not supposed to call producers directly, but not knowing any better, that's what I did. I looked up the phone number for NBC, called and when the operator answered, I asked to speak to the producer of *Laugh-In*.

Producer George Schlatter answered, and I told him I wanted to be on the show in the "Discovery of the Week" spot. There was a brief silence, and then he asked what I did. I told him I was working on an impression of a fork: there was more silence. Then he instructed me to come to NBC the following day and meet with him, which I did.

Once there, I was ushered into a room where George Schlatter and a team of writers were assembled. Two of the show's writers were Chris Bearde and Alan Blye, who would later play a large part in my pursuit to become known in show business.

I was asked to show them my impression of a fork and afterward, once again, there was brief silence. There was no response whatsoever as my mind suddenly plunged into a pool of embarrassment. I was thanked, told they would get back to me, and then ushered out of the room. I left NBC, positive I would not hear from them again. Not after that reaction. An audience of mimes would have responded louder.

But I was wrong. The following day they called and gave me a date to report to NBC to tape a segment of "Laugh In". I was ecstatic. They really loved me. I deduced that professional writers don't laugh at funny stuff, they analyze it. I was now convinced my impression of a fork would catapult me to stardom like Tiny Tim and I would soon be headlining in Las Vegas. Boy was I naive.

The taping day arrived, and I showed up at NBC where I saw cast members Goldie Hawn and Ruth Buzzi roaming about. I was star struck when Goldie actually talked to me and surprised when Ruth didn't. Okay, it was the other way around.

I was sent to makeup, and then George Schlatter guided me to the studio where I was put into position behind a curtain. He told me that when Rowan and Martin introduced me, I was to walk to a mark on the floor and perform my fork impression.

For some reason, I was not nervous, as I stood motionless waiting for my cue from a stage manager. I heard the director say "Action," and then I was introduced as "Beautiful Downtown Burbank's greatest impressionist," as Dan Rowan and Dick Martin read from cue cards.

DAN: So what talent did you find for us on the show tonight?

DICK: Wait until you see him. He's an impressionist.

DAN: Really and what does he do?

DICK: He does an impression of a fork.

DAN: A fork? And where did you find him?

DICK: What do you mean where did I find him? I was having dinner and he was lying next to my plate.

DAN: Can he do any other impressions?

DICK: Of course. Later he's going to do an impression of a knife... and stab himself with himself.

When my performance impersonating a fork was over, I was on cloud nine, ten, and eleven. I was finally in show business. The writers had come up with other impressions of a tube of toothpaste and a grandfather clock, which I performed later on the same show. I felt sure my appearance on *Laugh-In* was going to make me a star. I even took out an ad in "Variety," which read, "You've heard of Mack the Knife...Watch Murray the Fork tonight on *Laugh-In*."

On the night it aired, I gathered with friends to watch my first television appearance, and the following day I walked down the street with my arms in the air, trying my best to look like a fork, hoping people would recognize me. They didn't.

I really thought my television debut was going to be the beginning of a huge career. It was the beginning all right, the beginning of the end of my job at Universal Studios. When my boss found out I wanted to be a performer, he in no uncertain terms let me know that he was not happy with me.

My boss felt that if they were going to be training me to be a programmer then I should not be pursuing another career. I tried, in a nice way, to express to my boss that as long as I was doing my job, whatever I was doing outside of work was none of his business. My boss, in a not so nice way decided that it was his business and fired me. How rude.

I was now unemployed, but fortunately Roseann had found a job at the House of Fabrics, which I found coincidental since my mom opened her own fabric store in her home town of Bathurst.

In my mind, losing my job was an omen, so I decided to take time off and attack with fervor this elusive world of show business by doing what Bob Hope suggested. Even though I was petrified at the idea of standing by myself on stage, telling jokes, I would nevertheless attempt to become a stand-up comedian.

Comedy clubs were non-existent, and the only places you could see new comics live were at strip clubs. The most popular and well-known comics like Red Skelton, Bill Cosby, and Buddy Hackett worked in Las Vegas and other large venues around the country. The lesser-known comics on their way up performed at the Playboy Clubs.

So I went to the Playboy Club and saw my first stand-up comic in a live performance. His name was Paul Gilbert and he was amazing. I watched as he made the audience laugh for a solid hour, and thought to myself I could never do that. I was so impressed with his ability to remember so many jokes.

I approached him after his show and told him I was thinking of becoming a comedian, and he replied, "If you're thinking about it, it won't happen. You have to want it more than anything else." Then he surprised me by inviting me to join him at a coffee shop he frequented called Theodore's. It was a well-known late-night Hollywood hang-out on Santa Monica Boulevard, a place which would become my second home.

Paul Gilbert was one of the nicest guys you could ever meet. We met often at Theodore's, where he introduced me to many of the other Playboy comics. He also brought me to his house on Laurel Canyon, introduced me to his wife, and showed off his newly adopted daughter, Melissa. Thirty years later, I would meet Melissa Gilbert at a party and tell her I knew her dad. She was very touched, asking me questions about him, informing me that very few people knew that her dad was a stand-up comic. Except of course, her sister Sara Gilbert.

My ad in *Variety*, thinking it will catapult me to stardom.

e

:

.

n

s

y

e

y

r

.

s

:

.

f

...Ramos family is making preparations for Abuelita's funeral.

34 ENGANAME—Novela

8:00 4 ROWAN AND MARTIN

COLOR Guest: Liberace, who plays a psychologist, a screen idol, a scoutmaster and a dance instructor. Mod, Mod World salutes the kiddies; Alan Sues and Ruth Buzzi appear as George Washington and Betsy Ross; and the Discovery of the Week is a young man who does impressions of a fork. Judy Carne, Henry Gibson, Goldie Hawn, Arte Johnson, Dave Madden, Gary Owens, Dick Whittington, Jo Anne Worley. (60 min.)

11 HAZEL—Comedy

COLOR Steve is getting an inferiority complex: Hazel is constantly bragging

A mention in *TV Guide* of my fork impression.

1970

After a few months of trying to figure out how to be a stand-up comic with not much success, our bank account emptied. Roseann's income was not enough for both of us to continue to thrive, so I searched for another job, which was not going to involve computers.

I eventually landed a position at the Jane Arden Employment Agency as a recruiter. My job was to help other people find a job. It wasn't show business, but the office was located right on the corner of Hollywood and Vine, in the heart of Hollywood. At least my heart was in the right place.

Stores, shops, and companies listed job openings with us and we tried to match the listing with the right person. I was given a desk to which a name was assigned: Jim Allen. The reason was that the companies hiring through us would think they were always dealing with the same person. So whenever I would converse with anyone dealing with our agency, I was Jim Allen. The person before me was Jim Allen, and after I left, the next person was Jim Allen.

The receptionist was an attractive, sweet woman named Joy Farr. During one of our conversations, when I mentioned I wanted to get into show business, she told me that her husband had just worked in a Jerry Lewis movie. Wow! I thought that if I met her husband it would be almost like meeting Jerry Lewis. Joy also told me he was working in a film with several comedy stars including Milton Berle, called *Who's Minding the Mint?* Her husband's name was Jamie Farr. One day when he stopped by to pick Joy up after work, I met him and it was not at all like meeting Jerry Lewis. But he was cute and damn likeable.

Once upon a time, there existed a well-known comic personality known as George Jessel. If you are under sixty, you've probably never heard of him, but at one time, he was a very successful entertainer. One day while thumbing through "Variety" magazine, I saw an ad for a new restaurant/club that George Jessel was opening, and they were searching for new singers and comics to perform along with him. Auditions would be held a week before opening night, and though there would be no pay, there would be plenty of publicity associated with it. I was now ready to attempt stand-up comedy for the first time.

Paul Gilbert had told me that for a first timer, I should concentrate on putting together only five minutes of stand-up material, nothing more, and nothing less. I searched through several joke books, selected a few one-liners, combined them with a couple of my own lines, added my ridiculous impressions to the mix and voilà, I had five minutes of what I thought might be a funny routine. I stood in front of a mirror and rehearsed my five minutes over and over until I could recite those five minutes with my eyes closed. Okay, I have no idea what that means.

I was confident I had my routine memorized perfectly when I showed up at George Jessel's restaurant and signed up for the auditions. There were only about twenty people scattered at various tables in front of a tiny stage. George Jessel sat at a table in back while the acts were introduced. I stood almost numb, waiting for my name to be called. I couldn't believe I was actually going to do this. Inside I was petrified. Outside I was mortified, wondering, "Will I get crucified?"

After a few acts had performed, my name was called and I bounced onto the stage, enjoying the smattering of applause. I was shocked when the first joke out of my mouth worked. My opening line was, "They asked me to make you laugh for about five minutes, so I'll be up here about an hour." The small audience laughed. I continued and was amazed that every line I uttered, including my impressions, were received with laughter. When my five minutes were up, there was more applause and more shock when I was told I was one of five acts selected to officially open the club the following week. I was now convinced that stand-up comedy was going to be easier than I'd previously thought.

The official opening was more than I expected. The front was all lit up with photographers taking pictures of Mr. Jessel along with other invited celebrities. The place was crammed with people, and I was excited. I managed to get two of my coworkers along with my brother Gary, who was visiting me from Canada, into the show. They were all impressed. This was going to be my night to shine.

George Jessel began the evening with a rather extended comedy routine and had the audience laughing hysterically. As I stood outside the kitchen area waiting to be introduced, I kept thinking that all I had to do was to repeat word-for-word the five minutes I had previously performed. At the end of his set, Mr. Jessel then introduced a singer, who was well received, and then it was my turn.

When I was introduced, I strutted to the stage and opened with the same joke I had used in my audition. But this time there was no response. I moved to my next joke and again, nothing. I began sweating profusely as I launched into one of my stupid impressions, and this time I heard a laugh. It was my brother Gary's laugh and it was the only laugh I heard. He was trying to help me.

I didn't know what it meant to bomb but that is exactly what happened. My set ended with a spattering of weak applause. I was numb as I left the stage, feeling like a zombie. How could I kill at the audition and bomb at the opening? Was I that bad? What the fuck happened? My brother and my coworkers tried to console me but to no avail. I knew I had failed miserably. My conclusion was that I was not meant to perform stand-up.

During the following weeks, I wondered what my next direction should be. Should I just give up my dreams of being in show business? I thought about my idol Jerry Lewis who was largely responsible for me coming to Hollywood, and then it struck me. He had a partner, Dean Martin. That was it. I decided I would seek out a straight man and form a comedy team. Why didn't I think of that in the first place?

Through the comedy grapevine, I heard of a small restaurant called Ye Little Club in Beverly Hills, where they had talent nights. There, I met and befriended a tall, awkward-looking character named Jack Starr. I watched his attempt at stand-up comedy, which was not well received, but in my eyes he looked like the perfect straight man.

I convinced Jack to team up with me and we called ourselves, "Jack and Murray". Jack also worked a regular job, nevertheless, we began to spend many hours in our spare time at my place, working on sketches. They were mostly corny, but that's the kind of humor I was attracted to both then and now.

On the home front, Roseann was promoted to assistant manager at her job. She had developed a few friendships, and while I was off trying to find my way in show business, she seemed content spending time with them. I didn't know where we were headed as a couple, but as long as we enjoyed each other, everything seemed great. She seemed to understand the intense desire I had to go after my passion, though I don't recall her having much of a yearning for anything out of the ordinary. Of course, I could have had relationship blinders on, being consumed with my own ambitions.

One thing for sure was I had no interest in other women. Not that I didn't appreciate attractive ladies, but I had always been insecure around women, and Roseann provided me with what I felt was satisfying: sex, friendship, and companionship.

At Jane Arden, because we worked on commission, I wasn't earning very much, so I decided I'd use the agency to find another job for myself. I noticed a film company was seeking a publicist and that interested me, especially since the salary was quite substantial. I called the company as Jim Allen and highly recommended a young man named Murray Langston who had some experience.

When I met with the company executive, he seemed excited over the spirited recommendation Jim Allen had given him and hired me on the spot. I quit the agency, but unfortunately it only took a week before my charade was uncovered. The company arrived at a quick conclusion that I knew nothing about publicity and abruptly let me go, leaving me with no shot at being rehired at the employment agency.

Now out of work again, I had more time to work on my act with Jack. We began performing at various talent nights around the city and I liked that we had little interaction with the audience. For the most part, we performed sketches. We would quickly introduce ourselves, then Jack would say, "We want you all to know that we have a unique style." Then I'd say, "Yeah, Our style is... a lot of things we're gonna do, we're gonna think are funny as hell, but you'll find yourselves not laughing." Then Jack and I would say in unison, "But don't worry. That's just our style."

Then, we'd go immediately into a sketch, such as a scene from *Lawrence of Arabia*. We would crawl on our hands and knees like we were lost in the desert. Suddenly I would look ahead and yell excitedly to Jack, "Look I see a car!" Jack would look off into the distance, squint, and say, "No you idiot. That's not a car, it's a mirage." We would continue crawling when I would suddenly stop and yell out again, "Look, I see another car." Jack would stop, look, and mutter, "Mmmm... it must be a two car mirage".

Groans were inevitable, but small laughs would soon follow, and after several performances week after week, we weren't all that bad. We weren't all that good, but not being bad was good enough for me. It meant we were getting better. After a few months performing and perfecting our act wherever we could, we were offered a job in a small restaurant on Sunset Boulevard called "Knopows." It was named after its owner, Gary Knopow, and the salary being offered was a hamburger a night. We took the job. It was more than we were getting paid at the various talent nights. Hopefully one day we'd get a raise, like french fries.

Besides us, there were three other acts being showcased nightly. A folk singer, a stand-up comic named George, and another unique comedy team named Cheech & Chong. Tommy Chong was from Canada like myself but Cheech Marin was actually from Los Angeles and the son of a cop. Unlike Jack and Murray who were downright silly, Cheech and Chong performed sketches, which ran the gamut from satirical to outright raunchy. One of my favorites was when they would pretend to be two dogs. They would crawl around on stage on their hands and knees, sniffing each other's butts as they twirled in a circle.

At Knopows, we rarely performed to more than a dozen people and there were nights when there would be literally no one in the audience. On those nights, we would entertain each other by doing portions of each other's acts. Many a night, Tommy Chong prepared marijuana laced brownies in the kitchen for everyone, though I did not partake, worried that if I indulged, I would lose control of myself.

Knopows restaurant did not last long and neither did Jack and Murray. Jack found a girlfriend and felt his personal life was more important than our act, so we went our separate ways, and I never heard from him again. Within a year, Cheech and Chong would be seen by a producer, Lou Adler, who was instrumental in catapulting them to success with several hit comedy albums, followed by several hit movies.

No longer earning a hamburger a night, money again became an issue, so it was on to my next job, answering phones for a company which checked the credit of customers for stores and shops.

I was never afraid to work and neither was I ever unemployed for very long, so I decided to buy a house. Being a veteran, the GI Bill enabled me to purchase a home with nothing down, and I figured my monthly payment would be almost the same as the rent I had been paying.

My first house was in Arleta, which is part of "The Valley" and was only fifteen minutes from Hollywood. It had three bedrooms and two baths, and it sold for $19,000. Roseann and I loved our first new house, and soon after moving in, we installed a pool for $2,500.

One day, I noticed that a shoe store, across the street from the House of Fabrics where Roseann worked, was looking for a salesman. I applied, was hired, and quit my job answering phones. I thought selling shoes would be a hell of a lot more fun, especially during this time when miniskirts were all the rage. Visually, it was a great job.

However, it didn't last long. A couple of weeks after being hired, I went to lunch with Roseann. I was a couple of minutes late returning, for reasons I cannot recall, and Roseann was with me laughing as we entered the shoe store. My manager decided to chastise me for my tardiness, in front of several customers and my girlfriend. He looked at his watch, shook his head, and sarcastically said in a raised voice, "Mister Langston, I hope you realize that you're five minutes late."

Having been in the military and subjected to jerks who you knew weren't very smart telling you what to do, I was determined I would never let that happen to me in civilian life. If he had simply waited a few minutes, taken me aside, and politely asked that I be a little more punctual, I would have been okay. But he didn't.

Upon hearing him use that condescending tone of voice in front of everyone, especially Roseann, made my brain twitch and my voice get louder. I became angry and replied even more sarcastically, "Oh I'm so sorry, Mister Manager," my voice getting louder. I let the words flow very slowly out of my mouth, "Maybe you should take those five fucking minutes and stick them up your fucking ass, you stupid motherfucker." I grabbed Roseann's arm, my head held high, and stormed out the door as the customers and Mister Manager's jaws dropped—and I was again out of a job.

I was again looking through the show biz magazine "Variety", now a daily ritual, in hopes of finding an acting job, when I saw an ad looking for actors to be in a play called "Dracula Sucks."

I auditioned and was astonished when they gave me the lead role of Dracula. The play was a comedy spoof written and directed by Jerry Wheeler, and again, there was no money, but it was my first play. It was also fun playing Dracula as a slightly gay character, and my hope was to be seen and cast in an actual paying job. "Dracula Sucks" lasted a couple of months and did not lead to any other work, but I walked away with a perfected Dracula accent, albeit a slightly gay accent, which I hoped would help me in the future.

I was on a roll. I saw another ad in Variety seeking regular performers for a comedy/variety pilot called *Sight and Sound*, produced by Lloyd Thaxton—a well-known producer. Roger Miller, who was a huge country star, was to host it.

I responded and was told to bring a song to the audition and to lip-sync to it. I thought that since most people would probably lip-sync to a regular song, I should dare to be different. I remembered how Jerry Lewis lip-synced to an instrumental in one of his films and decided I would do something similar, but with a different song.

I found an unusual instrumental with blaring drums, trumpets, and saxophones running through it, and practiced for hours, mouthing the sounds and creating a visual of a guy slowly getting drunk, and then finally throwing up.

The producers were impressed, and I was signed for the pilot. It was great working with the legendary singer Roger Miller, who I found reserved, but very likable. One of the songs I lip-synced to was "Raindrops Keep Falling on My Head," with buckets of water raining down on me. Once again, I was convinced this was my time and stardom was very close by. Unfortunately, it was further away than I thought. The pilot didn't sell and I was back to looking for real work. But the job allowed for me to join AFTRA, the union for actors in television. Now, besides a mortgage payment, I would have to pay union dues every month.

I enjoyed my limited experience selling shoes, so I scoured the ads, and within days I landed another job at J.C. Penney's, in the shoe department. Well, it was "shoe" business, wasn't it? I seriously began to think that was as close to "show" business as I was going to get. But I still wasn't giving up. I had union dues to pay.

I heard of another club owned by a comedian known at that time by fans of party records. His name was Redd Foxx. When I saw him perform, I had heard he was dirty, but he was also brilliant. I began hanging out at his club, hoping to find another comedy partner and hit gold. Black gold. His name was Freeman King, a tall, charismatic black guy with a smile that could light up the night.

I was selling shoes during the day, but at night I would head right over to Redd's place, where besides Freeman, I met three other aspiring actors and comedians: Tito Scola, a chubby ex-priest; Maria LaMagra, a quirky, brash kind of woman; and Norma Miller, a talented black friend of Redd's who had been a popular dancer known especially in the black community as The Queen of Swing.

Norma had clout with Redd and wanted to break away from dancing and get into comedy, so she suggested the five of us form a group performing comedy sketches, and become Redd's opening act. We did, and became known as "The Foxy Players."

There was still no payday, but the chance of being seen and gaining experience was foremost in our minds. Just to see the various celebrities hanging out at Redd Foxx's place made it worthwhile. Many big stars of that era would frequent Redd's from the Temptations to Flip Wilson and Richard Pryor. I loved it. It wasn't until later that I learned that another reason so many celebs stopped by was because Redd's club was also the center for cocaine distribution—a drug in which they were all partaking.

Redd became known for his substance abuse, but regardless, I thought he too was one of the nicest guys in comedy, always out to help those he thought had talent. From those earliest days, he took a liking to Freeman and me and considered himself our mentor.

My main goal in teaming up with Freeman was that we would become the first black-and-white comedy team. As part of the

"Foxy Players," I concentrated on us performing many sketches together. Freeman also had a regular job, delivering telegrams during the day, but at night we would shine. The sketches we performed in together always received the biggest laughs.

Even though I was selling shoes during the day, my life felt exciting. Opening for Redd Foxx was a big deal to me. After our shows, the five of us would regularly head over to Theodore's restaurant and spend hours talking about our fledgling careers.

Other aspiring comics and actors would be added to the group. Among them were Fallstaff Wilde, an over-the-top gay comic, and another actor friend of Maria's who worked as a dishwasher at another restaurant called Figaro's. His name was Frederic Forrest and he would later star in many films including the Rose with Bette Midler. My comic buddy Paul Gilbert would continue to stop by when he wasn't on the road, and he was happy to see that I was gaining some momentum.

At J.C. Penney I was also gaining momentum as a shoe salesman. I was so good that the manager offered me a raise along with a promotion to assistant manager. I explained to him that I wouldn't be a good candidate for that position because my goal was to work in comedy and I hoped to one day make money at it, at which time I would have to quit. He respected my honesty and I was grateful that he didn't feel the need to let me go.

Roseann, who rarely joined me on my nightly excursions, finally showed up at Redd's to watch us perform. I could sense that she really enjoyed meeting Freeman and my new batch of friends, along with the various celebs that frequented the place. Though she didn't make a habit of it because she had to be at work early in the morning, she would make the occasional trek to hang out with us.

It had been another five years since I last saw my mom and dad, and I was overjoyed when they decided to drive from Canada to Los Angeles for a visit. They stayed with us at our new house, and while they were visiting, I took my mom to see Redd Foxx. Being a churchgoer, I was curious how she would react to Redd's foul language, though I warned her.

After his show, there was little doubt in my mind that she didn't understand most of his jokes. When we all gathered outside, I introduced Redd to my mom and he greeted her with a big smile saying, "Well, how did you like my show?" My mom, who was always known to say what she thought replied, "I think you need to wash your mouth out with soap." Redd smiled and responded, "You know, my mother used to always tell me that too... until I started sending her money." My mom, who had a great sense of humor joked back, "Well, if you have any extra, send it to me and I won't mention the soap again." Redd laughed, I laughed, and my mom laughed.

My first comedy partner, Jack Star.

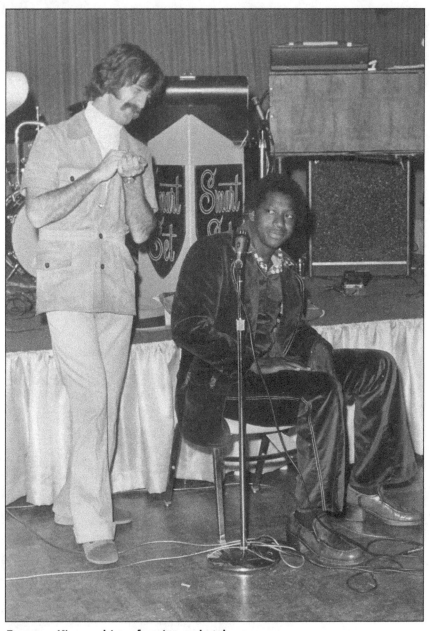

Freeman King and I performing a sketch.

1971

I wasn't laughing when my parents packed up and returned to their home in Canada. I wondered how many more years it would be before I saw them again. As we said goodbye, outward affection was still restrained, though I felt their love for me bubbling underneath. There was no hugging or the words "I love you" exchanged. Displays of love and affection were simply not a part of their makeup.

Without a doubt, having been raised in a home where hugs and verbal affection were limited had an effect on me. Amongst my new found friends, many of whom were exceptionally affectionate, if they made a motion to hug me, I would freeze, feeling awkward and uncomfortable. The same reaction occurred when people told me they loved me. No doubt, this emotional handicap also created underlying problems in my relationship with Roseann.

I wasn't about to be completely free of family for long when weeks after my parents left, my sister Annette came to visit. She confided in me that she was separating from her husband and was considering making a permanent move from Montreal to Los Angeles. She asked if she could stay with me until she was settled, and I of course, said yes. My sister and Roseann seemed to get along great and would often go out together.

Regarding my career, I was still at the bottom looking up, but a talent agent, named Sue Golden, spotted Freeman and I performing together at Redd Foxx's and was about to give us a push upward. She set up an audition for us to be regular performers on a new variety show which was going to premier in the summer on CBS starring Sonny and Cher.

Freeman and I arrived at CBS studios believing we had little chance, thinking there had to be hundreds of others also auditioning. When we were escorted into the offices of the producers, Chris Bearde and Allan Blye, I was pleasantly surprised when they recognized me as the "Fork" on *Laugh-in*; coincidentally, they were two of the many writers on Laugh-In who were in the office when I had auditioned years before.

That broke the ice, but when we were asked to perform the sketches we had prepared, the ice melted rather quickly. First of all, the sketches were relatively nasty because that was what Redd Foxx audiences expected and all we knew at that time.

We performed to silence. Memories returned of my first audition as a fork in front of these same writers who were now producers. They just stared at us, not reacting with even a smile. Afterward, they thanked us and as we left. Freeman and I were both convinced that our audition was a disaster. I was sure we didn't have a prayer in hell of getting the job, not that there were a whole lot of people in hell praying for us.

Though Theodore's was our nightly hangout, during the day, most of my friends and I were usually found bullshitting at the legendary Schwab's drugstore on Sunset Boulevard. At Schwab's, I had befriended a group of odd comic characters, from Joe E. Ross and Huntz Hall to Sally Marr—the mother of the infamous Lenny Bruce. Sally adored anyone who was into comedy and spent most of her life counseling and advising them in their careers. I spent many enjoyable hours sitting with her at "Schwab's" listening to her relate countless stories about the legendary comedians she had known.

It was at Schwab's, while having lunch with Sally, when the cashier yelled out my name that there was a phone call for me. I answered, and it was Freeman yelling into the phone that we got the job! Confused, I asked, "What job?" He screamed back that our agent Sue just called and told him the producers wanted to sign us for the *Sonny and Cher Summer Show*.

I was flabbergasted as I hung up and screamed out loud for everyone to hear. The news of being signed as a regular on a network television show was unfuckingbelievable. I grabbed the cashier, kissed her, and then ran through the place jumping up and down, letting everyone within earshot know that I was going to be on television—at least during the summer. My life was about to change Big Time.

This was no doubt going to be a highlight in my life. However, when there are highs, lows are usually not far away. My sister, who had been living with me for several months, told me she had something to tell me and it wasn't going to be good. With tears welling up in her eyes, she proceeded to inform me that she felt horribly guilty for something she had been keeping from me.

"What could it be?" I wondered, as she proceeded to tell me that on many of the nights she and Roseann went out, she had been having sex with several guys. I told her, even though she was still legally married, I understood. However, what she said next, I didn't quite understand. She said the tremendous guilt she was feeling was because she had also known that over the past several months, Roseann had been regularly cheating on me.

This was devastating news, especially when she continued telling me that Roseann was having sex with a multitude of guys from the seventy-year-old janitor at her workplace to a fifteen- year-old boy who lived next door to us.

I was emotionally crushed. If anyone ever asked if I thought Roseann would cheat on me, I would've laughed and replied with an emphatic, "No!" Why would she? We were a happy couple. At least I thought so. Cheating was something I never gave much thought to.

I knew I was going to have to confront Roseann, but first I wanted to understand why? I needed to talk with someone. I didn't have any close friends, but I did have a new buddy and partner in Freeman, so I went to him for some consolation and advice.

When I informed him what my sister had told me, Freeman lowered his head and blew my mind wide open when he admitted that he also had sex with Roseann. He apologized profusely, admitting it happened on the first night he met her at Redd Foxx's club. He said it was before we had become good friends and that he would never do something like that to me again. Not sure why, but deep down, I really didn't believe him. Then to cap it off, he disclosed that he knew of others who had sex with her, including one of the members of the singing group "The Temptations."

I had heard of the mental disorder known as "nymphomania" but thought it was a joke. It turned out the joke was on me. Once I had mentally digested everything, I confronted Roseann, and she became hysterical, begging me not to leave her, but I was too distraught to think rationally. I had received fantastic news about the *Sonny and Cher Show*, and now unforgiveable news about the woman I thought I knew for seven years.

My sister tried to comfort me, insisting that Roseann loved me, but couldn't help her compulsion to seek sex from other men, which, I later discovered, occurred from the beginning of our relationship.

Roseann became so grief-stricken knowing our relationship would not survive, that she committed herself to a psychiatric hospital. During that time, unable to comprehend the confusing emotions I was experiencing, I decided I needed to be on my own. One indiscretion I could forgive and forget, but the fact there were so many and for so long, I might be able to eventually forgive, but could never forget.

Looking back, I'm sure I probably had some input into Roseann's decision making. Women need to be told they're loved, and my upbringing certainly wasn't conducive in encouraging me to tell people I love them, even if I did. I'm not blaming my parents. It's simply a fact that we're all products of how we were raised.

Roseann eventually moved out and I moved on, giving notice to my job at J.C. Penney. The $1,000 a week I would be getting paid on the *Sonny and Cher Show* was big money to me, even though we were only guaranteed six paychecks.

My sister Annette found a job, met someone she liked, and moved in with him so I was back on my own again. Before Annette left, we talked about my parents and how it upset her that they never told us they loved us. I expressed how it didn't really bother me because I understood how their respective upbringings, lacking any demonstrative love, would have formed their thinking. I told her I never doubted their love, and to prove it I called home and told Annette to pick up the extension and listen in. My dad answered and I told him Annette was also on the line and that she was upset because we were never told "I love you," growing up.

My dad choked up a bit, and then responded with, "That's ridiculous. I love you Annette and your mother loves you too."

Annette was crying as she replied, "I love you too Dad, and I love Mom too." Not to be outdone, I shouted out, "Me too. I love you too and Mom too." It was too bad someone couldn't have taped the conversation. It was as funny as it was emotional. From that day on, whenever either one of us ever talked to our dad, he would always tell us he loved us. Who'da thunk that all it took was one phone call. My mom, on the other hand, remained reticent in expressing her love verbally, but I began saying "I love you" to her whenever we talked on the phone, and she would hesitantly reply, "...er...me too." I loved my mom.

On my first day heading to CBS for work, I'm thinking, "How could anyone call this work?" Freeman and I drove together and were both so excited, especially when we all gathered inside a rehearsal hall where we were introduced to Sonny and Cher. They seemed as insecure about this new venture as the rest of us.

Freeman and I were then introduced to the other regulars on the show: Peter Cullen was one—a Canadian with an uncanny ability to create sounds and cartoon characters with his voice. (Peter is currently known for being the voice of the Transformer in the movies of that title.)

Also from Canada were Billy Van—an extremely talented comic actor—and Ted Zeigler—originally from Chicago who became well known in Canada as Johnny Jellybean, a Saturday morning TV kid show host.

Everyone was surprised to discover that I too was Canadian. For me it was a coincidence, but for the others it was because the producer Allan Blye, also from Canada, hired them having worked with them before. Allan had also met his producing partner Chris Bearde, who was originally from Australia, in Canada. It seemed as though Sonny and Cher were the only ones who weren't from Canada, except for the one female regular who was an aspiring actress named Teri Garr.

Ted Zeigler would soon become my favorite of the cast members because he exhibited no inhibitions, always willing to do anything for a laugh. Like Jerry Lewis, he could contort his face into an endless array of comedic looks. I was an amateur working with professionals, but I was willing to do my best at whatever the producers asked me to do.

And the first was a song and dance routine with Art Carney. It was surreal rehearsing with him, my mind going back to when I was a kid laughing hysterically at him on the *Honeymooners* with Jackie Gleason. And now here I was, on television, performing with him. It was mind-blowing.

On the summer shows, I appeared in numerous sketches, sometimes without lines, but it didn't matter, I loved every minute. One sketch, which satirized CBS's detective show *Cannon* and its overweight star William Conrad, was so successful that several follow-ups were written with Tony Curtis and Jim Nabors in mind. These sketches were so much fun given that we wore "fat suits" and would spend most of the time bumping into each other and bouncing across the stage.

On the home front, I sold my home for almost double what I paid for it and purchased another house closer to CBS in North Hollywood. I thought real estate was a great investment.

Though Freeman and I had become close friends, Ted Zeigler was fast becoming my new best friend. I enjoyed talking, joking, and learning from him immensely. Ted also introduced me to Harvey Korman, who was a regular on *The Carol Burnett Show*, which was taped in the studio next door to us. I learned that Ted and Harvey had at one time worked as a Comedy Team.

An unusual coincidence occurred with Ted and I, which to this day still baffles me. Ted was in the process of getting divorced and moving out of their home. Because I liked him so much, I wanted him to be close by, so I looked throughout my neighborhood, hoping to find a house he could afford.

As I drove through the streets in my area, I spotted the perfect place, which had a "For Sale" sign out front. I called and a woman answered. She told me the price, which I found reasonable so I called Ted, told him I found a house for him, then said I would pick him up and take him there.

He agreed, and I called the lady back and set up an appointment. Upon arriving, we knocked on the door and an attractive older woman opened it. She looked curiously at the two of us, and then said, "Aren't you two on *The Sonny and Cher Show*?"

The show had only been on for a few weeks, so I was surprised yet gratified that we were already getting recognized. "Yes," I answered, "Are you a fan of the show?" "Yes," she replied, "especially since I'm Cher's mother, Georgia. I recognize you both because I've been to a couple of the tapings." It was mindboggling. What are the odds of such an occurrence? Regardless, Ted bought the house from Cher's mom.

The *Sonny and Cher Summer Show* was so successful it returned in prime time, and suddenly I was a regular on a hit TV show. We were now guaranteed twenty two more shows. In my mind I was going to be rich. In reality, at $1,000 a week, I was going to make $22,000. Still, a lot of money in those days. Not so much today.

There was little doubt that Cher developed and matured as a comedic talent during those years. One incident that showed me that she thought funny was during our first Halloween show. I had to play the part of a werewolf, spending hours getting made up with copious amounts of hair placed on every part of my body, including my face and the backs of my hands.

When I walked into the rehearsal hall dressed as the werewolf, I saw Cher with her back to me chatting with one of the dancers. I decided to try to scare her and slowly crept up behind her. I then gingerly placed my disgusting, hairy hand on her shoulder, expecting her to shriek when she saw it. Instead, she took one look at my grotesque, hairy hand and immediately yelled out, "Sonny, you're mother's here." Everyone laughed, and I knew then that Cher was not only a great singer but was equipped with a natural sense of humor.

We taped the shows on large sound stages in the lower halls of CBS studios, but our rehearsals took place on the upper floors in large cavernous rooms, furnished with nothing more than a few tables and chairs. During breaks, I would frequently visit other rehearsal halls and hang out with some of the cast members of other CBS shows. Next door to us was the number one show "All in the Family," and it was great fun getting to know its cast members. Carroll O'Connor appeared to be the most serious of the group, unlike Jean Stapleton, who was always giggling and greeting everyone with a warm smile.

Rob Reiner also seemed to take his work seriously, frequently coming off as aloof, but when he wasn't working on a scene, he was very friendly. He was obviously in a constant state of learning for the years ahead when he would direct some of filmdom's greatest films. One of my favorites: *Princess Bride*. When Freeman and I recorded our first comedy album—the first of one—we asked Rob if he would write a liner note for the back. He did not hesitate to offer, "This Album Sucks," which was prominently displayed.

One time, I strolled into their rehearsal hall while they were working on an episode of their show which centered on the Bunkers eating horsemeat. The producers wanted the show to always have the feel of reality, so actual horsemeat was brought to the set.

When Carroll O'Connor saw me, he offered me a hundred dollars if I would eat a piece of it. Though I found the idea of eating horsemeat disgusting, a hundred bucks sounded like enough for a great dinner later, so I agreed. It tasted terrible, nothing like chicken and he only gave me twenty dollars. He told me that was all he had and that he would give me the rest later, which never happened. And now that he's gone, I guess I'll never see it.

Sally Struthers and I developed a nice friendship, frequently having lunch together. From our conversations, I surmised that she was a troubled soul, unsure of her sexuality, though there were many wanting to share it with her, myself included. I had a crush on Sally, but I never asked her out. However, she asked me out several times— when I was in her dressing room.

I'll never forget Sally once telling me that she had no idea what it meant to be "horny." For a while, she even thought that she might be gay but that turned out to be short-lived when she developed a relationship with the director of *The Sonny and Cher Show*, Art Fisher.

Unfortunately, that relationship turned out to be volatile, with Sally frequently confiding in me that she had made a mistake when she moved in with him. They separated a few years later, and a few years after that Art was killed in a helicopter crash. Many years later, I often wondered if the reason Sally gained so much weight was because she was tired of sex being an issue with everyone she met and being overweight brought an end to that.

As the year came to an end, I was so grateful to be in the midst of this show business world I had yearned for, rehearsing and working with so many legends of show biz.... such as Jimmy Durante, Glen

Campbell, Merv Griffin, Glenn Ford, Tony Curtis, Dinah Shore, George Burns, Lorne Green, Tony Randall, Phyllis Diller, and Burt Reynolds, just to name a few. What a lucky guy I was.

Cast and crew of *The Sonny and Cher Show*. I'm forth from the left.

THE
SONNY & CHER
SHOW

Murray Langston

My *Sonny and Cher* script book.

Me and Art Carney in my first sketch.

Me in a sketch with Sonny & Cher.

My new best friend, Ted Zeigler.

Me as a werewolf.

1972

The word came to all of us: the guest on that week's show would be none other than Jerry Lewis. Up to that time, he was the one person I really wanted to meet, and now I was going to perform with him. This was going to be another major highlight for me.

The day of his arrival at the studio filled me with nervousness and excitement at the same time. I had read the script for that week's show and was thrilled that I was going to be in two sketches with Jerry Lewis.

When he entered the rehearsal hall, it was the Jerry Lewis I had anticipated and known from all the movies in which I had seen him in. Our producer, Chris Bearde, introduced him, and he was warm, funny, jovial, gregarious, and even handsome with his still slicked-down hairstyle. He might have been older, but to me he looked exactly the same.

The rehearsal sessions were great and Jerry seemed to be always on, joking and doing bits with all of us. He obviously loved the adoring attention we all showered on him. It wasn't just me: all of the regulars were charmed with the Jerry Lewis, with whom we had all grown up.

It was undoubtedly a highlight of my life working with Jerry, who also obviously loved working with us. At the end of the week, he showed his appreciation by giving us each a unique special gift: a yo-yo that lit up, with his name engraved on it. It was a simple gift, but we all loved it.

One of the writers on the *Sonny and Cher Show*, who was often called upon to perform in some of the sketches, was a then unknown Steve Martin. He was already performing stand-up at various local clubs, and he told me that Jerry Lewis also profoundly influenced him.

I recall one memorable encounter with Steve, which indicated he was a bit eccentric and sort of a loner. He noticed the camaraderie the regulars had with each other and mentioned to me and Ted that we should stop by his house to visit with him sometime. He gave us directions to his place, which was in the hills only minutes from us, and we told him we would soon take him up on his offer.

Shortly thereafter we did, and when we arrived at his place, Ted and I were puzzled by his unusual and reclusive personality. After knocking at his door several times, Steve opened it while playing a banjo. He continued to play it, acting a little surprised and said, "Hey guys, come on in."

Inside, his home was small but comfortable, with a woodsy feel. Upon entering his living room, he sat down and continued to play, not offering any real conversation. Ted and I joked and chatted about almost getting lost on our way to his place, while Steve continued to practice on his banjo, rarely looking up or saying anything.

I can only describe the feeling as awkward as Ted and I eyed each other at the way he was either intentionally or unintentionally giving us the feeling that we were intruding. His attention was obviously devoted to playing his banjo and he would only speak when we would ask a question. When Ted mentioned he was thirsty, he told him to get some water out of the kitchen, and never did release his precious banjo from his grip.

Ted and I, finally having had enough of this excitement, excused ourselves, telling Steve we had to go and would see him the following Monday at work. He smiled politely, said goodbye and continued to play, as we left thinking this guy Steve Martin was definitely a bit peculiar.

Perhaps that peculiarity was the basis for Steve having such an impact in the world of comedy, rivaling Martin and Lewis, Bob Hope, or any of the other comedy legends who become major stars.

When Steve first worked as a stand-up comic, very few people thought he was funny. Even his writing partner, Bob Einstein, who is the brother of Albert Brooks (a genius, whose real name is Albert

Einstein), told Steve that he would eat his hat if he ever made it as a comedian. According to legend, Steve handed Bob a hat to take a bite out of when he appeared on the cover of TIME magazine.

Because we were regulars on *The Sonny and Cher Show*, Freeman and I were quickly signed by the The William Morris Agency. They were responsible for getting us other work, opening for the Supremes, and appearances on a new late night show, "The Midnight Special," where the legendary Ray Charles introduced us. We made several appearances on the show, prompting the producer, Burt Sugarman to ask us if we'd be interested in starring in a television series with an established singer/songwriter named Paul Williams. He believed that visually, the three of us would be fun to watch. Freeman and I happily agreed, but unfortunately Burt Sugarman couldn't sell the network on his idea.

In our spare time, Freeman and I continued to work at night at various clubs in and around Los Angeles, honing our act. In public, Freeman was gaining more recognition than the rest of us, no doubt because he stood out as the only black on the show and he relished that fact.

At Schwab's, I heard that a new club called The Comedy Store, featuring comedians, was going to open on the Sunset Strip in a building which was formerly the home of Ciro's—a nightclub where acts like Sammy Davis Jr. performed. The Comedy Store opened in April, and was the brain child of comedian Sammy Shore and writer/performer Rudy DeLuca.

I was in the Comedy Store the night of its debut, having no idea it would be around for decades as a spawning ground for so many of the top comics of that era. Opening night, Sammy Shore hogged the stage to a mostly in-crowd, which irritated some of the veteran comics such as Jackie Gayle, who wanted a turn on stage.

The standout act of the evening was a comedy trio featuring three comic actors, Rudy Deluca, Craig T. Nelson, and Barry Levinson who performed hilarious sketches, which they had developed on the late-night, local television show, *Lohman and Barkley*. Rudy Deluca later became Mel Brooks's writing partner, Craig T. Nelson, a star of movies and television, and Barry Levinson, a hugely successful film director. Sammy Shore's credit was donating sperm for the future creation of Pauley Shore.

Freeman and I would occasionally show up at the Comedy Store and perform to small crowds. During the first several months, the Comedy Store struggled, not capturing the large audiences it sought. I was fairly certain it would not last very long.

On the personal front, I was single and still relatively bashful with women. At the ripe old age of twenty-eight, I had only been with a handful of ladies but thankfully, that was about to change. At a local market, I met Karla Purdy, who was adorable, cute, and possessed a smile that melted my heart whenever I saw her. I was ecstatic when she agreed to go out with me, and we quickly developed a relationship. But timing is such a bitch. In another time, she could have and would have without a doubt been the "One" for me—if I was not suddenly thrust into the female candy store known as show business.

Slowly but surely, I began to notice women were more attentive to me. My opportunities for dating beautiful ladies had suddenly multiplied tenfold. Great looks were not one of the gifts I was born with, but I was developing a rather charming, disarming sense of humor which many women seemed to be attracted to. Studies have shown that though men can be successful picking up women in a sports car, walking a dog, or pushing a baby carriage, none of them come close to becoming famous.

I loved my work on *The Sonny and Cher Show*, always one of the first to show up for rehearsals and the last to leave. Being punctual was very important to me and I'll never forget one horribly stressful incident which occurred after a long day of rehearsals. We had worked nonstop on a lengthy comedy sketch and were told to report to work the next morning at seven a.m. to begin taping and to not be late.

I arrived home exhausted, and after a bite to eat, laid down on the bed around six thirty and dozed off almost immediately. Waking out of a deep sleep, my eyes opened slightly to look at the clock and it was seven thirty. We were supposed to begin taping at seven a.m. and I was already a half an hour late. I freaked out, jumped out of bed, and like a madman without changing clothes, ran to the car and sped off toward the studio. It was still dark outside as I scrambled through traffic making my way to CBS. I just knew the producers were going to be angry and blame me for costing them tons of money for holding up production. As I neared the studio, I began to notice that it was not getting lighter, but darker. The sun was not rising, but setting. It was not morning, it was evening and I had only slept an hour before mistakenly thinking it was morning. I couldn't help but laugh as I turned my car around and headed back home. I felt like such a nincompoop, which is a word you rarely hear anymore.

As the year came to an end, a highlight was when I worked with many more celebrity guests, including Ronald Reagan and O.J. Simpson. Did I say, O.J Simpson?

A lowlight was when Freeman and I were invited to Sonny and Cher's Las Vegas show. Excited, we both brought dates, expecting to impress them with preferential treatment, but that was not to happen. In the thousand-seat showroom, we were placed in the last row, and after their show when we introduced them to our girlfriends, we were treated like bothersome groupies. My initial opinions of this dynamic duo, Sonny and Cher being kind, friendly, and likeable were beginning to fade.

Finally... Me and my idol, Jerry Lewis.

Me and Cher in a sketch.

That's me, not Sonny, in back of O.J. Simpson and Cher.

Me with cute, adorable Karla Purdy, who would have been perfect for me.

1973

My life was looking way up, up, and away. I was more than surprised when one of the sexy, shapely dancers on the Sonny and Cher show asked me out on a date. I accepted without hesitation and was even more surprised when she suggested we go to a pussycat theater to see a porno film entitled "Behind the Green Door." (In those days, porno films were shown in smaller theaters). As we sat there in the dark watching it, I couldn't help but think, "Well, I'm getting laid tonight." And I did.

I was still rather awkward around women and was attracted to our one female regular Teri Garr who I thought was cute and sexy. She had been in the Monkees film "Head," and she had already appeared in countless TV shows, so as I got to know her, I found her a little intimidating.

My friend Joe Battaglia, who made the kind of authentic spaghetti that could win awards, invited me over to dinner at his home. So I asked Teri if she liked Italian food, and when she said yes, I invited her to have dinner with me. I had not dated much, so when she agreed, I didn't realize she assumed I would take her to a restaurant.

At Joe's, I sensed Teri did not have a great time, and later at her apartment, we made out a little, but not for long. The next day, word got out about our date, and Sonny thought he'd have fun with it. First, he told me that Teri told him she thought our date sucked, and then he told Teri that I told him our date sucked. Though Sonny was kidding, Teri later told me that she thought our date was the worst she'd been on since she was a teenager. And from her perspective it might have been, but Joe's spaghetti was still better and less expensive than any restaurant.

But Teri was just a bump in the road on my new highway of relationships. I found out another beautiful dancer on the show, named Pam, who had been on the cover of Playboy, liked me and we dated for several months. I couldn't believe I was actually dating a Playboy cover girl. Pam was a wonderful woman, and after we stopped dating we continued to remain friends, and we are still friends to this day. Pam was an absolute doll, and had I not found myself on a new sexual merry-go-round, I might have pursued a more secure and lasting relationship. But at that time, all I was really interested in was a secure, lasting, meaningful one night stand.

After the demise of *The Sonny and Cher Show*, Pam went into management and signed up an aspiring actor whom she later married, a terrific guy named Greg Evigan. Greg later starred in several television shows including *B.J. and the Bear* and *My Two Dads* with Paul Reiser. Greg was later on the cover of *Playgirl* magazine, and it's prominently displayed in their home alongside Pam's *Playboy* cover. I doubt there's another couple in Hollywood who has such a claim to cover fame.

My love life began to explode in more ways than one. On one show Hugh Hefner guested along with twelve Playboy Playmates, and I hurriedly made my move, dating two of them. Even more rewarding for this kid from a small town in Canada was when the reigning Miss U.S.A. of that year, Amanda Jones, was a guest on the show and we began dating.

It was at about this time that my parents made the decision to temporarily move to Los Angeles, thinking the weather might be better suited for my dad's injuries. After a short stay at my house, my mom quickly got a job as an upholsterer and they found a small apartment not too far from me. My mom really liked Amanda, bragging to her friends that I was dating a beauty queen, but my relationship with Amanda fizzled resulting from her travelling on the road as the reigning Miss U.S.A. for most of that year.

I cherished having my parents around, not only because I had left home at such an early age but also because it gave me the opportunity to show off being on a national television show. They tagged along with me to the studio on several occasions taking pictures with Cher, Jerry Lewis, Harvey Korman, Jean Stapleton, not to mention Chas Bono who my mom held in her arms as a baby.

One of my favorite guests was a blind singer named Tom Sullivan. Tom had the ability to remember the sound of your voice years after meeting you. We were in the rehearsal hall when one of his friends, Sally Struthers, entered and yelled out, "Hey Tom, guess who?" Immediately upon hearing her voice, Tom yelled, "Sally Struthers...get over here and give me a hug." As Sally moved toward Tom, I stepped between them, letting Tom grab me and hug me tightly. As his hands moved over my body, it didn't take long before he realized I was not Sally. He threw me aside as everyone laughed at my little practical joke.

Tom Sullivan was an unpretentious, genuinely humble person who unbeknownst to him had a major impact on my life. After getting to know Tom, I made the decision that my life was so damn good and I was such a lucky guy that I had to give back a little.

With that in mind, for reasons unbeknownst to me, I sought out an organization which dealt with mentally challenged people and offered my services to help in any way that I could. My first assignment was to spend time with a fourteen-year-old boy that had the mentality of a six-year-old. His name was Alan Cook and he had been placed in a mental hospital after suffering brain damage in a trailer explosion which killed his parents. Because no existing relatives could be located, he became a ward of the state.

Initially, I would visit him once a week and spend time just chatting or playing board games. Later, I would take him bowling or to the park: anywhere that would take him away from his dull life at the mental hospital. It was a challenge, but one which I gravitated toward, enjoying the sense of sharing some of the success I had achieved.

On *The Sonny and Cher Show*, Jerry Lewis returned to guest a second time, and again fun prevailed. At the end of that week, another surprise for the regulars was when Jerry gave us each a check for $3.56 cents, knowing full well that none of us would cash it. Later, I had heard there existed cheap celebrities, who in restaurants would purposely leave a tip in the form of a check, believing that the waiter/waitress would not cash it, but keep it as a souvenir. I wondered if Jerry Lewis was among that group.

I had heard many rumors about Jerry Lewis being a self-absorbed egotist but it was never apparent to me. I did, however, observe that when he would bring one of his sons to the set, he would order him around like he was an employee. I remember thinking that I was glad I wasn't his son.

Others I was thrilled working with included Jimmy Durante, who often spit in your face as he talked, but you didn't care, because he was a legend. Bobby Darin was another super star I was fortunate to meet and was saddened to hear of his death only months after his appearance with us. Burt Reynolds who appeared several times was always a treat to work with, impressing everyone with his prolific sense of humor and fun personality, never taking himself or the show too seriously.

The hugely successful Jackson Five were guests on a couple of occasions, and Freeman and I became acquainted with them away from the show. At one point, we tagged along with Tito and Jermaine Jackson as they went house hunting. We were even invited to see them perform in Las Vegas at the Hilton Hotel. In retrospect, sitting in their dressing room, bullshitting, and joking with them as they prepared to go onstage, it didn't dawn on you that you were in a place where millions would have loved to have been. You just felt you were part of that show business family and it was where you were meant to be.

Michael Jackson, unlike his brothers, appeared shy and introverted but was always friendly, though he rarely uttered more than a few words at a time. I was thrilled when years later, Michael mentioned The Unknown Comic in an article in *The National Enquirer.*

At CBS, the Carol Burnett show was taped next door to us, which added an atmosphere of fun because Carol, Harvey Korman, and Lyle Waggoner were always friendly and ready to engage in practical jokes. Vickie Lawrence, on the other hand, seemed rather cold and standoffish.

One memorable prank that I played on Carol Burnett could have backfired, but thankfully it didn't. It was another Halloween show and I was again made up as a werewolf. As I was walking toward the set, I saw Carol Burnett in the makeup room lying on a lounge as makeup was being applied to her face. Her eyes were closed as our regular makeup man, Al Schultz, who incidentally later married Vicki Lawrence, was applying eyeliner to Carol.

Seeing the potential for fun, I tiptoed into the room and signaled for Al to hand me the brush. Al, always willing to have fun, quietly backed away as I took over applying the eyeliner to Carol. I then slowly lowered my hairy werewolf face closer to Carol's, at the same time increasing the sound of my breathing. Carol, sensing something, slowly opened her eyes, then upon seeing my hideous face, screamed so loudly that I almost crapped my pants. She bolted upward, obviously frightened, but when she realized it was me, she broke into her typical, loud laughter. Carol was a wonderfully talented woman who always appreciated a good practical joke.

On my days off, I continued hanging out at Schwab's where I met another funny person who was gaining recognition, Dom DeLuise. He was starring in a new TV series called *Lotsa Luck*, playing a bus driver. Dom was very likeable, encouraging, funny... and thin.

Back at *The Sonny and Cher Show*, Freeman and I were pleasantly surprised when our agent told us he talked Sonny into letting us be their opening act on some of their gigs.

The first show was awesome, when we performed at a stadium in front of ten thousand screaming fans. The laughs came in such tremendous waves that the twenty-minute set we had planned had to be cut down to ten minutes. Freeman and I felt we were really on our way up, being chauffeured from the hotel along with Sonny and Cher in a stretch limousine.

Unfortunately, the excitement was short lived when our next gig with Sonny and Cher was at Harrah's resort in Reno. This was 1973, and though racism was still a dominant social disease, I rarely felt the brunt of it, working with a black guy, until our opening night.

Freeman and I were on stage performing a routine where he tells me he's dating a new girl. When I asked what she's like, Freeman responded with, "She's a pain in the butt. All she does is nag! nag! nag!" I then replied, "Oh, she's a nagger, eh?" And Freeman would answer, "No, she's Italian."

It always got a great laugh, but a drunk in the front row, who obviously had too much to drink, yelled out, "That's not funny and neither are you guys." Freeman then used one of our standard heckler lines on him, saying. "Hey man, why are you bothering us trying to do our job. We don't go to your job and take away your plunger, do we?"

The audience was with us and laughed loudly as Freeman reached out to shake the guys hand to apologize, as he would usually do. However, the drunk replied in a condescending manner with, "I'm not shaking your hand." Freeman continued with, "Don't worry, it won't rub off," referring to the pigment of his skin, and again there was more laughter, but not from the drunk. He stood up, yelled something incoherent, grabbed his wife, and stormed out of the room.

We returned to our act, ending our set to thunderous applause, thinking we were winners. We were not. We later discovered that the drunk was a high roller who took offense, filing a complaint with the management. They in turn reported it to Sonny, who instead of defending us felt it necessary to fire us. I can't swear this was a black issue, but our agent later confided to us that the reason we were let go was because the high roller was offended at being insulted by a black guy. Wherever the truth lies, Freeman and I still felt betrayed that Sonny gave in so easily.

It's unfortunate, but the regulars on the show never really developed a fondness for Sonny, though we appreciated Cher. It became obvious that Sonny called the shots and Cher listened, rarely arguing.

In my opinion, Sonny was one of few people I had met in show business who, if you were not at their level, did not want to associate with you. It became evident that socializing with Sonny or Cher was not going to happen, unlike the regulars on The Carol Burnett Show, who became a family.

Sonny would also belittle the cast, by referring to us as "atmosphere." He did not show us any respect as supportive comedy actors and seemed to thrive on degrading us whenever he could. Though we rarely voiced our displeasure, having a great time despite Sonny's small-minded insults, we did eventually get the opportunity to respond.

Cher invited the cast to their mansion for Sonny's birthday party. After some discussion, we elected not to get Sonny a gift, feeling because of his disrespect for us, he didn't deserve one. On the night of the party, with studio heads and agents gathered, everyone celebrated Sonny's birthday with food and drinks. Toward the end of the evening, Sonny gathered the many gifts presented to him and, when they were all opened, he seemed surprised that nothing was brought to him from the regulars. He was quick to say, "How come I didn't get any gifts from the cast?" Ted, speaking for all of us yelled back. "Don't you mean 'atmosphere?'" Then he continued with, "I don't remember you getting any of us a gift on our birthdays." Sonny tried to laugh it off, joking that we were all going to be out of a job, but we felt confident that as long as we stuck together, there was little he could do. Luckily, that turned out to be the case.

Even though *The Sonny and Cher Show* was picked up for another year, I still wanted Freeman and I to continue developing our act. However, Freeman did not have the same desire, believing his television success would lead him into films. Nevertheless, I convinced Freeman that we should make a comedy album, which was released on Laff Records and sold in the hundreds. On one of the cuts of the album, I interviewed Freeman as the first black President—like that would ever happen.

Because I was concerned about Freeman and I breaking up, I began hanging out at the Comedy Store, wondering if I would ever get the nerve to again attempt stand-up. The owner, comedian Sammy Shore, feeling the Comedy Store was destined to fail, left it to his ex-wife Mitzi Shore, who took over its operation. Mitzi was always credited with the ensuing success of the Comedy Store, but I believe it really belonged to Johnny Carson. Timing is everything, and Johnny had made the decision to move the *Tonight Show* from New York to Los Angeles. In my view, had that not happened, The Comedy Store would not have lasted the remainder of the year.

What benefited the Comedy Store was that many of the bright, new comics of that day began to also move to Los Angeles. They knew that appearing with Johnny Carson could make them a star, and they needed a place to work out and/or get spotted by *The Tonight Show* scouts.

In New York, the Improv had been the place to be seen, but in Los Angeles the only club available was The Comedy Store which happened to be in the right place at the right time.

Suddenly, instead of the older comics who had dominated the scene at The Comedy Store, newer comics like Freddy Prinze, Gabe

Kaplan, David Brenner, Richard Lewis, and Jimmy Walker were showing up. Mitzi was suddenly overwhelmed with a new breed of young comics, and in a matter of months, the place exploded on the comedy scene.

Other stars I worked with on *The Sonny and Cher Show* that year: Chuck Connors, Howard Cosell, Dick Clark, Telly Savalas, Truman Capote, Jack Palance, Billy Jean King, Douglas Fairbanks Jr., Rick Springfield, Andy Griffith, Joe Namath, Robert Goulet, Tennessee Ernie Ford, Ed McMahon, Chuck Berry, Jerry Lee Lewis, Frankie Valli & the Four Seasons, Dennis Weaver, Danny Thomas, Kris Kristofferson and Rita Coolidge, not to mention "Lassie"—or did I just mention him, I mean her.

I was dating sexy *Playboy* cover girl Pam, now married to Greg Evigan.

One of several Playmates I got to know.

Miss U.S.A. of that year and me cavorting next to my mom.

Freeman and I in a sketch with Danny Thomas and Telly Savalas.

Freeman and I in a publicity picture used for the cover of our album.

Mom and Dad backstage with Cher.

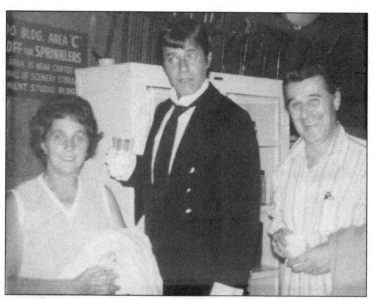

Mom and Dad backstage with Jerry Lewis.

Mom and Dad with Jean Stapleton of "All in the Family."

Alan Cook, the young man I began spending time with.

Ad opening for *Sonny and Cher*—check out the ticket prices back then.

1974

Fun times continued, working with such luminaries as Ken Berry, George Foreman, Paul Anka, The Coasters, Peter Noone, Neil Sedaka, Wolfman Jack, Vincent Price, Ted Neely, Dr. Joyce Brothers, Joel Grey, Ricardo Montalban, and the Righteous Brothers. I loved the Righteous Brothers.

I developed a crush on Cher's half-sister Georganne, spending many evenings at her apartment, but alas, though I was attracted to her, she did not feel the same way about me. She would later become involved with cute Brett Hudson of the Hudson Brothers, which still hurts to this day. Little did she know I would have married her if she would have asked me.

On the other hand, word was fast developing that the marriage of Sonny and Cher was falling apart and that they had separated. What followed was a nasty, very public divorce and the end of *The Sonny and Cher Show*—officially cancelled in May of that year. I was about to be out of a job. But wait! There was talk that Sonny would have his own show on another network and that the regulars, including myself, would be a part of it.

And so *The Sonny Comedy Revue* was launched. Cher also announced plans to star in a new variety series of her own. Critics, surprisingly, predicted that Bono would be the big winner and didn't think Cher's more musical showcase would survive.

On Sonny's new show, the powerhouse Jackson Five was again enlisted to boost the ratings, but the critics were wrong. After only six weeks, Bono's show was abruptly canceled and I was again out of a job. This became a time to ponder whether my career would stay alive and survive or perish and peter out.

So I'm back at Schwab's Pharmacy during the day and Theodore's restaurant in the evenings. I was invited by Cheech and Chong to see them perform at the Troubadour, and I was astounded at the huge reaction they were getting from the audience compared to the small doses of laughter they received at Knopows. I sat with Kris Kristofferson and Rita Coolidge, having met them when they appeared on *The Sonny and Cher Show.*

That year, John Lennon was kicked out of the Troubadour for being drunk and disorderly, apparently after he and Yoko had split up. Lennon showed up at Theodore's to sober up, sitting at the table next to me. By this time, I had reached a stage where being around celebrities had little effect on me, but I was majorly starstruck seeing John Lennon in person. It was obvious that all eyes were on him in the early morning hours eating with a couple of male friends, yet nobody approached him.

Being a huge Beatle fan, I knew I had to say something to him. I had finished eating and was ready to leave, so as I stood, I purposely "accidentally" dropped my check on the floor next to his booth. As I picked it up, I positioned myself so that when I stood up, I'd be facing him. I could see he noticed me, and I nervously mumbled a few words of thanks for all the great music he created for the world to enjoy. At first I felt I had made a mistake. Then, in a somewhat slurred Liverpool accent, he smiled and said, "Thank you... I couldn't have done it without your help...."

Not sure what he meant, but regardless of the altered state he was in, I left feeling the effects of meeting a legend. Years later, while working at NBC, I was introduced to Ringo, but it just wasn't the same. However, whenever I'm asked, "Which three people alive would you want to have dinner with?" Paul McCartney is always on my list. Bill Clinton and Richard Branson are the other two. There are so many questions I would want to ask them. However, lately, I might replace Paul McCartney with Ricky Gervais. I love his humor and views on religion.

Freeman's lack of interest in working on our act compelled me to once again work alone, so I took some of our routines, condensed them into a monologue, and returned to the Comedy Store. While working on my single act, I met another aspiring comic named Robin Williams who had arrived from San Francisco. I had already heard that he was as funny as he was outrageous and I had to agree.

Robin's uniqueness was his talent to improvise, or at least give the impression that everything he was saying was off the top of his head, which was not the case. Not that Robin didn't have the ability to improvise and create comedy on his feet, but what he possessed was an incredible bank of material which he could rely on when improv wasn't working.

He also possessed something which I did not. An all-embracing passion for performing which I had not seen in most comics. I would watch Robin onstage getting no laughs, and yet he would continue to perform, almost relentlessly, trying to illicit any kind of reaction from the audience. He wouldn't always succeed, but he would always try his utmost to at least suck some measure of laughter out of the many late-night, lackluster audiences that we faced at the Comedy Store.

Unlike Robin, if I didn't get laughs within the first few minutes, I wanted to get offstage as soon as possible, rather than submit myself to continued humiliation. Perhaps that is why Robin is where he's at and I'm where I'm at, which, by the way, for me is a phenomenal place. I believe we all either consciously or unconsciously design the destiny which best suits us and mine suits me just fine.

During that period, Robin and I worked together at the "Laff Stop" a comedy club in Newport Beach where I met Robin's first wife Valerie. She introduced me to her sister Leslie, and we developed a short-lived relationship. After Robin and Valerie separated, he and I would occasionally search out the ladies and double date.

It was exciting to watch Robin's meteoric rise, although during the *Mork & Mindy* days, he was getting chastised by many comics for stealing their material. I never thought Robin consciously stole jokes but might have unconsciously used lines belonging to other comics because of the pressure he was under to maintain the level of humor he had when he began Mork & Mindy. Robin was also getting deeper into drugs and alcohol, which could also have altered his reasoning. Still there's no doubt Robin was a genius, and the few jokes he may have lifted from others can in no way detract from that fact.

As with my friendship with Cheech and Chong, my relationship with Robin also faded as we saw each other less and less. One of my final recollections was when Robin invited me to his house in Topanga Canyon to celebrate the opening of his first film *Popeye*. It was not a huge success, but it certainly didn't hurt his future film career.

On the other hand, my career needed a major manicure, and for reasons I'll never fully understand, I decided to take what little savings I had left from *The Sonny and Cher Show* and invest it in a small nightclub/restaurant. It was located on the corner of Lankershim and Victory in North Hollywood, and I named it "Show-Biz." Not wanting to copy The Comedy Store, my plan was to showcase not only comics, but all types of entertainers, including singers and magicians.

The place I purchased had previously been a lesbian nightclub which led me to joke: "Before I bought this place, it was owned by lesbians. It was a tough club. It had a pool table with NO balls." That joke still works to this day. I suspect that my decision to get involved in this business was ego-driven more than anything else. Here I was, only twenty-nine and I had my own nightclub to show-case myself and my friends.

My menu featured four different kinds of ribs: American, Italian, Spanish, and Chinese. My parents were still living in Los Angeles, so my dad offered to be the cook and my sister Suzanne, who had recently made the move to L.A., became the bartender.

I had convinced myself that though I had virtually NO experience in the restaurant business, I was smart enough to make it successful. Sadly, that was not the case. I did however acquire a liquor license through a lottery, and instead of paying upwards of $20,000 I only paid $8,000.

Most of my comic buddies began showing up and performing, which caused Mitzi Shore of The Comedy Store to drop in to congratulate me, even though she was really checking out the competition. I was pleasantly surprised that within months, my club was doing great business on weekends, but that wasn't enough to pay the bills.

It was very difficult getting an audience in during the week. A few times, I took my employees and, along with a couple of entertainers, we'd form a line outside the front door hoping to make people passing by think that we were packed.

It worked on a few occasions when a couple would get in line, then we would all go inside, where they would then realize they were the only customers in the place. If they stayed, they were pleasantly entertained by us.

As my audiences built, comics who were finding it difficult to get good time slots at The Comedy Store began showing up at my place: acts like Kip Addotta, Vic Dunlop, Jeff Altman, John Barbour, George Miller, Skip Stevenson, and Charlie Hill. One talented duo, who routinely received standing ovations with their innovative musical/comedy talents, were known as The Junkman and the Carpenter (Granite & Carouso). Everyone thought they were going to be the next comedy sensation, but that didn't happen.

On Sundays, I presented talent night, which showcased newer, raw talents. One black female who always showed up was Shirley Hemphill, who reminded me of an earlier funny lady named Moms Mabley. Unfortunately, Shirley rarely elicited laughs because she mumbled and ran her words together so that it was difficult to understand her. But she was without a doubt a tribute to perseverance. A few years later, she succeeded beyond most of the other comics by landing a role on a hit TV series, *What's Happening!*

I've often said, "Achieving success in Showbiz is primarily based on being at the right place, at the right time, with the right look." Talent, though a plus, is usually secondary. However, what ensues is the more talent you possess, the longer you last in the business.

Another young comic with the right look, at the right place, just waiting for the right time, who frequented my club was Michael Douglas. Not Kirk Douglas's son. This Michael Douglas later changed his last name to Keaton for obvious reasons, supposedly because he saw Diane Keaton's name on a marquee and thought that it had a nice ring to it.

Michael Keaton had a lot going for him. He was talented, good looking, and had plenty of entertaining comedy material. I recall a very funny routine about dating and what it was like to wake up in the morning with someone you had picked up the night before, lying beside you asleep and drooling.

One unfortunate incident that happened to Michael at my club was when he told a joke about an aging actor named Durward Kirby, who used to appear on *The Garry Moore Show*. Unbeknownst to Michael, Durward Kirby's son Randy was in the club having a drink when he overheard Michael's put down of his father. What are the chances? After Michael's performance, Randy approached Michael and threatened to kick the crap out of him if Michael ever mentioned his dad in his act again. Randy was a bit of a jerk, and to my knowledge, Michael never repeated that joke. Years later I sat next to Michael on a plane and he was quick to recount that incident.

Another of my customers was Harry Colomby who managed a famous jazz musician, Thelonious Monk, along with a popular comedian of that era named John Byner. Harry told me how he loved John Byner but felt frustrated because John only wanted to work sporadically, then would disappear for months to an island he owned in Fiji. Because of this, Harry confided in me that he needed to find another act, and was interested in Michael Keaton. Harry eventually became Michael Keaton's manager and produced several of his films.

Even though we no longer worked as a comedy team, Freeman would occasionally show up at my place and we would perform some of our old routines. There was a method to his madness which was to pick up women, and he frequently succeeded.

Some of the many people who sang at Show-Biz included an attractive brunette Sunni Wells, who I had a brief fling with, and a very handsome young singer John O'Banion. John and Sunni fell in love and were married in my club, John entering from the men's room and Sunni entering from my office. A few years later John had a hit record called, "Love You Like I Never Loved Before," and made five appearances on *The Tonight Show*.

Another couple who met at my club and later married was the daughter of actor Jack Albertson, Maura Albertson, and singer R.B. Greaves, who had a number-one record called "Take a Letter Maria." Jack Albertson would often come into my club to see his daughter Maura sing at a time when he was getting ready to star in a new TV series, *Chico and the Man*, with a brash young comic, Freddy Prinze.

Another regular at Show-Biz was an actor named Peter Helm, who was dating sexy Joey Heatherton, a well-known actress/singer of that time who frequently joined him. Joey was delightful and I loved having her in my club. My feeling was that anytime anyone famous came in, the word of mouth would generate publicity attracting others.

One time cockeyed comic actor Marty Feldman got drunk in my place and tried to seduce my sister. When Marty Feldman had his eye on someone, he had his *eye* on someone! Fortunately or unfortunately for my sister, he was too drunk to follow through and she escaped unscathed. He was a really likeable guy and it was a real bummer to hear about his early death a few years later.

During those years, I developed an erratic friendship with a singer named Johnny Dark. As mentioned, I loved practical jokes, and on one particular night, Johnny was my target. When he sang a song, Johnny would always end them very dramatically, by holding the last note for what seemed an eternity, which would usually elicit thunderous applause.

Johnny was a nervous performer who would always wait outside the back door until just before being introduced. So while he was outside, I told the audience that after the singer I was about to introduce finished his song, do NOT applaud and we would all enjoy watching his reaction together.

I introduced Johnny who rushed onstage and began singing the Tom Jones song, "It's Not Unusual." At the end, he belted out and held the last note as long as he could and then shouted, "THANK YOU"! To complete silence.

The startled and confused look on his face when he received absolutely no reaction was seriously fantastic! He froze momentarily, his brain obviously trying to figure out what happened. Then a knowing look came over his face as he loudly screamed out, "Fuck You, Murray!" I laughed hysterically. The audience laughed hysterically. Johnny, being a bit sensitive, did not find it particularly amusing. Likewise, a few weeks later, he did not find it funny when he was singing onstage as Harvey Korman and Tim Conway, having had a few drinks, began heckling him.

Oddly enough, when most of us aspiring comics would hang out at various late night restaurants, Johnny was always the funniest one at the table, making everyone laugh. I would tell Johnny he was missing his calling, and subsequently, when others reiterated my belief, he began piecing a comedy act together. In the beginning it was mostly impressions, but Johnny quickly began getting recognition as a very funny stand-up comic.

Johnny would admit that back in those days, he had a drinking problem, which created a problem for me. One of many reasons my club did not survive was that I provided plenty of free food and drinks for the entertainers, and Johnny alone could polish off a bottle of scotch in one night. Being a novice night club owner, and not very good at math, I was not able to calculate that free food and booze to friends and performers was not good business.

Because I wasn't working on television, I had more time, which benefitted Alan Cook, the mentally challenged boy I continued to spend time with. I frequently brought him to my club, where he enjoyed watching the various acts on my stage. Most of my friends slowly became acquainted with him and always treated him in a very friendly manner. Of course they had little choice if they wanted to appear on my stage.

My friend Ted was responsible for one of the major highlights of my life, by convincing me to quit smoking cigarettes. I had been a smoker since I was fifteen, but thankfully less than a pack-a-day user. When I began smoking, its horrible effects on the body were still relatively unknown by the public, but now, Ted was helping spread the message. He showed me pictures of lungs blackened from nicotine comparing them to pictures of pink, healthy lungs. It wasn't easy to finally quit the nasty habit, but what finally persuaded me was my realization that I really enjoyed my life and didn't want it to end prematurely. Thank you, Ted.

I really did love my life, even though I was almost broke when I received a call from Chris Bearde, producer of *The Sonny and Cher Show*, offering me work on his latest project, *The Hudson Brothers Razzle Dazzle Show*. It was a kid's show, starring an up-and-coming teeny-bopper group The Hudson Brothers, who were three good looking young guys who were being groomed for stardom by network executives. It was to be shot in Toronto, Canada, for six weeks, which created a problem for me at Show-Biz, since I would need to be gone for that length of time. My problem was solved when two of my Show-Biz friends, R.B. Greaves and Peter Helm, offered to co-manage my club while I was gone. I gladly accepted their offer and left for Toronto.

Working with the Hudson Brothers, and being reunited with the other cast members from *The Sonny and Cher Show*, made for a great time for everyone. I also became friends with a new comic act who was added to the cast by the name of Rod Hull, who had a puppet bird named Emu. He was a very funny and talented guy from England and we hit it off from the beginning.

When the show was over, I returned to my club, and the first thing I noticed was blood all over the walls in the men's room which was a result of R.B. and Peter getting into a huge fist fight over who was in charge. During my time away, my business dwindled and I had to start all over again, trying to figure new ways to hustle customers into my place. Thankfully, R.B. and Peter subsequently made up, and we were once again a Show-Biz family.

My real family decided it was time to move back to Canada. Though my dad enjoyed hanging with the comics at my club, my mom and sister Suzanne were getting homesick and had had enough of the Hollywood life. Within weeks of their decision, they were dearly departed and I was left without a cook or a bartender.

One of the comedians, Michael Rapport, offered to cook, and I'm not sure if it was because he was a comic but the ribs always tasted funny. I also hired a female bartender named Dawn and fell madly in love with her. She was gorgeous, and I fell hard because, though I had been engaging in plenty of sex, she was the first to teach me about eroticism and boy did I get hooked.

About this time, a good-looking actor named Erik Estrada began hanging out at my club. He had just landed a role in the movie *Airport*, and he seemed like a nice guy. A few months into my relationship with Dawn, one night at her apartment after great sex, I noticed a picture of a guy on her nightstand. It was a publicity still of that "nice guy" Erik Estrada.

When I asked her about him, she told me that he asked her for a date and would I mind if she went out with him? I was flabbergasted and devastated at the same time, or was it the other way around? Either way, she then added that she was a free spirit who was not ready to be in a permanent relationship or settle down with anyone.

She suggested that under the circumstances perhaps she should quit working at my place as a bartender. I said, "No," probably thinking I could win her back, but she quit anyway and I never saw her again. I hope she and Erik had a great time together.................. NOT!

After cutting my wrist with a razor—okay, it was an electric razor—and dealing with a new emotional scar, I hired another "male" bartender. I was still trying to get audiences into my club and came up with the idea of holding celebrity "Roasts" at my place. I had seen them on the Dean Martin series of TV specials where celebrities were roasted, but where could I get a celebrity who would allow me to crucify them on stage?

A TV commercial, which played repeatedly, was for a car dealership owned by pitchman Cal Worthington. Everyone in Los Angeles knew of his antics, using animals from elephants to tigers to sell cars. I called and when I asked him if he'd like to be roasted at my club, he gleefully accepted immediately. All it took was a small ad in the papers and we were sold out for this mini event.

Cal was wonderful, arriving in his own limo, and the comics had a field day roasting him with joke after joke. Subsequently, I talked others like Frankie Avalon and Teddy Neely—of *Jesus Christ Superstar* fame—into also getting roasted at my club, and it became a monthly event.

Me and Andy Griffith.

Me and Kris Kristofferson.

Autographed Picture of Jerry Lewis for my club Show-Biz.

Mom and my sister Suzanne with Harvey Korman at my club Show-Biz.

My dad in the kitchen on a break from cooking.

Mom and Tim Conway at Show-Biz.

Mom with R.B. Greaves, Maura Albertson, and John O'Banion.

Mom and Dad with R.B. Greaves and me at Show-Biz.

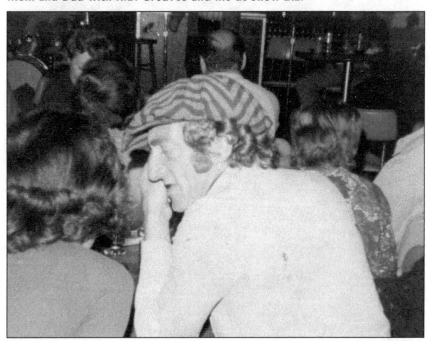

Marty Feldman at my club, flirting with my sister.

Frankie Avalon at my club being roasted.

Norma Miller roasting Frankie Avalon at Show-Biz.

Joe E Ross being roasted.

1975

Even though the monthly Roasts were successful, I continued to have a difficult time making ends meet. Unlike the Comedy Store, I paid my headliners the whopping salary of fifty dollars a week—a sum most of the struggling acts were grateful to receive.

One night, Johnny Dark, who was now fully engaged in performing stand-up, brought Freddie Prinze into the club. He had recently shot to fame with only one appearance on *The Tonight Show* and was starring in a TV series *Chico and the Man* with Jack Albertson, who was already frequenting my place.

On one occasion, Freddy showed up at my place with his girlfriend Kitty Bruce, daughter of comedy legend Lenny Bruce. One day, Kitty came to my club with a perky young actress named Linda Blair of *The Exorcist* fame. Linda was adorable, loved to laugh, and we became fast friends.

One incident, which showed her fun spirit, occurred after I had moved into a small apartment on the beach. Linda and my sister were supposed to meet me at my place, but I was caught in a traffic jam and arrived an hour late. They had already left, but not before Linda turned most of my furniture upside down and left a note which read "The Devil made me do it."

Years later, people assumed Linda and I were an item, but our relationship was more brother and sister than anything else. In fact, I became a source of comfort for her and she would seek advice from me when she had problems in her intimate relationships, which were plentiful. At that time, she was dating singing sensation Rick Springfield, and they would frequently join me for late-night breakfasts at Theodore's.

When Freddy Prinze ended his relationship with Kitty, I began dating her, which culminated in an invitation to the Academy Awards. The film *Lenny*, starring Dustin Hoffman, was nominated for several awards, and because Kitty was Lenny Bruce's daughter, she was invited, and she in turn asked me to be her date. It was a thrilling and memorable event, walking along the red carpet as we entered the awards ceremony with cameras flashing everywhere. The party afterward with all the motion picture stars of that era in attendance was also something to remember, though right now I can't remember it very well.

What I do remember, was calling my comic friend Paul Gilbert many times, inviting him to come to my club. He promised he would stop by but that was not to be. I was saddened when I received word shortly after I had last talked to him that Paul died of a stroke at the way too young age of fifty-six.

Also too young, were two girls who were caught drinking in my club where the legal drinking age was twenty-one. My bartender neglected to check their IDs when a man sitting at the bar identified himself as a representative of the state liquor board. He presented me with a fine of $500 when it was discovered the girls were only eighteen.

The girls apologized, and afterward, one of them mentioned that she was looking for a job. I needed an extra waitress, and because my place served food, I could employ people under twenty-one provided they did not serve alcohol, so I hired her. I learned that my new waitress wanted to be an actress and initially came to my place because she loved comedy. She told me that her last job was at a local theme park, Magic Mountain, where she had fallen off a tram, placing her into a semi-coma, after which she endured several months of physical therapy.

I thought she was really cute, and I especially loved her low, gravel-toned voice, which was magnified when she laughed—which was loud and often. Her name was Debra Winger. I really liked her and I could tell she liked me too, but I was not about to get serious after what I had just gone through with my ex-bartender.

By this time, I had given up my apartment at the beach because the distance from my club was just too far. Freeman had a two bedroom apartment on Laurel Canyon and suggested I share it with him so we could both save money, and I moved in. Debra Winger and I began spending more time together, having late-night meals, which would frequently climax at my apartment. After work, I would often drive her to acting classes, picking her up afterward.

In other news, it was great news for Johnny Dark when talk show host Merv Griffin spotted him at The Comedy Store and invited him to perform on his show. Debra and I went along with Johnny to support him, but his first appearance did not go well and we tried our best to console him.

Another comic who worked at my club was Jeff Altman, a funny guy with a volcanic delivery. Jeff possessed a few idiosyncrasies, one of which was to hypnotize girls and then attempt to seduce them. One time, I was in my office when Debra rushed in on the verge of tears, telling me that Jeff hypnotized her in the parking lot and persuaded her to remove her top, exposing her breasts. I told Jeff to leave the premises, but thinking back, with my limited knowledge of hypnosis, I'm not sure one can be made to do something that is out of character for them.

Though I liked Debra, I met another woman named Sandy Means who I liked even more. She was a Farah Fawcett wannabe, very beautiful, and I began seeing her at the same time. When Debra got wind of it, she terminated our brief fling, but you shouldn't feel sorry for her because many of the comics had mad crushes on her, most notably George Miller.

George did not succeed in his attempt to woo her, but another comic Gary Muledeer did, and they began a lengthy relationship. After Gary, she hooked up with comic Richard Lewis, whose heart she broke when she decided to move from comedy to film and began dating actor James Woods.

After our paths drifted apart, Debra was quick to land the role of Wonder Woman's sister on the television series, and shortly after that she starred in the film *Urban Cowboy* alongside John Travolta.

Was it a coincidence when Freeman told me that a young actor named John Travolta moved into the apartment next to ours? And what are the odds that while Travolta was living next to us, Gabe Kaplan would show up at my club while they were working together in the TV series *Welcome Back Kotter?* Los Angeles was indeed a small world unto itself.

One afternoon at my club, preparing for an onslaught of five to ten people for that night's show, a boyish-looking guy approached me and asked if I knew who owned the club. When I told him I was the owner, he told me his name was Jim Stafford, and I immediately recognized him because he was in the prime of his success with several hit records, "Swamp Witch," "Spiders and Snakes," and a very funny song called "My Girl Bill."

I was blown away when Jim told me he was in Los Angeles preparing to star in his own variety show on television and asked if he could return later that night to sing a few songs. "Of course," I replied, thinking I wished I had time to publicize his being there. He then asked if one of the writers he brought from Florida, who had never done stand-up in Los Angeles could also do a set and again I said "Yes".

Hours later, with a somewhat small crowd, Jim performed a lengthy set, the audience loving every minute of it. He then introduced his friend, a quirky looking guy with a hat, who bounded on stage carrying a large watermelon. His name was Gallagher and his set was met with hysterical laughter culminating in his hammering the watermelon with a sledgehammer, splashing everyone in sight. Though the cleanup was a mess, the night was a hit, and Gallagher returned to perform often, becoming one of my headliners, and earning fifty dollars a week.

A southern comedian who never reached headliner status at my club was Jim Varney, who performed his own down-home brand of humor, mostly telling stories rather than jokes, and though he did not garner huge howls, he always managed to charm the audiences with his slow southern drawl.

That southern drawl would later catapult him to national fame as Ernest P. Worrel in a hit television commercial campaign, which led him to star in several movies. Looking back, I can't help but find it gratifying that my funky little club would be a springboard for so many who were destined for comedic success.

Another young guy who showed up at my place, asking if he could work out his comedy material, was David Letterman. He had just arrived from Indianapolis with his wife Michelle, and they moved into an apartment a block from my club on a street called Oxnard, which was the source for one of his first jokes. Letterman:

"Yeah, I live on a street called Oxnard. Sounds like an animal disease, doesn't it?" He continued, "Yeah, my Ox has this ugly nard all around its nose...I think it has Oxnard."

My understanding was that my club was the ideal place for David to prepare himself before heading to The Comedy Store where his goal was to hopefully be seen by *The Tonight Show* staff. The dream of every aspiring comic of the seventies was to get seen on *The Tonight Show*, which would hopefully lead to a TV series. Everyone thought if it happened to Freddy Prinze, it could happen to many more of us.

My audiences immediately accepted Letterman's style. His jokes, always bathed in sarcasm, rarely bombed, and I knew he was going places. Though relatively new at performing stand-up, his stage persona exhibited total confidence, and though he most probably had performance anxiety as most of us did, you could never see even a hint of it.

Other lines he delivered at my club in his inimitable style: "Hey!" Letterman would mutter, "I picked up the Enquirer today. Yeah, the headline read, Why Robert Redford won't talk about his dead son???" A smirk crossed his face as he continued, "Now, there's a puzzler!" Then, pretending to talk to Redford, he asked, "Hey Bob...how's that dead kid of yours?" Then he answered for Bob, "I don't want to talk about it." It was sarcastic humor at its best.

He tried jokes, all original, on anything that seemed odd or out of place: a unique perspective, layered with his professional speaking voice from his previous years in television and radio as an announcer and weatherman in Indianapolis.

In those early years, Letterman appeared a bit aloof and not at all overly friendly, but he did eventually cultivate deeper friendships with other fledgling comedians such as Tom Dreesen, Jeff Altman, and, most notably, George Miller. He and I socialized occasionally with sporadic tennis matches and late-night conversations concerning the state of comedy. I also offered David the fifty dollars a week for headlining but he wouldn't accept it. One evening a stray dog walked in the back door of my club and Letterman, feeling sorry for it, took it home and named it Bob. I believe he later tried to teach Bob to perform stupid pet tricks on his late night show.

When David moved on to The Comedy Store, Jimmy Walker hired him and Jay Leno to write jokes for his act, and the two became mutual admirers and good friends until the late-show debacle.

Unlike the majority of aspiring comics, David quickly gained recognition as a talent to be reckoned with. Most comics spend years sharpening their comedy skills before getting noticed, but it truly did seem like Letterman became an overnight success. In a relatively short period of time, he was appearing on *The Tonight Show*, and the powers that be were paying close attention to David's comedy style. Few doubted that he was going to make it big.

My relationship with Sandra Means did not last for very long. Though she was a gorgeous hunk of woman flesh, I slowly came to realize that she lacked intellect. At least enough to keep me interested. There was very little stimulating conversation between us, which eventually resulted in the end of our relationship. I was on my own again and, needing a break from my club, Freeman and I decided it was time for one of our occasional trips to Las Vegas for a little fun and gambling. Upon arriving, we headed directly to the tables where we lost all of our money in a relatively short period of time.

Officially broke, we decided we would make it a short trip and drive back to Los Angeles on the same day we arrived. As we drove past The Desert Inn hotel, we saw on its marquee, "Bobbie Gentry." who gained fame for a huge bestselling record "Ode to Billy Joe." We had met and worked with her on *The Sonny and Cher Show*, and she had always been extremely friendly, often telling us that if we ever saw her in Vegas to stop and say "Hi!" Appearing as her opening act was comedian John Byner, with whom Freeman and I had also become friends with, so we thought it might be fun to visit both of them before leaving.

We made our way to the hotel, only to discover that the show had just ended. As the crowd was filing out, Freeman and I went backstage where a security guard was stationed, and I informed him that we were friends of Bobbie's. We gave him our names and moments later, he returned, smiled, and motioned for us to proceed to her dressing room. When we knocked, Bobbie opened the door and immediately gave us both a giant hug. With all the success and wealth Bobbie had achieved, she was one of the most friendly, down-to-earth women I had ever met: always making you feel she had known you for years. She had no idea that I would have married her, and not just for her money. She also owned several beautiful classic cars.

Once inside, Bobbie asked if we'd like drinks, then had us follow her into an adjacent room, telling us she'd like to introduce us to another friend of hers who had dropped by to visit. My face dropped when we found ourselves face to face with none other than The KING... Elvis Presley. I couldn't believe my eyes, ears, nose, or throat, when lo and behold, Elvis extended his hand to us.

"Nice ta meet cha," Elvis drawled in his inimitable voice. I was awed by his striking good looks. His flawless features and coal black hair were dazzling, and as we shook hands, my brain kept reminding me over and over that I was actually shaking hands with Elvis Presley. Right then, I changed my mind about marrying Bobbie Gentry and would have married Elvis, and not just because he was rich but because he was Elvis. Even though I had seen Elvis on a movie set years before, I was now in a social situation with The King... and loving it.

Freeman and Elvis were both from Mississippi, so that topic ruled the conversation until at some point I mentioned that I owned a nightclub. When Elvis asked how it was doing, I told him not very well and suggested that if he would appear at my place, it would improve my business. I told him I was paying fifty dollars a week, but jokingly offered him twice that amount if he would accept my offer. Elvis chuckled, saying he had once worked for less than a hundred dollars a week as a truck driver. While he continued to talk, my brain kept saying, "You just offered Elvis Presley a job."

As we chatted, I tried my best to joke around and every time Elvis laughed, my brain continued to shout out to my inner self, "You just made Elvis Presley laugh." This entire chance meeting was so surreal. After about twenty minutes, Elvis drawled, "Why don't we all go over to my place and have a party?" His place was a personal suite atop the Hilton Hotel where Elvis was appearing.

Freeman and I exchanged glances and without hesitation said, "Yes". Bobbie called to have Elvis's limousine sent to the back, and we all took the service elevator down toward the rear of the hotel where we met Elvis's personal bodyguard and friend, "Red" West.

Upon entering Elvis's suite, I was immediately impressed with its size and grandeur. It was more of a majestic penthouse with several adjoining rooms and an expansive living room, overlooking the lavish lights of Vegas. We were greeted by several of Elvis's cronies, one of them Elvis's half-brother. It didn't take long to notice that drugs were a distinct part of Elvis's lifestyle. Within minutes, we were offered various types of drugs, most of which were in pill form on small platters. We politely refused, and within a few minutes, Elvis's girlfriend of the time, Linda Thompson entered, draped in turquoise jewelry. She was beautiful, and I kept thinking there must be a way I can take her away from him. I'm still thinking that.

Within minutes, there was a knock at the door and in entered comedian John Byner, along with his manager, Harry Colomby. Bobbie had called John, telling him to meet us, and more laughs ensued.

It was clearly obvious that Elvis enjoyed a macho atmosphere amongst his group of guys. At one point, he told his buddies to show us the new gold-plated handguns he had recently given them as gifts, and they happily complied, retrieving them from their jackets. I could see a look of uneasiness cross John and Harry's faces as Elvis had them demonstrate their use.

Sometime later, Elvis wanted to give a karate demonstration to showcase his expertise, developed from his years of martial arts training. It suddenly dawned on me that only weeks before, I had had breakfast at Du-Par's Restaurant in Los Angeles with Elvis's previous martial arts instructor, Mike Stone. He was the guy who Priscilla left Elvis for, and someone Elvis would like to have had one of his cronies use their gold-plated pistol on. Again, such a small show-biz world.

Elvis changed into his karate outfit and asked me if I would play his opponent so that he could show everyone some new moves he had recently learned. Without hesitation, I obliged, as the small group of about ten gathered in a circle to witness this eccentric presentation. Elvis then proceeded to pinpoint areas on my body where he said, if provoked, he could easily disable me with a few quick blows.

I couldn't help but think that Elvis would rarely, if ever, have to worry about being provoked into any kind of action with the army of buddies and bodyguards constantly at his side. Elvis continued, pointing out three vulnerable areas on my body which he would go for if I attacked him. They were the eyes, the neck, and the groin. When Elvis reached down and pretended to grab my groin explaining the damage he could do, I responded with, "Well, when you grab my groin, do I at least get dinner and a movie with it?" Elvis laughed hard and again my brain said, "You just made Elvis Presley laugh again."

As the morning hours approached, Elvis decided to sing a few songs, and he motioned for one of his cronies to get his guitar. When it was handed to him, Elvis sat on the floor and placed it on his lap. The rest of us followed suit, also sitting on the floor and gathering into a circle. Again, I couldn't help but think back to the time at Universal when I pretended to sweep floors as I sang alongside him, wishing I were a part of his group. And now I was part of his group, sitting right next to him as he began to strum and sing.

The first song he sang was "Are You Lonesome Tonight" and as he sang, "Do you miss me tonight...?" I felt he was not singing to Linda Thompson, but every word seemed to be meant for his ex-wife, Priscilla. I couldn't help but think Elvis was still in love with her. It was unreal, surreal, and for real sitting next to Elvis as he sang several of his hits. Again, my mind went back to when I was a kid, watching the King of Rock and Roll on the Ed Sullivan show, shocking the world with his sexual, innovative style. And here I was singing with him.

This incredible in-house concert closed with Elvis singing a couple of religious songs, and it ended at about five in the morning. Feeling it was time to go, Freeman and I hugged everyone, thanking Bobbie Gentry profusely. We heartily shook hands with all the guys, ending with Elvis, who couldn't have been nicer, urging us to stay another night and come to his show as guests. Because Freeman and I were penniless and neither of us had a credit card, we had to decline the invitation, which I have often since regretted.

Some months later, I was happy to hear that Bobbi Gentry married one of the alumni from my club, Jim Stafford. What a small world... but I still wouldn't want to see it by bus again.

Back at my club, I was running out of funds to keep it alive, when one day, out of the blue, in walked Redd Foxx who had become a hugely successful television star with his own show "Sanford and Son." He had heard that I owned a small club, prompting him to stop by to say hi. When he walked in and saw me behind the bar, he smiled, hugged me, then handed me a check, asking if I would cash it for him. It was a check for $20,000—his weekly salary at the time.

My business began to improve when word of mouth went around that Redd would occasionally perform at my club, leaving my small audiences in fits of laughter. Redd loved hanging out with the new, younger comics, but more than that, my small cubicle of an office became a nest for him to satisfy his cocaine use.

Redd would often attempt to get me to try cocaine, saying "Murray, you gotta try this shit. You'll go home and fuck your old lady all night long." When I told him I didn't have an old lady at home, he continued with, "It don't matter. You'll fuck the sink and it'll be just as good." Redd always thought funny.

Before long, Redd began teasing me, telling me he was thinking of investing in my club and becoming my partner. I could only imagine how successful my place would be if Redd put his name on my marquee. Unfortunately, he never did follow through, and after a few months he stopped showing up. The beginning of the end of my club was imminent. I was broke and there was no job in sight.

But wait. I got another call from my old boss Chris Bearde who again wanted me to go to Canada to be a regular on *The Bobby Vinton Show*. The show, created by Chris and produced by Chuck Barris, would have me working for two months. This time I left my club in the hands of my old spaghetti friend Joe Battaglia, who promised to make it a happening place by the time I returned.

On *The Bobby Vinton Show*, I got to work with: Ethel Merman, Ted Knight, Barbara Walters, The Spinners, Donna Summer, Petula Clark, Lainie Kazan, Foster Brooks, Anne Murray, Loretta Swit, Adrienne Barbeau, and one of my favorite funny ladies from *Laugh-In*, Ruth Buzzi.

In one comedy bit with Ruth, I played Tarzan and she played Jane. It was a funny sketch but on the jungle set, where I was placed atop a large fake tree, I slipped, falling several feet. Luckily, my head broke the fall. Actually, I was momentarily knocked unconscious and awoke to see Ruth staring me in the face asking if I was okay. She was genuinely concerned and we soon became great friends.

Bobby Vinton, though, seemed to have the personality of a doorstop. I'd met people in the business who were aloof, but he was the aloofest. He rarely socialized with anyone, preferring to stay hidden away in his hotel room when he was not on the set. One of the producers of the show was a Canadian comedy writer named Alan Thicke, who for some reason wasn't fond of me to the point where he tried to get me fired. Fortunately, Chris Bearde did not agree with him and kept me onboard.

Two months later, I returned to Los Angeles and my club was a disaster. Under pressure, Joe did not possess an amiable personality and alienated many of the regulars. Even though I had made money from *The Bobby Vinton Show*, it was not enough to pay all my bills, so I decided I was going to sell the club and at the same time investigate whether bankruptcy might be an option.

The Improv owned by Bud Friedman was the original comedy showcase club in New York, and he decided to open a branch in Los Angeles. I dropped by a few times to see if I could learn anything, and what I learned was that I was not the type of personality who should own a club.

Though Bud Friedman was liked by many, it was mainly because of who he was and not because of his generous personality. In fact, many thought Bud took advantage of comedians because, like Mitzi Shore, he also refused to share the monies made off the comics who worked his place for nothing.

I also noticed that to make a club a success, you don't give free food and drinks to everyone or put people on stage because you like them, even though they lack talent. You have to be true to your overall goal of making money, which ensures a club succeeding. In other words, you have to be a prick, and that just wasn't me.

Bud had not yet acquired a liquor license, and when he found out I was about to file for bankruptcy, he offered me a small percentage of the Improv if I would transfer my license to him. I thought it was a great idea and was about to put the wheels in motion, when a buyer suddenly appeared who purchased my club outright.

With the few dollars I made from the transaction, I was able to pay all my bills and escape bankruptcy, but to this day, I probably would have been better off had I accepted Bud's offer. Once again, I showed I had little business sense. Well, at least I had common sense... or did I? Well, at least by years end, I was out of the night-club business... and out of money...

Newspaper Ad for Show-Biz.

Me and John Byner.

Me performing at Show-Biz.

Mom and Jim Stafford.

My sister Annette and Joe Battaglia.

Mom and my sister Annette with Frankie Avalon at Show-Biz.

Me and girlfriend Sandy Means.

Mom with Kitty Bruce, daughter of legendary Lenny Bruce.

My mentor Redd Foxx at my club Show-Biz with Herb Eden and John Barbour.

1976

The year started off great with another job, this time from Chris Bearde's producing partner from *The Sonny and Cher Show*, Alan Blye. Chris and Alan split as a team, and Alan joined forces with writer Bob Einstein. Together they produced and directed four specials starring sexy singer/dancer Lola Falana who was red-hot, selling out in Las Vegas.

A side note: As far as I know, Lola Falana was one of only two singers who headlined in Las Vegas, packing showrooms without ever having had a hit record. Can you name the other?............. It was singer John Davidson.

On *The Lola Falana Show* I was again hired to act in sketches. These four specials were not going to make me rich but at least they helped me pay my mortgage. Lola was a classy lady and fun to work with, and this time I had the opportunity to work alongside Bill Cosby, Muhammad Ali, Dick Van Dyke, and once again, my buddy Redd Foxx.

My earnings from *The Lola Falana Show* didn't last long, and I was once again in need of financial assistance. With nothing on the horizon, I began showing up at The Comedy Store, where Mitzi used me mainly as an emcee. I would open the evening's festivities with a couple minutes of stand-up, and then spend the rest of the night introducing the various comics. It was a thankless job, but I wanted as much stage time as I could get to further my experience telling jokes in front of an audience.

One of the comics told me about a new show that he had just appeared on called *The Gong Show*. He said it was an amateur talent/ game show and you could win $500. He also mentioned that he didn't win, but because he was in the Union (AFTRA) they had to pay him $250 anyway.

I was in the union, and making $250 for a few minutes of my time appealed to me. However, my immediate concern was the embarrassment of being seen on an amateur talent show after having appeared on so many episodes of various television shows. I didn't want my friends and family to suspect I was broke, and I felt it would have been demeaning to take a chance and get "Gonged" but I was under pressure.

Thankfully, pressure can be a great source for creativity. I put my thinking cap on and came up with the idea of putting a bag over my head and calling myself The Unknown Comic. The plan was to make a couple of hundred bucks and not get recognized by anyone who knew me.

Chuck Barris, who produced *The Gong Show*, also created *The Dating Game*, which I had appeared on several times. I had befriended the talent coordinator of *The Dating Game*, Ruth Goldberg, who also booked the talent on *The Gong Show*.

I watched a few episodes of *The Gong Show* then called Ruth, telling her about my idea of appearing with a bag over my head and calling myself The Unknown Comic. She liked it, then suggested that instead of appearing as a contestant and being subjected to getting "gonged," she offered an alternative way to earn the union fee. Chuck Barris had developed a part of the show which he referred to as "Curtain Closers." An act would be introduced and they would do something offensive or totally ridiculous which would cause Chuck to quickly close the curtain on them.

Since my single objective was to earn the $250 union fee, it sounded like a great idea. We talked it over and came to the conclusion that I would tell a couple of corny jokes, and then insult Chuck Barris, giving him a reason to close the curtain on me.

On the day of taping, I met with Ruth and the host Chuck Barris, who was already aware that he would introduce me as The Unknown Comic. I explained to him, that once introduced, I would tell a couple of bad one-liners, then ask him a question, and Chuck's response should be "No." He had no idea what the joke was going to be and didn't seem to particularly care.

The moment of my appearance arrived, and I was ushered

behind the closed curtain. The band was loudly blasting music when Chuck began. "We have a new act coming out who some people say is great. Unfortunately, those people are his mom and dad. His jokes are so bad; he wears a bag over his head.... Welcome..." Chuck then clapped his hands and slowly, but methodically, screamed out... "The Unnnnknownnnn Comic."

I rushed out, cigarette dangling from my fingers, looking every bit a hack comic with my pants too short and my jacket too tight, then delivered a series of one-liners, eliciting groans from the audience. I was really not sure where it was going, but all that really mattered was that I was going to make $250. Then I turned to the host and said, "Hey Chuckie baby... Do you and your wife ever make love in the shower?" Chuck's planned response was a quick "No." Then I hammered back, "Well, you should... She Loves It." The audience's response was quick and immediate; they howled with laughter as Chuck reacted to my insult by shoving me offstage and closing the curtain.

A soon as the show finished taping; Chuck came over and said, "That was great. Can you come back tomorrow and insult me again?" "Y... yes... sure" I stuttered, thinking how I had only planned on doing one show, but returning and earning another $250 was fine with me.

Sure enough, I showed up with another couple of bad one-liners followed by another insult. "Hey Chuckie, you have a very striking face." Chuck responded with "Thank you," and I quickly replied, "How many times have you been struck there?" Again a great response from the audience as Chuck shoved me through the curtain.

Chuck then took me aside and asked if I could do the show a couple of times a week, to which I of course responded with a resounding "Yes." That would be $500 a week—enough to pay my bills, plus there would be residuals when the shows were repeated. I soon realized that Chuck liked me insulting him because it gave him vulnerability that he felt he needed, since most of the time, he was slinging insults at the acts he was introducing.

Life was good again. I was making money on *The Gong Show* and still working on developing my single act. At the Comedy Store, Mitzi was still using me to emcee the shows, but that all came to an end when one night on my way to work (for no pay), I was stopped by a cop for a burned-out taillight. When the cop called in my plate, it came back that I had delinquent parking tickets with penalties totaling $300. He took me to jail, where I was told I would spend the night unless I could come up with the money. My immediate reaction was to phone The Comedy Store, knowing they must have cash on hand.

I called and was connected with the girl who worked in the Comedy Store office. I explained what happened and would she please ask Mitzi to loan me $300. I could hear Mitzi's voice in the background as she was told of my circumstances. Seconds later, the girl returned to the phone and told me Mitzi couldn't help because all of her cash was already locked in the safe. It was bullshit and I knew it, as my brain tried to grasp what had just occurred. I knew that Mitzi *must* have the combination but I hung up, knowing that the rumors I had heard about Mitzi being a "bitch" were not only true but, in my mind, she had been promoted to a "cunt."

My other option was to call Theodore's, where over the years I had cultivated friendships with the waiters and waitresses. When I informed them of my plight, without hesitation they all pooled their tips and bailed me out. I, of course, paid them back the following day, but not without profusely thanking them and forever after leaving them larger tips. Needless to say, I vowed to never again work at The Comedy Store knowing Mitzi was no friend of the comics, even if she was having sex with them.

I continued performing on *The Gong Show* on a regular basis, working hard at developing material and insults to throw at Chuck. Chuck was so impressed with my ability to come up with new bits that he asked if I'd like to be a writer on the show, supplying him with insults for his introductions of the acts.

I accepted and was given an office, with a time to come in and a time to leave. I worked alongside Larry Spencer, a nice guy, but after a few weeks, I decided I did not enjoy the confines of being stuck in an office and preferred being out amongst my buddies in the comedy trenches.

Chuck had no problem accepting my resignation, appreciating my continued bits as The Unknown Comic on *The Gong Show*. On one episode, I came out with a white bag over my head as The Unknown Preacher and asked if anyone in the audience needed healing. An audience member stood up—a friend—yelling out that he couldn't see. The camera cut to him and the audience saw he had a bag on his head, but without eyeholes. He was guided to the stage where I placed my hands over his head/bag and screamed out... "HEAL... HEAL..." then we both sang out... "The gangs all here, what the heck do we care...etc." I then grabbed the front of the bag with my hands and ripped it apart, exposing his face. He then shouted... "I Can SEE... I Can SEE"... as he walked back to his seat. Chuck and the audience loved it.

Another bit was when I brought my dog onto the set with a bag placed over his entire body except for his legs. As The Unknown Comic, I shouted, "This is my Dog. He's not a Boxer... He's a Bagger.... I was going to name him Chooser.... but baggers can't be choosers." Another time, my cat was placed inside in a bag... and I literally "let the cat out of the bag". It was silly, mostly juvenile, but the audiences loved it and I was making money.

Another job came my way when I received a call from Riff Markowitz, a Canadian producer who wanted to hire me as a sketch actor for another variety series starring the wonderfully eccentric Wolfman Jack. *The Wolfman Jack Show* was to be taped in Vancouver, Canada, and I would be needed for a month to work on twenty episodes.

Luckily, *The Gong Show* was going on a break at about the same time, so I'd only miss two weeks on that show, so off I went. Wolfman Jack was a total sweetheart, and one of the nicest guys I have ever met in show business. He also loved marijuana and did not hide the fact that he was a user.

It's always interesting to see the differences in celebrity personalities. Wolfman was a kind, sociable, generous human being who felt for anyone who was less fortunate that he was. He was very recognizable, and when walking through the streets of Vancouver, as we often did, many a homeless person would approach him and he would always hand them money. You could tell he enjoyed his celebrity status, and he reveled in its benefits without ever appearing like he was better than anyone else.

For me, it was blissful working with some of the world's greatest musical acts on *The Wolfman Jack Show*: Abba; Blood, Sweat & Tears; David Cassidy; Johnny Mathis; Jose Feliciano; B.J. Thomas;

Tom Jones; Wayne Newton; Del Shannon; Bobby Rydell; The Shirelles; Gary "U.S." Bonds; The 5th Dimension; Lou Rawls; Ray Stevens; Chubby Checker; Little Richard; Fabian; The Pointer Sisters; Freddy Cannon; Little Anthony & The Imperials; Bo Diddley; Manhattan Transfer; and Kenny Rogers just to name a bunch.

When I returned to Los Angeles, I immediately went back to performing my Unknown Comic antics on *The Gong Show*. At the same time, I worked out at clubs in an effort to improve my act, which had now grown to a solid twenty minutes of funny stuff. I occasionally performed at The Improv but preferred the newer breed of clubs in and around Los Angeles. The Laff Stop in Newport Beach, where I first opened for Robin Williams, paid their acts and included food and drinks, so I would make the hour drive to work there on a regular basis.

By now, I had more than thirty appearances on *The Gong Show*, and because I was slowly gaining recognition, I began to open my act with a couple of minutes with the bag on. I asked the emcees to introduce me as The Unknown Comic, slowly building that portion of my act up to four minutes, then five minutes.

The Unknown Comic worked great on *The Gong Show* in short two- to three-minute spurts, but in clubs I realized that the bag over my head was a gimmick, and the audience would only accept it for a short time. Until The Unknown Comic, I never noticed how much a comic relies on facial expressions to push over a joke, and with a bag on my head, I didn't have that luxury. I think that unconsciously I sensed this from the beginning, which is why I used my body in an almost manic way, jumping up and down, in an attempt to assist the joke I was delivering to get a laugh.

Life got better when I received a call from Barbi Benton, the then girlfriend of Playboy's Hugh Hefner. She told me that she saw me perform in a club and desperately wanted to have sex with me. Okay, that didn't happen. What she really said was that she had heard through a mutual friend that I wrote jokes, and she asked if I would consider writing a nightclub act for her, adding that she could pay me handsomely, though that was seldom how I ever got paid.

We met and worked together for several weeks, creating an act for her appearances in various Playboy Clubs, which were a guarantee since her boyfriend Hef owned them. Barbi was cute, sweet, and not the least bit pretentious. She came to my place a few times, but mostly we worked at the Playboy Mansion in Beverly Hills where I would dine with Hef and many of his guests. On one of our breaks, I played tennis with Bill Cosby, who by the way, was the opposite of Barbi when it came to being pretentious. Still, I consider Cosby to be one of the living comedic geniuses of our time. My favorite part of the Mansion was the Jacuzzi, designed like a large underground cave where Playmates would cavort in the nude. The stress of writing jokes for Barbi forced me to spend many hours lounging in that area. Writing for Barbi was a tough job but somebody had to do it, and I was grateful that somebody was me.

Toward the end of the year, after more than fifty appearances on *The Gong Show*, I was beginning to realize I had a character I might be able to capitalize on. I actively began seeking out other television programs, and suddenly I was appearing as The Unknown Comic on several talk shows of that era: Merv Griffin, Dinah Shore, Mike Douglas, and John Davidson. Subsequently, there developed a widespread curiosity as to who The Unknown Comic really was. Many people thought it might be Steve Martin or Bill Murray playing a prank on the public.

Then I received a career-changing call from a man named Jack Eglash. Thank God I paid my phone bill. He was the talent booker for the Sahara Hotel in Las Vegas, and he asked if I'd be interested in working in their lounge for a two-week gig. The Sahara was where all the comedy greats like Johnny Carson, Don Rickles, Bob Newhart, and Jerry Lewis headlined. I couldn't believe it, especially when he offered me $5,000. I had never come close to earning that kind of money for two weeks work. When I repeated incredulously, $5,000 for two weeks, he corrected me, saying the $5,000 was not for two weeks, but *per* week. Holy Shit! "YES" was my immediate response.

What I wasn't prepared for was Jack informing me that they needed a one-hour show twice a night. I didn't tell him that I had perhaps thirty minutes of material, but that certainly wasn't going to stop me from accepting the job. I simply needed to figure a way to extend my thirty minutes to an hour. I knew that somehow I was going to have to make sure my opening night in Las Vegas would be BIG.

At my club, I had used a young piano player named Steve Thoma—a talented, spunky guy—and I called him, saying I needed to put a three-piece band together to add music to my show in Vegas. I figured music could fill a portion of the hour. My plan was to have them also wear bags on their heads and call them The Brown Baggers.

Steve wrote a clever opening song, which went:

Show me a comic with a face that's unknown... and I'll show you a brown paper bag.

He may be handsome and then maybe he's not. You see it's all just a part of the gag.

He's got a million jokes from A-Z... guaranteed to keep you in hilarity.

He's original, sensational. He's one of a kind. He's The Unknown Comic...TooooNight.

The melody was infectious and I was sure it would work perfectly. Next, I hired two girls to dance and sing the opening song before introducing me. They would be called "The Baggettes." I wanted my show to kick ass.

Ted Zeigler, my coworker from *The Sonny and Cher Show* who I now considered one of my best friends, suggested he become my manager. Up to that point, I had never given the idea of being managed any thought. Ted proposed that we try it for a few months, and if I didn't feel it was working out, he would understand. I trusted and respected Ted wholeheartedly, and so I agreed.

A few days before my opening night we—me along with my crew of three band members, two dancers, and Ted—made our way to Las Vegas. I obtained rooms for everyone at my expense, but I was pleasantly surprised when, upon my arrival, I was given a massive suite with a bar stocked with liquor, all paid for by the Hotel. My dressing room in back of the lounge was also stocked with liquor, and I felt I was being treated like a headliner rather than a lounge act. In my mind I was a gimmick, and my act was to comedy like Tiny Tim's act was to music. But I was I grateful.

Stand-up was never what I had originally intended for myself, so I was extremely apprehensive about whether I could pull off entertaining an audience for an hour. I decided the first half of my act would revolve around The Unknown Comic, using my band and two dancers as filler. In the second half, I would remove the bag from my head and perform the remaining thirty minutes as myself.

On opening night, needless to say, my insides were churning, wondering if I would succeed or bomb so badly that I would be fired after one show. I feared that I might relive my opening night at Georgie Jessel's club.

It was twenty minutes before show time when I left my room after rehearsing all day. I was trembling as I approached the lounge, and I was surprised to see a line of people that stretched out through the casino and around the blackjack tables, waiting to get in to see me. My first show was going to be a sell out! I was thrilled and at the same time nauseous from the heightened anxiety I felt in my bones and other places. This was going to be "do or die," the beginning of a new career... or the End of one.

Then it was show time. The band and girls, all with bags over their heads, were flawless in their musical introduction of The Unknown Comic. When I charged onto the stage, the audience went crazy, which catapulted my energy to places I'd never experienced before. They screamed at my one-liners, laughed at my silly magic tricks, and applauded the bag impressions I had created. I introduced my grandfather in the audience, and Ted, with a wrinkled bag over his head stood, causing the audience to explode with more laughter.

One of my dancers, now bagless and in the audience, pretended she was an ex-girlfriend of The Unknown Comic and rushed to the stage yelling that I was the father of her baby. When I responded, "You can't prove that," she replied "Oh yeah?" then held up a baby (doll) with a bag over its head. More laughter.

Twenty minutes into the act, the audience was shocked when, without warning, I ripped the bag off my head. This turned out to be a treat for them, having no idea what I looked like. I said "Thank you," took a bow, and promised to be back in a few minutes, then exited the stage to thunderous applause as my band played me off with a song.

Backstage, as my band continued to eat up time playing another song, I quickly changed from The Unknown Comic outfit into regular clothes. When the second song was over, I was reintroduced as Murray Langston, rushed out, and performed the second half of my show. Though lacking the initial excitement, I was still pleased that the audience was with me all the way, laughing at the rest of my act minus the bag. Opening night was a smash success and the reviews were terrific.

At the end of my two week run, Jack Eglash offered me a long-term contract, guaranteeing me twenty weeks with the Sahara Hotels in Las Vegas, Reno, and Lake Tahoe. This was, as they say, Life Changing. I was getting paid to make people laugh, which in my mind officially made me a stand-up comic. Clubs like The Comedy Store and The Improv did not pay the comics, considering their venues to be colleges for comedians. As far as I was concerned, I had now graduated comedy college, and with little help from their pseudo schools for comedians.

One statistic, which has always fascinated me, was that back then, I was one of less than one hundred comics existing in the entire country who were getting paid to make people laugh: from the top comics like Don Rickles, Bill Cosby, Buddy Hackett, and Redd Foxx to the new group who were on the upswing like David Brenner, Cheech and Chong and Freddy Prinze. I was now a part of *that* small, select group. Unfuckingbelievable.

Me and "Chuckie baby" on *The Gong Show*.

A group shot of my band, the Brownbaggers, and my dancers, the Baggettes.

BAG-MAN K.O.'S VEGAS, UNKNOWN COMIC WOW'

Mon., July 24, 1978 COMEDY STORE
NITERY REVIEW

The Unknown Comic;
(Comedy Store Mainroom;)

After brown-bagging it for a couple of years now (and over 100 "Gong Show" stints), the Unknown Comic is finally exceeding his monicker. As the vociferous audiences at the Comedy Store Mainroom demonstrated, he's very well known, at least in his papered alter ego, and very well liked.

The name Murray Langston may not strike the same chord of familiarity, but it's the persona that's now emerging from underneath the sack. In last week's four-night stand, he did only a brief turn as the Unknown Comic, and the rest of a 70-minute set as himself.

Wisdom of this unveiling is vouchsafed by the continual laughs Langston is able to evoke even without the bag jokes. The style remains the same: rapid-fire oneliners, cornball humor, horrendous puns and blatant sight gags, all sprayed across the house like verbal machine-gun fire.

Langston is in some ways the '70s heir to Henny Youngman's comedy approach: squeeze in so many jokes that the clunkers sink rapidly away, while the audience is still convulsed over the previous zinger. It works because, for the most part, the material is fresh, zany and original.

Trimming down of the baggy jokes takes away some of Langston's unique appeal (such, as a doggy bag impression), but addition of the Bagettes, two femme dancer-singers (Sunni Welles and Randi Meryl) and the Brown Baggers (drummer Larry Vineyard, organist/musical director Steve Thoma) makes for a more well-rounded set.

★★★★★★★★★★

Langston is especially adroit at audience manipulation, an easier task since attendees seem to be ardent camp followers. X-rated material abounds, always with a subtle twist that takes off the rough edge. Props are also well utilized, such as a blue blanket that becomes a sea for a Mark Spitz impresh. Langston is also one of the few comics able to use double-talk patter and make it work.

So while the bag gags may be missed, Langston is clearly headed for bigger and better things. That may disappoint his diehard fans, but it should also open him up for a new, non-"Gong Show" oriented crowd.
—— *Poll.*

LAS VEGAS

Monday, February 6, 1978

VARIETY

NEW ACT REVIEW

The Unknown Comic
(Comedy; 55 min.)

Las Vegas, Feb. 5 — Whether direct or indirect from video's "The Gong Show" as hyped, the Unknown Comic (Murray Langston) moves into another medium with the same absurd artfulness which could well introduce a cult following.

Langston is great in the Sahara Casbar with a slew of brown-baggers carrying signs and responding to Langston's giggling ripostes with similar burbles. But there is careful thought behind the foolishness and an act put together with attention to detail.

Two hyperactive girls called Bagettes sing and romp through some fast contempo body action and steps backed by organ and drum duo (Brown Baggies).

The act moves fast and is integrated well, but the attention is upon Langston and his torrent of puns, cornball jokes, impressions, hoke puppetry using "Sad Sack" and other extensions of the brown-bag theme.

Without the sack over his head, Langston comes on even stronger as a comic character with a fine communications knack, playing off-color when punches are required for extra visceral sock. He is young, looks at ease and, what is very important, gives out vibes of thoroughly enjoying his word noodles, zany zigs and zags and bizarre bagged role. *Will.*

→ SAYS--- HE'S A HIT !

My act is reviewed in *Variety*.

1977

I decided I needed to spend more time with Alan Cook, who was now sixteen. He had been moved into an old age home because mental institutions were being phased out, and I felt I had to do something more for him. Most of his time was spent sitting in his room and listening to the cries and complaints of the aging residents.

I set up a guest area in my house and moved him in with me. Alan had befriended my comic buddy Tom Dreesen's son Tommy, and they began spending time together. I even purchased a motor scooter for Alan and taught him how to ride it, which enabled him to drive to local stores and shops. I was determined to teach him how to take care of himself.

I was now a Las Vegas performer earning the unbelievable sum of $5,000 a week, but not really. After deducting the salaries and costs of hotel rooms for my band members and dancers, I personally was only earning a few hundred dollars a week. But that was fine with me because I figured it was an investment that would benefit me in the future.

One amazing benefit which I did receive from the Sahara Hotel was known as "Power of the Pen," which was usually only given to headliners and wealthy gamblers. It meant you didn't have to pay for anything the Hotel had to offer, from limousines and room service to meals at any of the restaurants located on the premises. All you did was sign for it.

Because I was gifted with this "Power of the Pen," I would frequently have parties in my suite, ordering booze and the best food, with the tab often reaching $1,000 or more. I simply signed for it and would never get charged. I loved it. It really made you feel important.

Also important was my friend Ted Zeigler, who had been acting as my manager. He introduced me to John Mucci, an accountant who formed The Unknown Corporation, to ensure everyone was paid properly, including my taxes to the government. To handle any contracts, he hooked me up with one of his friends, an entertainment lawyer named Tom Rowan, the son of Dan Rowan from television's *Laugh-In*. He also suggested that perhaps Tom could draw up a contract for Ted to officially become my manager.

Unfortunately, introducing me to Tom Rowan turned out to be a mistake for Ted. One day Tom called me into his office and told me that though he considered Ted one of the nicest guys he knew he doubted his abilities as a manager. He then suggested I sign up with a well-known management team of Milt Suchin and Danny Moss, who had on their list of client's comedians Rip Taylor and Phyllis Diller. Because of his alleged friendship with Ted, he suggested that I not mention any of this conversation to him.

I felt that telling Ted I no longer wanted him as my manager would break his heart, but Tom convinced me it would be the best for my burgeoning career. When I informed Ted of my plans, he gracefully acknowledged that this management team might be better suited for me, but months later I discovered that he was extremely hurt by my decision. If he only knew it came from someone he considered a friend. That was my first taste of the backstabbing that goes on in Hollywood. There would be more.

I suggested that, like Ted and I had done, the management team should also proceed with a trial period before I signed with them, and they reluctantly agreed. The first show they asked me to appear on was a Canadian variety show starring a young singing sensation Rene Simard. I was being offered $1,000, which I would have gladly accepted until I discovered that it was being produced by Alan Thicke, who tried to have me fired from *The Bobby Vinton Show*.

I asked my managers to find out what their top fee was, and when they told me $5,000 I demanded that I be paid that amount. My managers were quick to inform me that amount was for major guest stars, not upcoming comics. I stood my ground, telling them to inform Mr. Thicke I would only perform for $5,000, fairly confident they would turn me down; and they did, but I still felt a feeling which felt really good. One good turn deserves another. Or is it one good turn gets most of the covers? Whatever!

I was still earning nice paychecks appearing on the *Gong Show*, having performed on well over a hundred episodes thus far, and I was getting more guest spots on various talk shows appearing frequently on *The Merv Griffin Show*. I was even flown to Philadelphia where *The Mike Douglas Show* was taped, and after one of my appearances, a young guy introduced himself to me as an aspiring comic. He was a nerdy, gangly-looking guy and asked for my advice on getting into comedy. His name was Bob Saget and my advice was to try telling jokes with a box over his head and move to Los Angeles. He took my advice; not the box over his head, but the moving to L.A. part.

I also travelled again to Vancouver, where I was invited to perform on a Canadian talk show hosted by Alan Hamel. Also guesting was Paul Williams, whom I'd previously met on the Midnight Special, plus he was a Judge on the *Gong Show*. Prior to taping, Paul and I were having lunch in the cafeteria, watching television, when suddenly we heard breaking news that Freddy Prinze was dead of a gunshot wound to the head. I was shocked, but Paul was visibly upset telling me that over the last couple of years, he had become close friends with Freddy. Paul immediately rushed back to Los Angeles where he was one of Freddy's pallbearers. Freddy was only twenty-two years old.

Another of Freddy's best friends was a young comic named Alan Bursky, who was not liked by many because of his abrasive personality. Shortly after Freddy's death, he joked, "Freddy's comedy album had just become number one... with a bullet." According to Alan, Freddy's suicide was a result of drug use and jealousy over the success of another teen idol who replaced him on the covers of most of the teen magazines. Coincidentally, they worked next to each other at NBC. He was the star of the new series *Welcome Back Kotter*: John Travolta.

I have a theory that those who become too successful too young, especially during their teen years, do not adapt well to fame. I believe their brains have not matured enough to understand that their success is largely due to LUCK. Instead, they begin to believe that they are larger than life and because they're special, they deserve all the accolades that are showered upon them by their fans. The result is an ego, which grows out of proportion. Others, who I believe fit to some degree in the same category, were Elvis, Cher, Jerry Lewis, and Whitney Houston, who all became famous while in their teens.

On the contrary, those who become famous later in life *are* usually aware that their fame is largely a result of being in the right place, at the right time, with the right look, and the right talent. In other words, "Lucky." However, "being in the right porn film" can also lead to fame. Can you say, "Kardashian?"

Though some are lucky becoming famous, others become unlucky *because* they're famous. I was sitting in Schwab's, when a waitress rushed in telling everyone she'd just heard that Elvis died at the age of forty-two—the same age his mother died. He apparently suffered a heart attack while engaging in a bowel movement, the stress on his deteriorating drug infested body finally ending his life. When you die at forty-two, that's unlucky. Once again, I regretted that I did not accept his invitation to see his show, and like most of my generation, Elvis's death brought home to us all the fact that life is short, and even shorter if you're unlucky enough to become a drug addict.

In other news, a new buddy of mine, Scoey Mitchell—a talented black comic—landed his own late-night talk/variety show called *90 Tonight*. He asked Freeman and I if we would reunite and be guests on his show. Appearing with us was pop singer Tony Orlando, with whom we struck up a nice friendship which lasted many, many weeks.

On that same show, I met a young attractive blonde who was promoting a book of love poems she had written. Finding her sexy, I flirted with her, but that came to an abrupt end when she told me she had a Canadian boyfriend named Alan Hamel: the same Alan Hamel on whose talk show I had recently guested. Her name was Suzanne Sommers and we struck up a nice friendship which lasted many, many hours.

One friendship that lasted longer than a few hours was with an attractive new young comedienne named Melanie Chartoff. I saw her perform, liked her a lot, and helped her get her first paying nightclub gig resulting in our dating for a short time. She was talented, and it didn't take long before she became a regular on a new series which was designed to compete against *Saturday Night Live* called *Fridays*. Because of her, I landed a guest spot on one of the episodes hosted by Valerie Bertinelli, and she introduced me to her hubby, Eddie Van Halen. They were a strikingly beautiful couple and made me realize that I had never been part of a strikingly beautiful couple.

One night, Ted, Freeman, and I were having lunch in a restaurant when we noticed the strikingly beautiful Burt Reynolds, seated in a booth chatting with friends. Though Burt appeared with us a few years earlier on *The Sonny and Cher Show*—and as much as we wanted to say hi—we decided we wouldn't bother him because we doubted he would remember us. Especially since his naked centerfold in *Cosmopolitan* magazine shot his penis and his career through the roof. To our surprise, as Burt prepared to leave, he suddenly strolled over to our table and said, "Hey, are you guys too stuck up to say hello?" We shared a few laughs about the good times he had working with us, and when he left, we looked at each other and agreed, "What a hell of a nice guy!"

I continued performing in the lounges at the Sahara Hotels, fulfilling my contract, and I was slowly developing as a stand-up. However, I was still insecure about my abilities. I knew I had the energy, which I used to the utmost, but felt limited when it came to writing great jokes. Much of my material was derived from simply having fun wherever I went. If I made someone laugh by ad-libbing something, be it a waitress or a friend, I would put it into my act that night. Like most comics, you discover certain jokes which kill almost every night, suddenly lose their impact because of their age or it was related to an issue which did not remain relevant. Eventually, I began buying jokes from writers who would submit them to me.

I'll never forget the day my dad called and told me he came up with the perfect joke for The Unknown Comic. He then proceeded to tell me I should tell the audience, "I have a joke that's going to blow your mind." And then, in front of their eyes, have the bag explode. When I asked how I was going to have the bag explode without hurting myself, his reply was, "Hey I just write the jokes. It's up to you to figure out how to use them." Gotta love my dad.

As a stand-up, I was definitely getting better, and my initial twenty minutes of material began to approach forty, then fifty minutes. I began to think that, one day, I might actually be able to perform without my dancers or band and actually make money.

One of the weeks I worked in the lounge, I found out that Jerry Lewis was also scheduled to perform in the Main Room. I was flabbergasted, to say the least—to say the most would take longer.

On opening night, prior to going on stage for my late show, the maître d' informed me that Jerry Lewis had reserved a booth to watch me perform. I was petrified and elated at the same time. Elated that this legend in my life, who was responsible for the world I was now living in, would actually see me perform. On the other hand, I was terrified that I might have an audience that sucked, which happened every once in a while. This would always send me into a state of depression. Please, I pleaded to whatever was in heaven or hell or even purgatory, "Don't let this be one of those nights."

As my show began with the band playing, I peered through the curtain looking at the reserved booth, which was empty, causing me to wonder if Jerry was going to show up in the middle of my show, near the end... or not at all.

Once introduced, I rushed on stage, and in between the onslaught of one-liners, I kept looking at that empty booth through the holes in my bag. I was only on a few minutes when I saw Jerry Lewis and his entourage being escorted to the waiting booth.

Upon seeing him, something in me sparked, my energy soared, and I worked feverishly in an effort to impress him with my comedic abilities. I sweated and joked and pulled every comedy trick I could think of out of my bag of material. And it worked. At the end of my show, I was awarded with a standing ovation by an audience who for that hour loved me.

I was now excited to acknowledge the presence of Jerry Lewis, giving him a flowery and appreciative introduction, prompting the audience to also stand and applaud him. Trying to think of some comedic way to end on a high note, I asked him, "Do you mind taking a picture?" Jerry screamed back in his inimitable voice, "A Picture? Of course not."

I kept a flash camera on the piano for a bit I did where I would tell the audience I loved them and wanted to take their pictures so I could take them to bed later and have an orgy with them. I would run through the crowd picking people I liked and take their picture, telling each how they were to participate in my imaginary orgy.

So, when Jerry said he wouldn't mind a picture, I yelled to my piano player Steve to bring the camera to me. He rushed over, gave it to me and I quickly handed the camera to Jerry. I then placed my arm around my piano player's shoulder and prepared for Jerry to take our picture.

It only took a second for Jerry and the audience to realize what I was doing. Jerry took our picture, the camera flashed and everyone exploded into laughter. I returned to the stage to bid all a farewell, and after the show, Jerry and his entourage came to my dressing room where he showered me with compliments, giving me supportive advice on how I could improve my act. It was a *great* evening.

Back in Los Angeles, I met a talented comedienne and writer, Merrill Markoe, who on occasion would come to my home where we talked about comedy. She was interesting and very intelligent, which in those days scared me. I was not used to being around really smart and articulate women, which is why, I suppose, David Letterman began spending a lot of time with her. David's career was really blossoming with appearances on the *Mary Tyler Moore Variety Show* and even as a judge on *The Gong Show*. But his appearances on *The Tonight Show with Johnny Carson*, who loved David's acerbic act, gained him recognition with top television executives.

To most of us, it was just a matter of time before Merrill would become involved with Letterman, and shortly after his divorce, which was already imminent, they moved in together. It was obvious David respected her abilities as a writer, using her to hone his own act. She later became one of the driving forces behind Letterman's early television shows, garnering her an Emmy.

At my house, I had a pool table where another comic, Jay Leno, would stop by and shoot a few games with his then live-in lover Adele Blue, an aspiring singer. Jay, always a nice guy, practically lived at The Improv when he wasn't on the road perfecting his act. One time, when I was booked in Hawaii, I suggested he should try to get a gig there, and he replied that he was not interested in palm trees and sand. He loved bricks. Like Robin Williams, it was obvious that Jay worked harder at his craft than most other comics.

It was on this same pool table that I began dating actress Jackie Giroux, who had starred in a film with Pat Boone and Erik Estrada called *The Cross and the Switchblade*. Jackie was also a professional photographer, and one day I came up with the idea to mimic Burt Reynolds's naked centerfold. Jackie shot a similar pose of me: naked on the pool table with a bag over my head and a very long bag used for wine bottles strategically placed over my groin suggesting a rather lengthy penis. If truth be known, I had to fold my penis in half for it to fit into that bag.

The Naked Poster became a hit, and was one of the nation's top sellers along with a poster of Debby Boone, who had a smash hit record that year with "You Light up my Life." Unfortunately, both Debby and I were robbed of any monies from those sales, as the poster company filed for bankruptcy when it was time to pay up. Naturally, they later reopened a similar company using a different name. We both knew the cost of lawyer's fees to go after them would far exceed any monies we might get, but I still enjoyed walking by various shops on Hollywood Boulevard and seeing my naked poster displayed in their windows.

It seemed like work for me was always just around the corner, when my old mentor Redd Foxx gave me a call, wanting me to guest on his new variety show, cleverly called *The Redd Foxx Comedy Hour*. I performed on several episodes as The Unknown Comic, working alongside the extremely loveable Billy Barty and another favorite, Billy Saluga—also known as Raymond J, "But ya' doesn't hasta to call me" Johnson.

When I wasn't working, I would take my band and whomever I was dating, and head to Maui where we would have a blast. I paid most of the expenses and it soon became an annual event. I was never really cognizant of the money I was earning. My managers were taking care of my finances along with my new business manager, and I was getting the feeling that money would no longer be as much of a problem as it had been for most of my life.

For me, a defining moment indicating I had achieved some measure of financial success occurred when I realized I no longer had to look at the "Price" side of a menu. All my life, whenever I ordered in restaurants, I would always look at the side of the menu which listed the cost first, concerned about what I could afford. Though my goals then and now were never to become extremely wealthy, for the first time in my life, I was beginning to think that money would no longer be a major problem for me.

However, on the home front, problems were arising with Alan Cook, when I discovered he and one of his friends were involved in the theft of a bicycle. I soon realized that Alan couldn't be left alone when I was on the road. I was also having problems with him becoming sexually mature, finding pornographic magazines and material in his room. My desire to help Alan have a better life was worsened by the fact that I wasn't always there to help him develop a better life. I became worried that Alan would get into serious trouble if I didn't find professional help soon. I spoke with the managers of the old age home he had previously lived at and worked out a deal whereby Alan would be given a paid job, working as a handyman. This gave him a feeling of importance, and our relationship remained constant, with Alan frequently driving to my house on his scooter to hang out.

My best friend and manager Ted Zeigler with my sister Annette.

Me and Alan Cook.

Me and Melanie Chatoff.

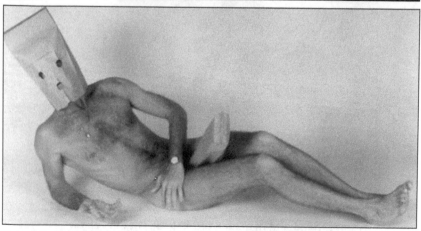

Naked Picture of The Unknown Comic.

1978

I was at Theodore's restaurant when another comic friend, Roger Behr, entered with a beautiful young eighteen-year-old girl named Jeri, and I couldn't take my eyes off her. She was gorgeous but way too young. I was thirty-four, but that didn't stop me. The next thing I knew, she was living with me, which was a huge mistake and deep down I knew it. Several months later, she left me with a broken heart. Not sure if that was my third or fourth broken heart, but it was worth it while it lasted.

About this time, I heard about a new comedy venue opening in Hermosa Beach called The Comedy & Magic Club, owned by Mike Lacey. I began performing there regularly, packing the place, as my Unknown Comic character continued to gain more fame and recognition. Because I was earning money on a regular basis, I sold my home in Studio City, which I had lived in for four years, and moved upward, buying a brand new house in an area above Hollywood called Mount Olympus.

I was still making *Gong Show* appearances—now totaling about 150—when I ran into David Letterman, who was booked to be one of the judges. David was making big money from a long-term network deal he had signed, and he had just purchased a small house in Malibu, where homes were very expensive. By then, David was fully entrenched in his relationship with Merrill Markoe, and during our conversation he told me that if I was ever in the Malibu area to stop by and see his new home.

Weeks later, I was at the beach and decided to pay them a visit, so I called and Dave gave me directions. His house was one of the lower-priced homes in the celebrity studded neighborhood and only blocks from his idol Johnny Carson's hidden estate.

Dave and Merrill had been living in his new home for many months, so I was taken aback when I walked in seeing virtually no furniture, except for a few odds and ends and a mattress to sleep on. We sat on a few pillows scattered around the living room and engaged in some light chitchat, mostly about how they hadn't had time to look for furnishings because of their heavy schedule preparing for David's new morning television show. Before I left, David invited me to be on *The Tonight Show* with him on a future date when he guest hosted for Carson.

True to his word, I appeared on the show and my set was well received, especially the subsequent banter when Dave and I kidded with each other. At first, I was upset when David didn't ask any of the prepared questions, instead preferring to ad-lib, which sort of threw me. But when I later looked at the tape, I realized that David's genius was in his ability to take an interview out of the realm of mediocrity by moving it into any direction he felt he could solicit laughs. He knew he had to rely on his abilities rather than his guests if he was to make it big as a talk show host.

While on the show, I met Paul Block who booked the comedy talent for *The Tonight Show*, and some months later, Paul felt it might be the right time to book me with Johnny Carson. On that night, though my set received six applauses from the audience, Carson was not impressed. I later learned that he was not a fan of gimmick comics. I was disappointed, but life must go on, and the life I was leading was still a fun adventure with so much more to be explored, appreciated, and enjoyed—and not necessarily in that order.

I was grateful to Paul, who put himself on the line getting me on *The Tonight Show*, and I knew he still liked me because months later he called again, wanting me to audition to be a regular on a new afternoon talk show called *Everyday*. And he wasn't interested in The Unknown Comic. He wanted Murray Langston to be a part of this new show, but first I had to audition for the producers. The show was designed to combine music and comedy with serious discussions of issues and topics of the day.

I was flown to Philadelphia for a week of testing, along with several other comics and personalities. By week's end, I was notified that I was selected as the main comic to be teamed with a group of other talented people. Our hosts were an engaging duo: Stephanie

Edwards, an experienced, local talk show host; and John Bennett Perry, an actor and the dad of a then-young Matthew Perry.

The *Everyday* show afforded me the opportunity to work alongside a wonderful cast of talented performers. Among them was Bob Corff, a gifted singer who had starred in *Jesus Christ Superstar* and *Hair*; Ann Bloom, a cute blonde comedic actress who appeared in countless commercials; and Tom Chapin, an extremely likeable folk singer whose brother Harry Chapin had many hit songs, most notably "Cats in the Cradle." For me, one of the most precious moments on the show was when the entire Chapin family guested and sang a medley of songs.

On this new show, I also got to meet many famous comics with whom I had not yet worked with. Among them was Phyllis Diller, who was such a classy lady. As part of the show, we were all invited to her gorgeous mansion in Beverly Hills for dinner. She was an absolute delight and everyone had a great time.

I'll never forget when, months later, I was working in the lounge in Vegas, and Phyllis was appearing in the main room of the Hilton. She came to see my early show on opening night but didn't come backstage to say hi, so I convinced myself she must have hated my act. I was surprised when people at my shows began telling me they came to see me because they saw Phyllis at the Hilton, and at the end of her show she told her audience to make sure they saw my act before leaving Vegas. She did this every night of her engagement. That kind of encouragement was not at all typical of most comics. Most consider each other a threat but not Phyllis Diller. I would have married Phyllis Diller and not just for her money. She also has a great house and a lot of jewelry.

More thrilling moments occurred on the *Everyday* show when I performed in sketches with legends Milton Berle and Bob Hope. I was able to share with Bob Hope the time I was in the Navy and he told me that one day we might work together. It finally came to fruition. Unfuckingbelievable.

Of the newer breed of talent, John Ritter—of *Three's Company* fame—was also one of my favorites. I was given the opportunity to interview him, and together we had a lot of fun trying to outdo each other performing ridiculous impressions.

The loveable Foster Brooks and I worked on a fun sketch together, and others I got to work with were: fellow Canadian Loren Green, Anthony Quinn, Kurt Russell, Barbara Eden, Olivia de Havilland, Lauren Bacall, Eartha Kitt, Peter Marshall, Connie Stevens, and more, but I would only bore you, if I haven't already.

Our show was also the first to showcase a young flamboyant Richard Simmons who had a small gym (The Anatomy Asylum) and health food restaurant (Ruffage) located in Beverly Hills. He was fun, wild, and appeared with us many times, prior to moving into the big time.

Another highlight for me was when I was asked to sing on television for the first time. I sang the Tennessee Ernie Ford classic "16 Tons" with a live band, but of course I had to add humor to my version.

I also got to work with many hot-looking women like Victoria Principal, who Bob Corff and I found stunningly attractive. Bob and I did everything in our powers to get a date with her, but alas, she turned us both down. Bob (the good-looking singer) and I (the not-so-great-looking comic) would often compete to date some of the fun and attractive ladies we worked with. One such lady was Lucie Arnaz.

The first time we met her, we decided she was date bait, and Bob was the first to take her out. Undaunted by Bob's initial assault, and because I thought Lucie and I had much more in common, I asked her out and squealed with delight when she agreed. By the way, I still squeal when I'm delighted.

I developed a great affection for Lucie and we began seeing each other on a regular basis. One of the highlights of our time together was rehearsing at my house for her starring role in Neil Simon's play "They're Playing Our Song." I spent many evenings helping her memorize lines, and on opening night it was exhilarating to see my girlfriend Lucie in front of a star-studded audience, as I watched her onstage displaying her wide range of talent.

In her dressing room afterward, I met Neil Simon—a momentous occasion considering his résumé—and we joked about his brother, Danny Simon, also a writer, who coincidentally was working with me on the *Everyday* show. But that paled in comparison with meeting Lucie's mom: Lucille Ball, the star of the most watched sit-com of all time, *I Love Lucy*. Staring in the face of a comedic legend and sharing time with Lucille Ball was undeniably a treat to treasure.

Dating Lucie was always a new adventure. One time, she took me to Merv Griffin's ex-wife's house to play tennis. Mel Brooks and his wife Ann Bancroft were visiting, and I was surprised when Ann Bancroft recognized me, telling me she'd been sick in bed for a week and watched me daily on *Everyday*.

Unfortunately *Everyday* lasted only six months. Our numbers in most markets were pretty good but then we were placed opposite a relatively new popular talk show, *Phil Donahue*. Our ratings dropped dramatically and our show was cancelled.

Luckily, I was still making money with my act in Vegas/Reno/Tahoe and continued making more TV appearances on various shows such as Norm Crosby's *Comedy Shop*.

Back at the lounge in Vegas, the maître d' told me that Joan Rivers had been in to see me perform a couple of nights in a row. However she never came backstage to say hello, which was sort of unusual for comedians. By this time, Joan was a big comedy star and I was still a novice. One of the things I noticed about many of the comedy giants of that time was that they were not that funny off stage. Rodney Dangerfield was a classic example. Comedy seemed to be a serious business to these giants, but for some reason it was not to me. I loved being playful and silly every chance I got. I was, however, not always successful, occasionally making mistakes in judgment, resulting in embarrassment.

That most certainly could have happened on another night when the maître d' informed me that Joan Rivers was back to see me again, this time with an entourage including her husband Edgar, Edie (of Steve and Edie Gorme), and film producer Ross Hunter, who gave us such films as *Airport*.

After my show, I was in my dressing room chatting with my band, when I heard knocking on the door. I opened it, and there in all her glory was Joan Rivers with the aforementioned group by her side. She introduced them individually, and I politely greeted each with a handshake, telling them how grateful I was that they took time to come to my show. Then, for some unknown reason, in my mind thinking it might be funny, I quickly turned to my band and said, "So anyway, as I was saying..." and mid-sentence, I abruptly slammed the door in the face of Joan Rivers and her group.

Instinctively, I knew it was a comedy gamble, but I wanted to do something funny for Joan. But was it funny? It seemed like minutes passed, but fortunately it was only seconds before I heard them all burst into laughter on the other side of the door.

Relieved, I immediately opened it, and as they entered they were all very complimentary. Joan then invited me to see her perform at Caesars Palace on my next off night, which was the following day. I was surprised, as we sat backstage before her performance, when she told me she was nervous, knowing that I would be watching her. It was gratifying to think that she had placed me at her level, since in my mind, I still had much to learn about stand-up.

I learned a lot about playing pranks and having fun though. One practical joke that I concocted, occurred when I was alternating shows with a very funny and nasty ventriloquist act performed by Wayland Flowers and his puppet Madame. It was rumored that Wayland was gay, a rumor that, by the way, he started. We got along great, frequently exchanging jokes, especially the dirty ones. Wayland's puppet Madame was a very unattractive woman with a foul mouth which audiences loved.

Backstage, our dressing rooms were at opposite ends, and one night after my show, as I was passing Wayland's dressing room, I saw our entertainment director, Jack Eglash, entering the area. Before he could see me, I ducked into Wayland's dressing room, with the intention of possibly scaring him. Then I noticed Wayland's large wooden puppet, Madame, lying on a chair with her mouth wide open; I immediately unzipped my fly, took out my penis, and placed it in Madame's mouth and began moaning. Jack looked in, and when he saw me in that perverted scenario, I acted embarrassed, quickly putting my dick back in my pants. Before he could say anything, I shouted, "Jack you gotta' try this. Madame is one great cocksucker."

Jack laughed hysterically, and the next day I received a call from Wayland telling me that Jack told him what he had witnessed. He proceeded to tell me that he was jealous and swore he could do so much better than Madame. I replied that I was sorry for letting Madame suck my dick because the next morning I woke up and my groin was covered with termites. This was one example of many; I would do just about anything for a laugh.

Though I considered Ted and Freeman my two best friends, I welcomed two new best friends into my life, Ruth Buzzi and her husband Kent Perkins. Like myself, Ruth would also do almost anything to get a laugh, and her husband Kent and I could find fun just hanging out. He was a struggling actor, who earned extra money buying and selling exotic cars, especially Rolls Royce's. With my career on the upswing, he sold me a beautiful six-year-old Rolls Royce Silver Shadow for the same cost as a regular new car. I loved it, and I figured being in my thirties it was time to show off a little.

A new restaurant/bar opened across the street from The Improv called The Moustache Café. Its name was inspired by the owner, Fernand Page, who sported a handlebar moustache. Fernand loved parking my Rolls in front of his cafe along with other hot-looking cars, telling me that his dream was to one day own one. Within a year, his place was so successful, he bought a brand-new Rolls Royce— not a used one like mine.

His place became my new hangout because not only was the food great but he also hired gorgeous waitresses. One waitress/actress who I dated briefly was also working part-time on a soap opera, the beautiful Deidre Hall who later gained star status. I think I liked dating waitresses because, like myself, most of them came from poor backgrounds. Let's face it, very few kids of the rich waited tables.

Once again, I was offered a job to perform in my hometown of Montreal on a variety show called *Julie*, hosted by a talented female Canadian singer, Julie Amato. Arriving at the studio, I was struck by the fact that I was on the same walkway where I had met Jane Mansfield and her daughter when I was a kid so many years before.

Appearing on that same show was another upcoming comedian, Billy Crystal, who was already much more successful than I was. He was on a popular TV series *Soap*, and I looked forward to meeting this talented guy. However, I should have looked backward because when I approached him, congratulating him on his newfound success, if ever I met a cold shoulder it was attached to Billy Crystal's arm. His response was meager at best, showing zero interest in getting to know me and, from my observations, anyone else appearing on the show.

Though I was disappointed, I had to assume that perhaps he was having a bad week, and I shouldn't judge him. Just because he didn't want to engage in chitchat with me should not necessarily mean he's a dick. I was willing to accept the fact that some people just don't always connect with others.

When I returned to Las Vegas, I heard horrible news circulating among the entertainers that it was the end of "Power of the Pen." In every hotel, even big stars were told they could no longer sign for everything. Howard Hughes had purchased seventeen hotel casinos and he singlehandedly brought an end to "Mafia" control of Las Vegas. However, even though the Mob bosses left town, they did have some of their clean-cut guys with protestant backgrounds remain, buying into some of the smaller hotels.

Still, the days of unlimited hidden gambling profits were mostly over. Hughes thought himself an astute businessman and wanted each department in every hotel to be financially self-sufficient. However, he never made the profit margins he had hoped for, and four years after his initial involvement, Hughes sold everything and left Vegas. Small pockets of Mob influence would reemerge but for the most part, he had changed the dynamics of Vegas forever.

Though I didn't love Vegas, I liked it a lot, and one of the reasons was because I developed a relationship with a couple who lived there named Jimmy and Judy Delisse. Jimmy was of Italian descent, and you sensed he was someone you wouldn't want to cross, but as you got to know him, he had such a likeable and generous personality, you could never imagine wanting to cross him. Jimmy managed one of the smaller hotels in Vegas almost within walking distance of the Sahara, so on many days I would visit with him and we would spend hours bullshitting and playing video poker.

What I grew to love about Jimmy was that, unlike myself, he showered his affection on anyone he felt close to. He would always greet everyone with a huge hug, which I was not used to, usually stiffening when anyone would make an attempt. With Jimmy, if you were his friend you got used to being hugged, whether you liked it or not... and I grew to really like it. Likewise, if he felt close to you, he wasn't afraid to tell you he loved you, and again, I grew to love that too. Without question, Jimmy was the most significant person who taught me to be unafraid of telling those I cared for—

man; woman or child—that I loved them, and that was a gift that I could never repay. It didn't take long before I sensed we would become best friends, which would make him number four: behind Freeman, Ted, and Kent. I considered myself exceptionally lucky to have four best friends.

As the end of the year approached, Lucie asked me to join her for Christmas at her mom's home in Beverly Hills. I tried not to show it, but I was excited beyond belief at the thought that I was going to spend Christmas Eve with Lucille Ball.

When we arrived, I was a little surprised that her house was nowhere near as palatial as I had expected. It was modest rather than ostentatious. The interior looked more like a large dollhouse, adorned with comfortable but plain furniture. As we passed a large, decorated Christmas tree, Lucille Ball welcomed me with her low, gravel-sounding, smoker's voice and offered me a drink. She then lit a cigarette and seemed to puff the life out of it as she introduced me to her husband Gary Morton.

We sat, engaging in light conversation, and just like my night with Elvis, I found myself thinking back to when I was a kid, watching *I Love Lucy* on a black-and-white TV. In those halcyon days, I would have never imagined that I would someday be spending Christmas Eve with Lucille Ball.

Lucie's brother Desi Jr. showed up, and after more small talk, they exchanged gifts. After a few hours, Lucie told her mom we were invited to another party at a friend's house, so we all wished each other happy holidays, and after a few pecks on the cheek, Desi Jr., Lucie, and I left.

I couldn't help but think of the millions of people who would have loved to have spent Christmas Eve with this special lady, Lucille Ball... and yet, I did. And now we were leaving her alone with no crowds, no parties, and no family except for her husband, a few drinks, and a few cigarettes. Somehow I felt that was the way she wanted it... At least I hoped so.

My new girlfriend, Jeri Ott.

The cast of the *Everyday* show.

Is Lucie Arnaz's friendship with the "Unknown Comic," Murray Langston, just for laughs? Everyone knows "relationship" with Jim Bailey was.

LUCIE ARNAZ' TOP BANANA
Dating up a storm with comic.

Me and Lucie Arnaz in gossip magazines.

Working with Bob Hope on the *Everyday* show at Christmas.

Me with the adorable and funny Phyllis Diller.

My Rolls Royce.

My new best friends Ruth Buzzi and her hubby Kent Perkins.

Me kissing the host of the Canadian variety show *Julie*.

1979

Driving down the strip in Vegas, I was returning for a two-week gig in the lounge at the Sahara, when I saw Jerry Lewis on the marquee with his opening act, Joey Heatherton. As I checked in, I was sad to hear that they had closed the previous night and I was slightly bummed, thinking I might have hung out with them.

That night in my room, I responded to a knock at the door, and a bellman brought in an enormous supply of flowers, and he told me they were from Miss Heatherton. Attached was a card that read she was sorry she couldn't be there to see my show and wished me luck on my engagement.

I tipped the bellman and admired the massive amount of flowers—shocked that Joey would go out of her way with such a nice gesture. Then, after a closer look, I couldn't help but laugh when I noticed the flowers were all dead. She had taken all the flowers that she had received on her opening night two weeks earlier and sent them to my room as a practical joke. I loved it.

Working at the Sahara was truly a treat for me because most of the big-time comedians of that era appeared there. Between my shows, I would slip into the back of The Main Room and watch everyone from Buddy Hackett, George Carlin, Bill Cosby, and Flip Wilson—who offered to take a picture with me in his Geraldine Outfit. Others who I watched nightly included Don Rickles, Bob Newhart, Dom DeLuise, and Johnny Carson.

I found Carson's act to be slightly disappointing, his routine more like a professor discussing humor than a comedy act. Johnny undeniably was unequaled in his abilities as a talk-show host, but he did not shine performing stand-up. The two biggest laughs he received from the audiences were when he used the word "shit" twice. Johnny, who was known for his clean-cut comedy, literally shocked his audience into laughter with the mere mention of that word.

A favorite main-room act of mine was the always-jovial Dom DeLuise. He and I maintained a nice friendship, which lasted for decades. I was invited to his house many times, where he would cook and serve massive amounts of food, mostly Italian. Dom had many celebrity friends and one we shared was Ruth Buzzi, who was like a sister to him. They met and worked with each other, performing in theatre in New York City, long before either of them gained any fame.

What I loved about Dom was that he was really just a regular guy, but a bit eccentric. He relished going to garage sales looking for bargains, but to most of his friends, Dom himself was the best bargain anyone could have.

When you were with Dom, he always seemed to be "on," wanting to entertain. I think Dom's fondness for me was that I was the same way. But when you got to know him better, you sensed there was a deep inner sadness, which, I learned from conversations with him, stemmed from a loveless relationship he had had with his father. Throughout the years, I'd heard rumors that Dom had gay tendencies, but I could care less whether they were true or not. Dom was simply one hell of a fun guy to be around.

A favorite story of Dom's, which he once related to me, was about an older, sophisticated friend of his who asked him if he could recommend a hair stylist. Dom suggested a lady he had known for years who worked in a Beverly Hills salon. As the story goes, this refined gentleman was seated in the chair, an apron covering his body from his neck down to his lap, as the stylist went about her work. When she had finished and began blow-drying his hair, she couldn't help but glance down to this gentleman's lap and was appalled when she saw an up and down motion going on under the apron.

Shocked and angry at such a perverted action, the stylist screamed at the gentleman, then proceeded to whack him with the blow dryer. As she did so, the apron fell away, revealing that the up and down motion was caused by the gentleman cleaning his eyeglasses. Classic! I always thought that incident would make a great scene in a movie.

Another great scene in a movie would have been what took place when I got a call from Jack Eglash, who told me he wanted me in The Main Room as the opening act for Charo—a headlining attraction at that time. I was thrilled at the prospect of performing on the same stage as all those famous comics I had watched.

On opening night, as usual, I felt a mixture of excitement and anxiety. Jack was there, along with Rip Taylor, who I had become buddies with since we both worked the same lounge. Just prior to the show, I peeked out through the curtain and saw a nearly packed room, which made me fairly confident that I was going to have a great show. As the opening act, I only had to do twenty minutes so, though I was a bit nervous, I felt ready for the big-time.

At showtime, I was introduced, and as the audience applauded, I rushed out, bag over my head, grabbed the microphone, and delivered my first joke. "Hey, it's great to be here. I just flew in from Chicago. What a bummer. I got airsick... and nobody knew." The audience was silent. I delivered my next line. "They gave me a room here but what a weird hotel. I called the desk clerk and told him I gotta leak in my sink... he said, 'Go ahead.'" Now this line *always* got a laugh, but this time, again nothing.

As each succeeding line failed to elicit any kind of response from the audience, I realized I was bombing horribly and began to sweat profusely. Through the eyeholes in my bag, I looked to the side of the stage and saw Rip and Jack looking in my direction. I figured Rip must be laughing and feeling sorry for me at the same time, and Jack must be thinking I was not ready for The Main Room.

The remainder of my set was pure torture. The more energy I put into my performance, the more useless it was. As I finally reached the end of my act, I forlornly staggered to the dressing room where Jack and Rip were waiting. To my surprise, they were both laughing hysterically.

I was practically in tears when, through their laughter, they sputtered something about the audience for Charo being an invited crowd of Spanish-speaking people who did not understand English. Those bastards knew I was going to bomb and didn't warn me, preferring to watch me suffer. Still, I had to give them credit for playing a great practical joke on me.

The rest of my shows were great, and in the following months, Jack had me open for other headliners such as my old boss Lola Falana and a very unfriendly lady with a monotonous act, Helen Reddy. I wasn't the only one who felt that way about her either; every comic I talked to who opened for Miss Reddy disliked her. Besides her cold personality, her boring act became a joke in Vegas which went, "Helen Reddy was arrested for loitering in front of a band."

One person who was never boring was Joan Rivers, who called and invited me to perform at a charity event she was hosting, and I willingly agreed. At the event, Joan was introduced, told a few one-liners, then introduced several speakers who for several hours, solicited donations. Between speakers, a charity auction was held, then dinner was served, and then finally, I was told I would be next.

With the many hours that had passed, I could tell the audience was tired and ready to leave. I instinctively knew I was not going to do well, and I was right. The audience was inattentive, my set was not well received, and once again I felt I had "bombed," even though to the best of my knowledge everyone spoke English. After that unfortunate performance, I never heard from Joan Rivers again. Considering I was performing for nothing, it put a bad taste in my mind about accepting future charitable events.

There's an old saying: "There's no such thing as a bad audience," which is bullshit. If you have a raunchy comic perform his act in front of a crowd of nuns, they're going to be a bad audience for him. I will admit that most audiences can start out great, but there are many variables which can turn them from a good audience into a bad one. If the lighting sucks and/or the sound system are barely audible, causing the crowd to strain to hear what you're saying, it can turn them into a bad audience.

One person can easily turn a good audience into a bad one, simply by "groaning" after each joke. The audience will slowly be psychologically convinced that person must know something and begin to agree with him. I've seen it happen many times. Comedy can be a risky business, which I can attest to, having had ash trays and chairs thrown at me.

Hecklers can turn an audience against you if you don't have the experience to deal with them. In one show, I had a drunk customer grab onto my microphone cord, in an attempt to intimidate me. I slowly yanked on the cord and told the audience I was fishing, and I'd just landed a huge asshole. The audience loved it but he didn't, and he tried to come onstage after me until a couple of employees grabbed him and tossed him out of the club.

Even as a comic, I realized I was not always a good judge of comedy talent. So much relies on the audience. One night at The Improv, I was watching a comic do his set to little reaction. In my mind, I thought the guy wasn't very good, yet the next night, that same comic with the same material, had the audience in hysterics. This taught me that a comedian should never be judged on one performance.

Comedy is very much like having sex, with the audience being your lover. If you have a great lover, the chemistry can lead to an awesome experience, but if your lover is inexperienced or too drunk or too boring, the result can often end up meaningless and futile.

An incident which taught me not to take bombing so personally was when Johnny Dark and I were booked to work a club in the mountains. It was a "favor gig," so though we were both being paid, it was well below our normal fee. As with most bookings, after being ripped off once, I required that I always get paid prior to my last show.

We were booked for two shows with Johnny opening, and the first one was fantastic, the laughs nonstop. However the late show was quite the opposite. The majority of the sparse crowd was in a drunken stupor and prone to excessive heckling. Johnny was bombing miserably, the crowd shouting rude remarks after every joke, "That's not funny," etc.

When Johnny finished his set, he was visibly pissed off as we passed each other, and now it was my turn to take the stage. I kept thinking, I'm The Unknown Comic and I'm going to win this war. However, as soon as I uttered my first joke, I wished I'd had a white flag to wave. I tried valiantly to perform to the best of my ability, but within minutes I knew I was doomed. I was heckled mercilessly by this drunken, uncaring crowd of idiots.

Only minutes had passed, and realizing I had another fifty minutes remaining, I quickly made the decision to end the evening's festivities. I removed the bag from my head and shouted to the boisterous crowd, "I've got a great house, great friends, money in the bank and I drive a Rolls Royce. I don't need this shit." I then bounded from the stage, signaled for Johnny to follow me, as we charged through the back door, hopped into my Rolls, and headed for home.

From that day on, I made a decision to never let "bombing" bother me again. In the past, I would get depressed for hours, sometimes days afterwards, but this time, a negative had being turned into a positive because I was positive I would never allow a bad audience to upset me again.

For most people, making someone laugh is not easy, and that was true for another new TV show called *Make Me Laugh*. The object of the show was for a comic to make a contestant laugh, and if they didn't laugh they won money. It was a fun show, and I appeared on it many times both as The Unknown Comic and as myself. Other then-unknown comics who also appeared on the show were: Bob Saget, Howie Mandel, Gallagher, Gary Mule Deer, Yakov Smirnoff, Bruce "Baby Man" Baum, and Garry Shandling.

One day, when I was back at Schwab's, I heard my named called and it was the unique, scruffy voice of Debra Winger. She introduced me to an actor she was dating, James Woods, who had been in an episode of *Welcome Back Kotter* and just made his mark in the film *The Onion Field*. Debra was excited about a film she was about to begin filming entitled *French Postcards*. She looked great, and I wondered if we would still be together if I had become serious with her, though I seriously doubted it. Debra was determined to become a great actress and/or a big star. I wasn't sure which, but I certainly did not doubt her determination or her abilities.

I also bumped into Bill Hudson, who I hadn't seen in many years, since we worked on the Hudson Brothers kid's TV show. I knew he'd had a relationship with Ali McGraw of *Love Story* fame, but he told me he was now married to Goldie Hawn. He further informed me that Goldie had recently given birth to their daughter and invited me to their palatial home in Beverly Hills.

Goldie was still as gorgeous as ever, and I was touched when she remembered our first meeting when I imitated a fork on "Laugh-In." They escorted me to their nursery, where Goldie lifted out of a crib a wide-eyed, beautiful baby girl they named Kate. Goldie, who was in fabulous shape, was egged-on by Bill to show me her

Cesarean scar. She finally agreed and handed little Kate Hudson to me. As I nervously cradled her in my arms, Goldie lowered just enough of the top of her skirt to expose that famous belly adorned with a petite scar. I often wonder what ever happened to that little girl of theirs.

During the summer, I got a call from Mike Lacey, owner of The Comedy & Magic Club. He told me he was having trouble keeping his club afloat and asked if I would work below my normal fee to help him out. I agreed and once again performed there on several occasions, packing the place. One of my opening acts was a young comic/magician Harry Anderson, who only two years later was starring in his own TV series *Night Court.*

On another summer night I was at The Comedy Store, sitting in the back watching the genius of Richard Pryor onstage. Suddenly, Robin Williams joined him and they engaged in some improv comedy banter. Then Stephen Stills and Mick Jagger leapt onstage to join them in more comedy antics. It was a momentous evening, watching those talented people cavort onstage in front of an audience of less than a hundred people.

Unfortunately, it was shortly after that night when I joined in a strike against The Comedy Store. It's owner, Mitzi, refused to pay any money to the hundreds of aspiring comics who were responsible for her becoming wealthy off *their* sweat and talent. All that was asked was a measly twenty-five dollars for each comic per night, but she refused. She simply could not understand that though a few comedians who worked her place would become major stars earning great wealth, they were only a small fraction. Most would struggle for the rest of their lives, never attaining the success they craved.

For five weeks, most of the comics—including Jay Leno and David Letterman—staged protests, picketing in front of the club, while a few crossed the picket line. The comedians involved formed a union called Comedians for Compensation. Mitzi alleged that her place was more of a college for comics. However, she was making a fortune while many comics—including Leno and Letterman—were occasionally forced to sleep in their cars. She was making so much money that she purchased the place next door and opened a larger comedy room, allowing her to make even more, and yet she wouldn't pay any comic one single dollar.

The Comedy Store along with the Improv, which was the first to agree to pay the comics, did eventually give in. After the strike, though many comics—including myself—refused to step on the stage of The Comedy Store again, Mitzi made sure others, who were instigators of the strike, were no longer *allowed* to perform there.

One comic, Steve Lubetkin, was so distraught over the strike that he committed suicide in front of the building by jumping off the roof of the Hyatt Hotel next door. He left a note that read: "My name is Steve Lubetkin. I used to work at The Comedy Store." I wonder if Mitzi ever thought making all that money was worth his death.

When all was settled, I was hanging out at the Improv, when one night I saw Billy Crystal again. And once again I said "Hi," wondering whether he would recall us working together in Montreal. If he gave me the cold shoulder the first time, this time his shoulder was made of ice. He responded with a snobbish and weak "Hello," and then quickly turned to continue chatting with others, who I'm sure could do more for him than I ever could. Billy was the only other person I had met who reminded me of Sonny Bono, who also had no interest in befriending anyone who he felt was beneath his stature. At first I thought perhaps Billy just didn't like me personally, but I began to hear from many others who had negative opinions of him, along with a couple of writers who worked on *The Tonight Show*, who confided in me that most everyone dreaded when Billy would appear on their show. I decided it wasn't just me that Billy didn't particularly care for, but he simply wasn't interested in socializing with anyone who wasn't at his level or above.

At my level was my sister Suzanne, who called from Canada and asked if two of my nieces, both thirteen years old, could come to Hollywood and visit with me. When I agreed, they were ecstatic, in their minds believing I was a Hollywood celebrity. I hadn't seen them since they were infants, and they really didn't know me so I thought I'd have fun with them.

I talked my friend Kent into helping me pull a practical joke on them. We would take my Rolls Royce to pick them up at the airport and Kent would pretend he was my driver. Kent donned a chauffeur's cap, and as we left for the airport, we had a blowout. As we hurriedly jacked up the car on the side of the road, cars were honking at us and we knew they were chuckling to themselves, watching two guys changing a tire on a Rolls Royce.

We were late arriving at the airport, and as Kent came to a stop in front of my waiting nieces, he rushed to grab their luggage. I acted like it was his fault we were late, and screamed at him, while Kent kept apologizing. I continued to berate him and when he tried to apologize again, I slapped him on the side of the head, telling him to never look me directly in the eye when he talked to me. My nieces were obviously appalled and shocked at my behavior, and as we entered the back seat of my Rolls, I could feel the pity in their voices as they tried to calm me down saying, "It's okay, Uncle Murray," and "we don't mind you being late." From the driver's seat, Kent continued apologizing, and I continued slapping him on the back of the head.

My poor nieces were almost trembling when I threatened to fire him and screamed for Kent to close the glass partition between us, so we wouldn't be subjected to his stupidity. Finally, when Kent pretended to sob and I saw my nieces going into a state of shock, I realized I had to end our practical joke. When I let them know it was all just a gag, my nieces were so grateful and we laughed all the way to the bank... I mean home.

It was Thanksgiving week, and I was feeling lonely working again in the lounge in Vegas. For the past year, I had been seeing Lucie Arnaz whenever we could get together, which was sporadic due to both our working schedules. On this Thanksgiving night, my spirits were lifted when Lucie called but they lowered slightly when she told me she was having turkey dinner with many of our mutual friends at her place. We chatted a bit, and then she wished me luck on my shows and passed the phone around so everyone could say "Hi" and tell me they wished I were there. And I did wish I was there.

Hours later, as I stood backstage preparing to go on, I peeked through the curtains to see the size of the audience. The front row was lined with several people with bags on their heads. This was a common occurrence, and I would usually introduce them as members of my family: my sister Baggy Sue, my brother Sad Sack, and my cousins Scum Bag, Dirt Bag, and, of course, Douche Bag.

At showtime, I ran onstage, and as usual, performed the first fifteen minutes with a bag over my head. Then, as usual, I shocked the audience by quickly removing my bag, allowing them to see what I look like. I then told the front row it was their turn to remove the bags from their heads. They acted reluctant, so I reached down and pulled off one of the bags, and I was dumbfounded when it revealed it was my friend Bob Corff from the *Everyday* show. The others followed suit, removing the bags from their heads, revealing more friends along with Lucie Arnaz. Apparently, after our phone conversation, she missed me and took it upon herself to fly everyone to Vegas to surprise me...and indeed, she succeeded.

After my show, we all proceeded to my suite where I provided food and drinks for everyone. A great time was had by all, but the partying must have gone a little too far. Lucie arrived at the conclusion that I was not ready for a serious relationship, and when I awoke the next morning, she was gone. However, she did leave a sweet note saying that she would always consider me to be someone special but for now it was time for both of us to move on, and we did.

Lucie moved to New York, and I moved into film when I was asked to appear in a movie both as myself and as The Unknown Comic. The film, called *Skatetown U.S.A.*, was about the roller skating craze that was sweeping America, and it starred a new actor in his first role: Patrick Swayze.

Coincidentally, my friend Linda Blair was also filming a skating movie called *Roller Boogie* directly across the street from where we were shooting, so we spent time visiting on each other's sets.

Others in our cast included Scott Baio, Ron Palillo, Flip Wilson, and in a small role, a stunningly beautiful sexy, Canadian, Playboy Playmate/centerfold named Dorothy Stratten. She and I shared a scene where I had to pinch her ass. I worked it out with the director, Bill Levey, so that I had to redo the scene several times.

I still vividly recall subtly flirting with Dorothy before our scene, and her responding that she shouldn't be talking to me because her boyfriend was jealous. She discreetly pointed him out and I saw him staring in our direction giving me "the evil eye." Sadly, shortly after filming, Dorothy was murdered by that same boyfriend, all later recounted in a film about her tragic ending: *Star 80*.

For me, shooting *Skatetown U.S.A.* was a lot of fun, and I noticed it was even more fun for many on the set who were using cocaine, which seemed ever-present. Personally, I still had no interest in drugs, preferring to live in the real world, which I was enjoying so much.

Back then, the "word" on cocaine was that it was not addictive. That "word" was later changed to "Bullshit." Most people seemed to use it to stay up and party as long as they could. Another actress in the film was an alumnus of *The Brady Bunch*, Maureen McCormack. She later wrote that cocaine was everywhere on the set and that she had a severe addiction to it. After much coercion from friends, I finally tried it, and the only noticeable effect it had on me was when I wanted to sleep I couldn't, which was reason enough for me to never try it again. I loved my sleep.

Like many comics of that era, I did a lot of jokes about cocaine: "I tried snorting coke, but the carbonation wrecked my sinuses;" or "I tried cocaine one time but it had no effect on me... except the next morning, I woke up on the inside of my waterbed," followed by "talk about wet dreams."

Because of the hyper personality I exuded on stage, many in my audiences were convinced I was a druggie. Frequently, after my shows, they would surreptitiously hand me different kinds of drugs. Those went directly to my band members, who did not hide the fact they were indulging on a regular basis.

On the set of *Skatetown*, I met Connie and Lou, two cute wannabe actresses who shared an apartment. Initially, I developed a crush on Lou, but later I discovered that Connie had a crush on me and before long she and I were dating.

Connie was beautiful, exuberant, friendly, funny, and laughed at everything I said or did—a prerequisite in those days for me to date someone. I still love when women laugh at me, even while having sex. What I don't like is when they laugh and point at the same time. Before long, I was falling in love with Connie, or at least I thought I was. What I didn't know then was that Connie withheld a secret from me that could easily destroy our relationship, which I was to discover later. And no, she didn't have a dick.

Me as the Unknown Comic with Flip Wilson.

My good friend Ted and I, performing a boxing sketch.

My girlfriend Connie.

1980

My personal life changed dramatically with Connie becoming part of it, and I could easily envision a serious relationship evolving. She was still living with her girlfriend Lou, and they had taken on a new roommate, Karen Hall, a sweet, immensely shy young thing from the south, accent and all. Karen was only supposed to visit them for a short time, but ended up moving in.

Karen wanted to be a television writer and was obsessed with the TV show *M*A*S*H*. Whenever I was at their place, Karen was always in her room feverishly writing scripts, and then sending them out to various producers "on spec." Connie and Lou were of immeasurable help, aiding Karen in any way they could, and we all became sort of a mini-family. Knowing Karen was struggling, I would occasionally give her money to type material for me.

Thankfully I wasn't struggling, when one day, driving my Rolls through North Hollywood, I came to a stop and noticed a brand new Rolls Royce pull up alongside me. I looked over and there sat Tommy Chong, smiling at me, proud as could be in his gorgeous automobile. He shouted, "Hey, can you spare a hamburger?" Life had sure changed since the days when we worked for a hamburger a night at Knopows.

Though I was not making anywhere near the kind of money Cheech and Chong earned, I was grateful for my biggest payday to date, which occurred when I was offered a two-week gig at the Sands Casino in Atlantic City, paying me $15,000. With that kind of money in one lump sum, I decided to pay off my parents' house in Canada. I contacted their loan company, and discovered the mortgage was $14,000, so I wrote them a check. My parents were shocked, staggered, surprised, stunned, stupefied, and speechless all at once. It was a thrill for me and not a big deal. After all, it was only two weeks work, which would make their lives easier for years to come. To this day, it was the best money I've ever spent from my showbiz earnings. So far show business had been very good to me financially. At least that's what I thought.

I was having lunch with some of my comic buddies, discussing show business, when Tom Dreesen said something that hit home with me. He artfully articulated that if you're in show business, you not only have to take care of the show but also the business. He continued to say that too many people who made lots of money in our business ended up penniless, and that was not going to happen to him. I decided that wasn't going to happen to me either.

I had never really given my finances much thought and was known to be exceptionally generous, always picking up the check at restaurants or taking groups of friends to Hawaii. I had been working fairly consistently and decided it was time to meet with my accountant and investigate how much I was worth. I hoped it would be fairly substantial, even though I had a band, an accountant, an agent, a lawyer, and two managers who were all taking a piece of me.

To my dismay, my accountant informed me I was living month to month and had virtually no savings. I insisted he explain where every dollar was spent, which he proceeded to do. I understood the cost of my band, my accountant taking five percent and my agent ten percent, however, I was not happy when I discovered my managers were not only taking fifteen percent but, on top of that, were charging me for phone calls, paperwork, taxis, and their airfares when they would fly to see me perform. What really ticked me off was while I flew coach to Atlantic City, I learned that *they* flew first class, charging it to me.

As I searched through my financial statements, I noticed I was charged $250.00 for my lawyer to look at contracts for each of the many talk shows I had appeared on (Merv Griffin/Mike Douglas/ Dinah Shore etc.). A major flaw existed because I was getting paid $300 per show, which meant minus my lawyer's $250 fee, I was only receiving $50. That was not right: in fact it was downright wrong.

I was furious and went to my managers, asking them to explain why they were charging so much. They told me it was standard procedure and they operated in the same manner with their other clients Rip Taylor and Phyllis Diller. Well, in my mind, I thought it was wrong and decided then and there I no longer wanted them acting as my managers and ended our relationship.

I then approached my lawyer and asked why I was charged $250 for shows that only paid $300, especially since the contracts were standard and didn't really need a lawyer's attention. His response was a meek: "It must have been a clerical oversight." Clerical oversight my ass! Though he was not prepared to reimburse me, he did allow for me to receive a credit of $5,000 against future representation. What a guy!

Tom Dreesen was right. This was a major revelation about how Hollywood can take advantage of someone who is new and/or naïve. I was extremely disappointed and, right or wrong, I also decided not to re-sign with my agent. From now on, I was going to be the only one to make deals on my behalf. This experience opened my eyes to how so many people who became famous and wealthy, years later end up broke.

Back in Vegas, a young guy named George Pecoraro began hanging around my band and I. He was raised in Vegas and was a huge fan of comedians, especially Jerry Lewis, and though he was still a kid in my eyes, our mutual interests in comedy led us to become buddies. His passion for show business was infectious, and though he loved comedy, he knew performing was not where his talent laid. Instead, he wanted to be an agent for comics, and I was one of his first bookings.

The first gig he got me was at UNLV, the local college, to host a wet t-shirt contest. It was low paying, but I wasn't about to turn it down, thinking this could be fun and sexy, or vice versa, or who cares? My job was to introduce each girl, who would then stroll over to a large container of water and dip their breasts into it, after which they would display their visibly chilled and straining nipples to the screaming throngs of male students. Did I enjoy introducing these young nubile girls, parading their clinging, wet titties? Of course, until I was told I would be needed to assist a girl... who had NO arms and NO legs. This is not a made-up story.

Though I was injecting funny one-liners into the festivities, I had no joke for this brave young girl, as I lifted her torso and carefully leaned her far enough into the water until her breasts were soaked. I then held on to her, parading her full breasts and extended nipples in front of the cheering crowd. I was happy that she won second prize for her courage and sense of humor, and this unusual job turned out to be the first of many which George would get me, but never as a signed agent, only as a friend.

My contracts with the Sahara ended, and instead of continuing to work as a lounge act, I wanted to move into an upward direction. George obtained a meeting with the entertainment director of the Landmark Hotel about putting a show into their main room. We subsequently met with them, selling them on the idea of an all-comedy show, which would feature myself as the headliner with new, upcoming comics opening for me. Long before comedy clubs such as the Comedy Store and the Improv opened in every other hotel, I'm proud to say I was the first to bring the concept of having several comedians on the same bill to Las Vegas.

On my first show, I enlisted my best friend Freeman, who was gaining more recognition as a regular on a new TV show called *Dance Fever*, to emcee. The first two comics I booked to open for me were a very funny comedy team, Roger and Roger—who specialized in impressions—and an extremely funny lady, Elayne Boosler.

The show was well received, and though I remained as the headliner, I changed my opening acts every two weeks, using other talented comics like ventriloquist Willie Tyler and Lester, Wil Shriner, and many more. Our comedy show lasted several months, when the hotel decided it wanted to bring in a larger production show featuring naked ladies. I was upset, but I had nothing to do with the Landmark being blown up a few years later. Still, I was again out of a job, but this time with no agent or manager... I still had this new kid and budding agent, George.

It was time for more change, and I purchased a brand new home in the hills overlooking Hollywood. One gorgeous California morning, while shaving and listening to birds cough outside my bathroom window, I didn't realize the close shave I was about to get.

The shrill sound of my phone ringing pierced the tranquil setting and I rushed to my bedside to pick up the receiver. Placing it to my ear, I returned to the bathroom, dragging the long cord behind me. "Hello!" I muttered, and then jokingly added. "Who is this and why are you calling and what makes you think I'm paranoid?" It was then, and still is, a rare occurrence for me to answer the phone in a normal fashion.

"Is this Murray Langston?" a gruff-sounding voice bellowed into my ear. "Hold on a second," I answered, "Let me check my underwear." I paused for a moment to give the impression that I was actually checking them, a scenario I had used many times before, and then continued, "Yep, it says Murray Langston right here next to Fruit of the Loom."

The voice on the other end did not find my humor amusing. "Listen you asshole, this is Frank Sinatra," was the reply. "And if you ever mention my name on television again, I'll break your fucking head into a million tiny pieces…you got that you cocksucker?"

"Joe… is that you?" I replied, thinking this was my long-time Italian buddy Joe Battaglia. I was sure the gruff-sounding voice combined with the foul language could be none other than Joe. As I laughed into the receiver, the voice on the other end immediately responded, angrier than before, "This is not fucking Joe, you fucking idiot. This is Frank Sinatra and I'm telling you that you better never mention my name anywhere ever again or I'll smash your fucking face all over the fucking pavement, you little prick."

Again, I laughed out loud, thinking that, to my knowledge, I had never mentioned Frank Sinatra's name on television or even in a joke because no part of my act made any mention of him. Even if I did mention his name, which I was certain I hadn't, Frank Sinatra would certainly NOT be calling me himself, in the flesh, on the phone. And most importantly, if he really knew me, I mean, really knew me… he would never refer to me as a "little prick."

"You can't fool me Joe because you're the one with the little prick…" I joked, as I continued, "What the fuck do you want?" The voice on the other end became even angrier… "Listen you asshole, I'm telling you for the last time that this is Frank Sinatra." The voice was now furious as I shouted back…" Oh yeah, Mr. Sinatra… Well, sing… 'My Way'."

"You cocksucker" were the last words I heard as the receiver on the other end slammed down, jolting my ear with its force. I hung up and noticed the remaining shaving cream on my face had almost completely evaporated, so I squirted another dose into my palm as curious thoughts ran rampant through the hollow channels of my mind.

"What the hell was Joe up to? When is he going to call back? Did he really think he fooled me with that lame Sinatra impression?" As I applied more shaving cream to my face, the sudden sound of the phone ringing again brought to an end any more of those burning unanswered questions. "Ah ha!" I chuckled to myself, "Joe is calling back." I picked up the phone and spoke calmly, "Yeah Joe, what do you want now?"

"Is this Murray Langston?" The voice on the other end said, only this was a different voice, a higher pitched and familiar voice. This was now confusing, as Joe never really mastered the art of doing impressions because his voice was so gravelly that all his impressions sounded alike. "Yes, this is Murray Langston," I answered, now trying to figure out to whom this familiar voice belonged.

My curiosity was quickly squelched as the voice replied, "This is Milton Berle." He then asked, "Do you recognize my voice?" Without a doubt, I knew this was not an impression but the actual, distinctive voice of the onetime King of television. Coincidentally, I had just worked with him in a sketch a few months earlier on the TV show *Everyday*. "Listen," he continued, sounding reasonable, "Sinatra just called me and apparently you didn't think you were talking to him, did you?"

"Wwww... hat... duh... wh...," I stuttered, mumbling incoherently. My brain became numb and my heartbeat increased, "T... that was F... F... Frank Sinatra on the phone?"

"Yes," Milton replied..." That was Frank."

"But," I responded, "I've never mentioned him on television." I managed to calm down. "Why was he cursing and threatening me?"

Milton was nonchalant. "Ever since he became a grandfather, he gets very upset if anyone jokes about him anywhere, anytime, especially on television."

I responded, "But... I've never mentioned his name on television. I don't even do Sinatra jokes in my act."

It became obvious that Milton was on my side as he continued. "Frank told me you did a joke about him on a comedy show. Something about a halfway house?" Then it hit me like a bolt of lightning. A year earlier, when I had performed numerous times on the show *Make Me Laugh*, I had used most of the jokes from my act and was trying to come up with new material.

On one show, I decided to read comical news items from a newspaper. I now recalled the joke: "Frank Sinatra recently opened up a halfway house.... for girls who don't go all the way." Thinking back, it seemed like a relatively harmless joke, but I guess Sinatra thought otherwise.

I explained to Milton how I'd forgotten about that joke and that Sinatra must have seen it on a rerun. I also asked why Sinatra didn't have someone call me and ask me politely, rather than cursing and threatening me the way he did. I certainly respect people in the business and would have politely apologized, but the lack of respect he showed me was way out of line. Milton agreed, but reiterated Sinatra's paranoia was unfortunately getting worse with age and added that he would call Frank back and try to calm him down.

After hanging up, I thought I should call George Foster, the producer of *Make Me Laugh*, and suggest that if they reran that episode again, perhaps he might edit that joke out of the show. When George answered, I immediately said, "George…you'll never guess who just called me?"

Without hesitation, he answered, "Frank Sinatra." Surprised, I asked how he knew, and he quipped, "Who do you think gave him your phone number?"

I was shocked and questioned further, "Why did you give him my number?" He sort of chuckled, and then replied. "Because I didn't want him to have my legs broken."

Fortunately, nothing ensued, and I believe my one saving grace was that this story made it around Hollywood rather quickly, and *if* anything did happen to me, Sinatra would surely have been blamed. Some years later, I received a phone call from Kitty Kelley, who was writing Sinatra's unauthorized biography. Through the grapevine, she had heard about my phone call from Sinatra and asked if she could include it in her book. I denied the incident occurred because by this time, I had already decided that I would one day prefer to have this story in my book... By the way, I did eventually finish shaving but with several nicks and cuts on my face and neck.

Despite the Sinatra episode, it was a good year for me. I was invited to appear with Andy Williams on the *People's Choice Awards*, and also appeared on *Don Kirshner's Rock Concert, The Mac Davis Show, The Pat and Debbie Boone Show,* and *Jack Jones at the Palace*.

In Los Angeles, I booked myself at the Roxy on Sunset, which normally showcased music acts, including a newcomer Bruce Springsteen. It was a fun experience with my band opening the show, playing several of their own original tunes before introducing me to the packed house. The audience applauded wildly as The Unknown Comic rushed to the microphone, but they were suddenly confused when another Unknown Comic, also with a bag on his head, leaped onstage and began chasing the first Unknown Comic. Within seconds, the second Unknown Comic grabbed the first Unknown Comic and ripped the bag off, revealing it was none other than Ruth Buzzi. Ruth screamed and began whacking me with her bag, then rushed offstage, leaving the audience laughing hysterically. It was a great beginning to my show.

Next, I was back in Las Vegas, appearing at the Aladdin Hotel, opening for Gladys Knight and the Pips. While working with them, I developed a horrible flu bug sending my temperature soaring and forcing me to stay in bed until right before show time. I'm still not sure how it happened, but once I was introduced, my energy surged and I was able to get through my twenty-five-minute performance effortlessly. However, minutes after my set ended, I would rush to my room, collapse in bed, and painfully wait for the next night's show.

During that week, Buddy Hackett stopped by to visit me in bed, and a few days later, he joked with Carson on the *Tonight Show* about my predicament. When Hackett told Carson about my high fever, Carson asked if he took my temperature and Hackett replied, "Yes, and guess where I had to put the thermometer since he had a bag over his head?" Funny stuff.

As we approached the end of the year, Connie, Lou, and I were excited. Their new roommate Karen Hall had sold her first script, an episode of *Eight is Enough*. It featured one of the lead characters wearing a bag over their head working as an Unknown Stripper in a club. I wondered where she got that idea?

I scheduled a party at my new house on the night the show was to air, and friends gathered to celebrate Karen's first big break. This was going to be exciting, and hopefully it would kick off her career as a writer.

As we all prepared for Karen's episode of *Eight is Enough*, laughing, eating, and drinking in front of the television set, everything came to a sudden halt. A voice on television announced "This is a special news report" and we were all shocked into silence with the somber news that Beatle John Lennon had just been shot dead. Karen's episode was pre-empted and was not shown that night.

Me and Connie.

Connie's and now my new friends, Karen and Lou.

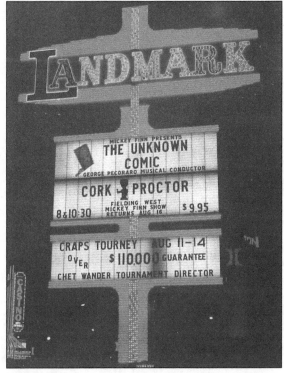

The Landmark sign in Las Vegas featuring my show.

An ad for my Landmark show in the paper.

A publicity photo with Elayne Boozler, Roger & Roger, Freeman, and me.

Me and Elayne Boozler with Norm Crosby who visited us backstage.

Me and Gladys Knight on a poster.

1981

John Lennon's death at the age of forty certainly affected me. Once again, like Elvis, your own mortality rears its ugly head. And once again, I decided I needed to enjoy every single day. I was also saddened to hear of the sudden car-crash death of my friend Tom Chapin's brother, Harry Chapin. Not the way to start a year.

But life goes on, and I flew to Florida where I opened for Melissa Manchester at the Diplomat Hotel. Melissa was a dynamic singer, and I watched every one of her performances, never getting bored. She was that good.

My first night opening for Melissa, I felt my own show was not that well received, and at the party afterward, I was slightly depressed until a smiling Olivia Newton John lifted my spirits when she told me she enjoyed my act. Also at the first show and party afterward, was legendary singer Liza Minnelli, who for the most part seemed to be in some sort of stupor. I couldn't tell whether her bizarre behavior was derived from substance abuse or that was simply the real Liza.

Next, I was again off to Canada, appearing on Alan Hamel's talk show, with his wife Suzanne Summers guesting. Also appearing, was a famous '60s singer from my teen past, Dion, "The Wanderer." Though I rarely indulged, that night we smoked a joint together in his hotel room. I found it somewhat amusing that several months later, I saw Dion on a talk show, admitting to once having had a drug problem, but insisting that he hadn't smoked a joint in over ten years—hard to believe that a celebrity would lie about their drug use.

Once again, I was asked to return to my sketch acting roots and worked with two giants of comedy, Don Adams and Don Rickles, in a Showtime special called *Two Top Bananas*. It was an attempt to recreate the burlesque era, and among the many sketches we did, I especially liked playing a gay guy with the two Dons. Appearing on the same show were two ladies I grew very fond of, the lovely Rhonda Shear and the sexy Carol Wayne—known for her many appearances on *The Tonight Show* as the Matinee Lady.

Back on the club circuit, I was performing in San Francisco, when Lucie Arnaz called and told me she was in town and wanted to see my show with her new boyfriend, actor Lawrence Luckinbill. It was great seeing her again and realizing there were no hard feelings between us. Months later, I was even happier to hear that she and Lawrence got married.

Many months later, I was positive there were no hard feelings between us when Lucie had me flown to New York to test for a lead role in a television pilot she was to star in. Unfortunately, that series never got off the ground, but I did get a chance to have a fun visit with Lucie and her new husband.

When I returned to Los Angeles, I was stricken with the flu bug again, which lasted weeks. I began noticing that I was getting sick on a regular basis, and every time I would visit my doctor—ironically named Dr. Sugarman—he would prescribe antibiotics. Even after I recouped from the flu, my nasal passages would continue to run for hours each and every day, and my doctor informed me it was allergies.

For some reason, I didn't believe him, and I was getting sick of being sick so I took it upon myself to read several health-related books beginning with "Sugar Blues". It detailed the harm sugar can have on your immune system and there was no doubt my diet consisted of bountiful amounts of that sweet substance.

I decided to give up all forms of sugar for as long as I could, and I lasted almost a year. The results were immediate. Within a week, my nose stopped running, my energy soared, and during the ensuing year, not a single cough. I wasn't going to give up sugar completely, but I was going to lower my consumption drastically because I wanted to enjoy life to the fullest, and I was still young with lots of things to accomplish. Let's face it, without your health, life really sucks.

My career was still very healthy when I received a call to bring my All Comedy Show to the Hacienda Hotel in Las Vegas. Some of the acts I used to open for me at the new venue were Johnny Dark, Sean Morey, Johnny Yune, Jimmy Brogan, and a new Russian comic, Yakov Smirnoff, who I thought would become my best friend number five... until he treated me like number two.

While at the Hacienda, my agent George called and told me to watch a young juggler on the Merv Griffin show, named James Marcel. When I saw him juggle three electric chainsaws, I was blown away and immediately booked him. Speaking of blown away, one night, superstar Liberace came to our show and was absolutely delightful, both as an audience member and as a person.

After the show, Liberace showed up at our dressing room, which had a small piano in the corner. We joked and laughed for a long time, whereupon everyone became so comfortable that I said to him, "Hey Lee, why don't you play a little piano for us?" Though I was joking, to everyone's amazement, he played several tunes for us all. Before leaving, he gave me his phone number, saying he'd love to invite us to dinner at his Las Vegas Mansion. Little did I realize that when Liberace said "invite us," he really meant my opening act James Marcel who just happened to be an extremely attractive young man with an incredible body to match.

Apparently Liberace couldn't wait for dinner, because the following day, James told me that Liberace called him at the hotel and offered to take him on the road as his opening act for a substantial amount of money. Obviously, we were all aware of Liberace's homosexual lifestyle and this worried James, who at the time had a girlfriend.

Compared to what I was paying James, it was the kind of money he couldn't turn down, so he took the job and, as a protective measure, brought along his girlfriend. It worked, but not completely because according to James, on the occasions when his girlfriend couldn't be with him, Liberace would make late-night calls to his room with numerous sexual propositions. Luckily, James was able to humor him while denying him. His gig lasted for close to two years until James decided he wanted to become an actor.

My show at the Hacienda was receiving good reviews and even David Letterman called asking if I would use a mutual friend of ours, George Miller. George was one of my first comedy friends, and though Dave and I both knew he had a substance abuse problem, I nevertheless hired him.

Since I had signed a six month contract with the Hacienda, I decided to buy a new house in Las Vegas, which was only minutes from the hotel and my friends Jimmy and Judy. Back in Los Angeles, I sold my home in Mount Olympus, making a profit of over $100,000 for a place I owned for only four years. Not wasting any time, I purchased another house at the end of Lankershim Boulevard, within walking distance of my old work place, Universal Studios. It was an older home and I was anxious to fix it up. My newly found love was making empty living spaces look like happening places.

At year's end, my life took a turn for the worse when I was asked to be the host for the "Miss Nude America" contest. I was forced to share the stage and dressing rooms with over twenty naked ladies. It was a low-paying job, which I found disgusting and demeaning, but nevertheless, I hosted it … every year for the next three years.

My house on Lankershim, which Princess Stephanie considered buying.

Me and Melissa Manchester together at the Diplomat in Florida.

Me hosting Miss Nude America.

1982

Meanwhile, my *All Comedy Show* at the Hacienda was running smoothly when I was informed that they wanted to bring in my old buddy, Redd Foxx. It turned out to be good news because Redd only wanted to perform once a night, so I was moved into the early slot at eight while Redd performed his triple-X-rated show at ten.

Grateful for my success, I said yes when I was asked to appear in a charity commercial for "Hard to Adopt Kids." In the commercial, I first appear as The Unknown Comic, asking for help from the viewing audience to find parents for the many hard to adopt children in Las Vegas. As I talked, lined up in front of me were bags of all sizes and shapes, resembling kids of all ethnicities: a black bag, a tall bag, a fat bag, a bag with slanted eyes, even a bag with an Indian feather attached. Toward the end of the commercial, I removed the bag from my head and made a further plea as myself, Murray Langston.

This commercial provided me one of my all-time favorite accidental practical jokes. It occurred one night when I still owned my Rolls Royce. After one of my shows, I noticed a young woman in her twenties, crying softly, standing outside the hotel, and I asked her what was wrong. She explained that she came to Vegas with a girlfriend and was excited because it was her first time, but from the moment they arrived, her friend had not stopped gambling.

Feeling sorry for her, I asked if she'd like to see some of the sights of Las Vegas with me and pointed to my Rolls, which I kept parked in the front. For some reason, she assumed I worked for the hotel as a valet attendant and asked if I would get into any trouble. Once I realized this, I went along with it, telling her that I was on a break and it wouldn't be a problem. She then gladly accepted my offer, and as I escorted her into the back, I hopped into the driver's seat and off we went. I drove all around the strip showing her the various hotels and sights, explaining their origins as best I could.

Later, feeling frisky, I asked if she'd like to join me at a friend's house for some drinks and a Jacuzzi. She agreed, and off we went to my home, all lit up and looking very inviting. She asked if I was risking my job, so I told her I would call the hotel and have a friend take over my shift.

After my fake phone call, we drank, laughed, wound up in the Jacuzzi naked, and, later in bed, we enjoyed each other to the fullest extent of my penis. Afterward, I turned on the television and we began watching a little Letterman when suddenly my aforementioned commercial appeared. She leaped forward upon seeing The Unknown Comic, telling me how she loved him and asked if I had ever met him. I told her once or twice, knowing that in a few seconds The Unknown Comic would remove the bag, revealing that it was the same guy she was lying next to.

After a few more seconds, The Unknown Comic slowly began removing the bag as she leaned forward, eager to see what he looked like. When the bag was removed, her mouth dropped and she performed the only "triple take" I had ever seen, her head swinging back and forth from me to the television set at least three times before realizing I was The Unknown Comic.

It was a fantastic night, highlighted by the fact that I was booked to appear on a local talk show the next morning. They sent a limousine to pick me up and I brought her along, and then afterward had the driver take her back to her hotel. She thanked me profusely for showing her a night she would long remember. It truly was a special evening for both of us... and as I write this, I only wish I had asked what her name was.

One name which I never forgot was actress Karen Black, known for her varied film roles, especially *Five Easy Pieces*. We met on one of my many appearances on *The Alan Hamel Show* in Vancouver, which were becoming an annual event. On the show, Karen was eccentric yet very funny, and the following day we flew back to Los Angeles together. We laughed through the entire flight and decided to meet for a drink at the Improv the following evening.

The following night arrived, and as we sat in the lounge area of the Improv, enjoying a drink, I was shocked and delighted to see Cher walk in with her flavor of the week boyfriend. I pointed her out to Karen, who didn't seem impressed—in fact she appeared rather peeved. In spite of her reaction, I excused myself and strolled over to say "Hi" to Cher. Upon seeing me, she gave me a big hug and introduced me to her date, actor Val Kilmer. In my attempt to impress her that I was with someone who was also well known, I told her I was with Karen Black. Cher then sarcastically responded with "Well keep her to yourself," and proceeded to deliberately avoid looking her way.

When I returned to Karen, she explained to me that she appeared with Cher in the play, *Come Back to the Five and Dime, Jimmy Dean, Jimmy Dean,* which was later turned into a small film, and they did not get along at all. Karen didn't want to get into the reasons why, which I respected.

A couple of months later, Karen and I coincidentally hooked up again when we were both working in London, England, on different shows. While there, we met for dinner at a quaint, proper English pub, where we were asked to quiet down or leave because we were laughing too loud and too much. Too bad. If you're wondering if Karen and I ever became intimate, the answer would be no. We simply enjoyed each other's company and did not see each other again for many more years.

Once back on U.S. soil, I ventured into cable television, writing and putting together a comedy show entitled *The Unknown Comedy Hour* for the Playboy Channel. It was a combination of sketches and stand-up material performed by myself, Johnny Dark, and my young buddy James Marcel, the juggler.

The show became Playboy's second-highest-rated show that year, and once again, I was put on the "list" of invitees to the mansion.

When you were on the "list," you could visit the mansion anytime and watch movies with Hef, where current films were projected onto a large screen. For me, one of the best perks was the food, which was available twenty-four hours a day because chefs manned his kitchen around the clock. At the mansion, you also became aware that Hef was always in a robe: morning, noon, or night. My guess is he always wanted to be prepared for bed, because having sex available 24/7 from plenty of gorgeous ladies had to be exhausting.

Still, my sex life, though nowhere near as plentiful as Hef's, continued to flourish. However, I knew my philandering ways were about to end because I was getting serious with Connie, and we decided she should move in with me. Connie was a beauty and had posed in a sexy bikini for a poster for an oil company which appeared everywhere.

One day, I took my car to a mechanic for some repairs, and plastered on their wall was Connie's poster. Proudly, I mentioned to the mechanics that the girl in the poster was my girlfriend. They looked at me... and laughed, convinced I was joking. I guess the joke was on them... or was it on me? Whatever!

1983

I was saddened to hear that after fifty-one years of service on Sunset Boulevard, my home away from home, Schwab's closed down because of financial difficulties. An auction was held and everything, even the rolodexes with celebrity names like Judy Garland, Sylvester Stallone, Danny Thomas, Goldie Hawn, Al Pacino, Shelley Winters, and many unknowns—myself included—went to the highest bidder.

Meanwhile, my girlfriend Connie's ex-roommate Karen's writing career was soaring, as she went from writing more episodes of *Eight is Enough* to working regularly on the highly acclaimed series "*M*A*S*H*." More kudos to her when she was credited as one of the writers on the final episode.

Great news for Connie, when she got a job as a model on a new game show *Sale of the Century*, making close to $2,000 a day, working one or two days a week. In the past, Connie had been travelling with me most of the time, but this new job brought a swift end to that.

A red flag erupted in our relationship when I was appearing at the Hacienda. My piano player, Steve, had a girlfriend Lynn, who became good friends with Connie, and whenever we were out of town, they frequently hung out together. One night after a show, Connie and Lynn called, telling us they were invited to a party at the Playboy Mansion and asked if we would mind if they went.

Steve told Lynn that he preferred that she didn't go but that it was her decision to make, and I told Connie the same thing. Days later, Steve told me Lynn chose not to go, respecting Steve's feelings, but Connie did go and her lack of respect for me evidenced itself even further in that she went in my Rolls Royce.

Meanwhile, my friend Kent had befriended a film producer Bill Osco, who was going to make a horror film, directed by his wife, Jackie Kong. I learned Osco had made millions writing and producing porno films, which were shown in movie theaters. He had huge moneymaking hits with his porn versions of films like *Alice in Wonderland* and *Flesh Gordon*, but he wanted to break into more mainstream legitimate films.

Kent was hired as a coproducer and offered me a small role. The movie was called *The Being*, and was to feature three Academy Award winners: Martin Landau, Dorothy Malone, and Jose Ferrer. (FYI, Jose Ferrer was married to Rosemary Clooney, was the father-in-law of Debby Boone, and was the uncle of George Clooney.)

Unfortunately, those actors must have accepted the roles because their careers were on a major downward swing. The only horror in this movie was it was *horror*-ble. It was a terrible film, and I was fortunate getting killed within the first few scenes.

Another performer I had the kinky pleasure of meeting on that film, was a very eccentric comedy singer/author Kinky Friedman, known by many for his song "They Don't Make Jews Like Jesus Anymore."

After eight months, my gig at the Hacienda came to an end, and I had to seek out other opportunities. I was not used to working regular comedy clubs, but I decided to accept a few offers from around the country.

My first shows on the road were well received but that didn't matter. I was not a fan of being in a distant city where I'd perform a show nightly, then have twenty-three hours to kill in a place where I knew no one. Though I was making good money, I was not enjoying myself. My passion in life had slowly evolved and veered away from show business, stand-up comedy, and comedy acting. My new passion was to simply enjoy my life to the fullest, and being away from my girlfriend, home, and friends was not appealing, gratifying, or fulfilling to me.

However, I didn't mind working Las Vegas, which was always like a second home, especially with one of my best friends Jimmy always willing to share great conversation and wine. Jimmy was more than my friend. He was really more like my brother, even though I had both a younger and older brother in Canada.

I believe because I left home at such an early age, I never felt much of a connection with my older brother Ronnie, who lived in Montreal, though I did enjoy my rare visits with him, his wife, and their six kids. My brother Ron and I really were distant relatives in more ways than just living miles apart.

I don't place blame on either one of us. It was what it was and is what it is. I believe our lack of closeness might be due to the fact that Ronnie was a year older, and at the age of twelve he left home for a Catholic boarding school. Going the religious route was completely alien to my thinking, which was more in tune with finding out what girls looked like naked. My relationship with my younger brother, Gary, though somewhat closer, did not evolve to any great degree either.

On one of my visits to Montreal to visit my brother Ron and his family, he told me that he had never seen stand-up comedy live. So I brought him and his wife to a small comedy club, where they were amazed watching a young unknown talent named Jim Carrey. Though I found him lacking in material, he easily captivated the small audience with his unbridled energy and array of incredible impressions, bringing the crowd to their feet with a standing ovation at the end of his set.

After Jim's performance, I congratulated him on a great job, and just as I knew that Robin Williams would make it to the top when I first worked with him, so did I feel this same kind of intuitiveness about this young performer.

Months later, out of the blue, my producer buddy Chris Bearde called again, offering me another job. He asked if I would be one of the lead performers on a couple of specials for The Playboy Channel, to be called *The Sex and Violence Family Hour.* My immediate response was "Hell Yes!" Anything to get out of working the club circuit.

The show was again shot in Canada, and when I arrived at the studio, I was sent to the rehearsal hall where a sign was posted on the door which read "Closed Set. Do Not Enter." The director, Harvey Frost, whom I had not yet met, was in the middle of rehearsing a sketch using several topless ladies. I slowly entered and crept to the back of the hall, enjoying the sexy scenery.

The director spotted me out of the corner of his eye, and believing I was an intruder immediately brought the action to a halt, yelling,

"What the hell are you doing here? This is a closed set." When I explained that I was The Unknown Comic, his demeanor suddenly changed, and he excitedly grabbed me and paraded me to everyone, especially the topless ladies. I just knew this was going to be another fun job.

He then introduced me to a new young comic hired to work with me named Jim Carrey. Who knew that the kid I had just seen in a club a few months earlier was now going to be in the same TV show with me. You could see that Carrey, though appearing in his first television show, possessed a unique style, delving deep into a character causing you to forget Jim was even in the room. Getting to know this young newcomer, it was obvious he was totally consumed with perfecting his craft, determined to make it big. We performed several sketches together, most notably one where I played a cocaine addict.

I couldn't help but feel mesmerized at Carrey's abilities as a comic performer, even though by now, I was supposedly the more seasoned professional.

Once back in Los Angeles, I was happy to be home with Connie and my friends. I was convinced that I was falling in love with her and she with me, so we decided to get engaged. However, in the back of my mind, I was worried. Blame it on my insecurity, which I've felt dating back to my teen years: the insecurity that led me into show business, which can provide love, not from just one person but from hundreds, thousands, even millions of people, depending on your level of success.

My problem with Connie was that I felt I was always there for her, but seldom felt she was there for me. It seemed that she was more interested in partying with a group of people than being alone with me. I was also confused with how she could spend the $2,000 a week she was earning as fast as it came in. Still, our personalities seem to gel and there was always plenty of laughter, which I believed was the glue which kept our relationship together. But I could have been wrong. It could have been crazy glue.

Me and Connie with my good friends Ruth and Kent.

Me and Johnny Dark at Jimmy & Judy's house.

1984

The laughs continued, and the new year began with more work when I was asked to star in another sketch TV pilot entitled *Uncensored*, which was later released as a video. We filmed in and around Las Vegas, including at my new house. The show also featured a young actress/comedienne, Cassandra Peterson, who later gained recognition as horror hostess Elvira, Mistress of the Dark. I managed to also get my girlfriend Connie involved in the show, and she proved herself worthy in the sketches she and I performed in.

It was also the year I decided to unbag myself. One of my comic buddies, Skip Stevenson, who had frequently performed at my club "Show-Biz," was one of the hosts of a new network television show called *Real People*. Skip suggested I should debag on the show for publicity, and I agreed because I felt my Unknown Comic act had pretty much run its course. So off came the bag, and the reaction was neither good nor bad.

One nice consequence was a call from Bill Dana, known for a character he created, José Jiménez, which dated back to *The Ed Sullivan Show*. Dana was a prolific writer of humor and wanted to do a joke book about The Unknown Comic, offering an advance of $10,000. It took me seconds to respond, and we met to discuss the book, which was later published and sold in the tens, perhaps even twenties.

It was a financial loss for Dana's publishing company, convincing me that I was right about The Unknown Comic character having run its course, but Bill and I, nevertheless, became good buddies. I was tiring of the character anyway and felt it was time to move in another direction. The slogan "Change is Growth" had been my motto, and I felt it was time to move forward not backward, but I still worried about going downward.

People often told me that I was lucky coming up with The Unknown Comic character but I never looked at it that way. I often thought that if I had never created the bag character, I might have actually garnered more success as Murray Langston. Of course, the answer will never be known and my life has been so much fun, I wouldn't change places with anyone anyway.

I was happy to hear that The Unknown Comic was still in demand in other places like Australia, where I was invited to appear on several TV shows. A lot of people are not aware that *The Gong Show* originated in Australia. Having never been there, I was excited that I would be paid and flown to this new and fun vacation spot. Unfortunately, because of Connie's work schedule on her game show, she couldn't join me.

My back was aching after the long flight, and when I checked into the hotel, I asked the desk clerk if they had a Jacuzzi. In his heavy Australian accent, he replied, "Just a minute, mate," then proceeded to leaf through a book on the counter. After turning several pages, he looked up and said, "No sir, he must have checked out." "What?" I responded, "Who checked out?" "Your Mr. Jacuzzi" he replied, "He's no longer registered here." "No, I'm not talking about a Mr. Jacuzzi," I said, using my hand to make circular motions, "My back is sore from the long flight and I was hoping to get into a hot Jacuzzi." He then understood, saying, "Ah, we call those whirlpools, not Jacuzzis." Okay, it's not a hysterical story, but it is cute... and true.

The next morning as I sat in the coffee shop waiting to be picked up, I heard a familiar voice behind me. I turned to see that it was another teen idol from my childhood, Ricky Nelson. I introduced myself and was surprised when he and his band members had heard of me. They were also booked on the same television shows I was scheduled to appear on, and within minutes our ride showed up. Though my time with Ricky Nelson was limited, my impression was that he was a super nice guy whose life tragically ended a few months later and way too soon.

My week in Australia was a combination of work, travel, and fun, and then it was back home, where I tried to figure out where my personal life was headed. It seemed to be slowly unraveling, with red flags surfacing on a regular basis. During a conversation with a friend, he let it slip that a comic friend of ours, Kevin Nealon, had been at my house a few times alone with Connie when I was in Australia. I had previously noticed some flirtation between the two of them when Kevin and I worked together, but let it go, not wanting to appear jealous.

When I asked Connie about it, she responded that he was JUST a friend. I explained that if he was stopping by to visit with her while I was out of town, he was NO friend of mine. And he wasn't. He was an acquaintance at best. A few nights later, I saw Kevin at the Improv and emphatically let him know I didn't want him visiting my home when I wasn't there. I don't believe I was upset because I was jealous but rather because, in my view, Connie was disrespecting our relationship by allowing someone I barely knew to be in my house alone with her.

And there was bad news for Connie when she was fired from her game show. Apparently, when I was on the road, Connie stayed up late on several nights partying, and then sent her girlfriend Lou in to replace her at work, telling her producer she was sick. It didn't take long for her bosses to figure out what was really going on, and after one too many times, they replaced Connie with Lou permanently.

I discovered that the reason for Connie's dismissal was her addiction to cocaine, and the money she had been making was going up her nose. She apparently had been an addict for years and unbeknownst to me was actively engaged in drug use when we first met on the set of the film *Skatetown*.

Addicts want to be around other users, and since I was not into drugs, Connie decided it was time to end our relationship. Believing I was in love with her, I didn't want it to be over, but I soon learned that she'd been doing coke regularly with the owner of an auto dealership with whom she left me for. The truth was that she was not really leaving me for anyone, but for more access to that white powder that she craved. Cocaine had become her true lover.

As I pondered my predicament, I came to the conclusion that ending a relationship was similar to quitting smoking. The first weeks, your thoughts are consumed with the loss and it's on your mind constantly. Then after about a month, you notice that you're not as consumed, but you still think about it regularly. Then after a few more months, you become grateful that your pain is only sporadic, and finally, after more time, you look back and think, "Why did I allow that unhealthy relationship (with a person or cigarettes) to almost wreck my life in the first place?" And you realize that life for you can only get better.

"Happiness is a running stream and not a stagnant pool," a quote, engrained in my brain, thankfully led me in the right direction. I knew I had to find something to keep me busy and get my mind off my breakup with Connie. I had to get back in that stream and not allow myself to wallow in that stagnant pool.

Bill Levey, the director of the film *Skatetown U.S.A.*, and I had become buddies, so I convinced him that we should write a film script about The Unknown Comic. He agreed, and for the next several weeks I was gratefully fully engaged in working with Bill, taking my mind off of Connie. Our film would feature me as an inept cop who moonlights at night as an unknown comedian, wearing a bag over his head. We named it *Night Patrol*.

In the meantime, I took a local gig at the Ice House, where I met a strikingly attractive woman named Gayle, who I hoped would also take my mind off of Connie. She was a head-turner in skin-tight jeans, and she seemed very proud of her bountiful bosom. We spent that first night together, and within days I was smitten with this gorgeous hunk of woman.

I was keenly aware I was on an emotional rebound but regardless, within weeks, Gayle was spending virtually every night with me. Could it be that she really liked me when she told me that she was falling in love, or could it be that having recently lost her job, I could be a nice asset until she got back on her back... I mean feet?

Gayle's sensuality and sexuality were especially convincing when she told me she was unhappy living with her roommates and hinted that she wanted to spend all of her time with me. Though my "inner voice" was telling me not to get serious, my outer extremities were convincing me otherwise.

One night, while we were having dinner in a restaurant, to my surprise, Connie entered with a girlfriend. Spotting me, she came over, and I enjoyed the jealous look she gave Gayle, who couldn't have looked any sexier if she'd been naked. The following day, I received a phone call from Connie telling me she looked back at our break-up as a mistake but my thinking was that getting back with Connie would be a mistake. I was anxious to see if my relationship with Gayle would improve, and once again I felt like I was one lucky guy. But was I?

As months passed, if I thought little red flags were popping up with Connie, those flags seemed much larger with Gayle. I couldn't put my finger on it, though I had many times, but telling me once too often that she was going out with her girlfriends, or suddenly hanging up the phone if I walked into a room unexpectedly, made me a tad suspicious.

When I told my friend Kent about my suspicions, he had known Gayle long enough to have an opinion, and his was that she was trouble. Coincidentally, Kent had been pursuing work as a private investigator and told me that he could hook up my phone with a small tape, record her conversations, and possibly find out her true feelings for me. He was also quick to let me know that I should be prepared for the worst.

The thought of secretly recording her was nerve wracking, but I decided to try it during my next gig out of town. Johnny Dark and I were working a weekend in Arizona, and I asked Gayle to drive us to the airport that Friday morning. Because we were returning at midnight that Sunday, I told Gayle that Johnny and I would take a cab back.

The tape was set, and after Gayle dropped us off, Johnny sensed I was agitated and asked why. When I explained what was going on, Johnny said I was being ridiculous; he said that Gayle was madly in love with me, and he was sure nothing incriminating would be on that tape.

Over the weekend, my phone conversations with Gayle were sprinkled with "I love you" and "I miss you" dialogue, causing me to think that Johnny was right. I swore to myself that if nothing was on that tape, I would never, ever do that again. When we returned, my nerves were on edge. The cab dropped Johnny off first, and I couldn't wait to get back to Gayle's arms, feeling a bit lonely and ashamed of what I had done. I was sure it was my own insecurities being blown out of proportion and nothing would be on that tape.

It was well after midnight, and once inside my house, I tip toed to my room where Gayle was soundly sleeping. My first thought was to crawl into bed and worry about what was on the tape the next day. My second thought was "That's not going to happen." I quietly rushed to where the tape was hidden, grabbed it, snuck outside into the dark, and got into my car. My heart was pounding through my chest as I sat there and pushed "play."

The first thing I heard was a phone ringing. After several rings a click, then a man's voice, "Hello." Next, Gayle's voice, "Hey Danny, I just dropped Murray off at the airport. I can't wait to see you and jump your bones. We're going to have a fuck party tonight." The male voice replied, "Sounds great. I picked up a bottle of tequila; now get your ass over here pronto." There was more sickening, descriptive dialogue, but I was numb as those red flags burst into flames. I felt ill, like I was going to throw up, then anger replaced the sickness as I sat stunned, trying to gather my thoughts before heading back into my house.

Once inside my bedroom, I purposely jumped into the bed next to Gayle. She seemed irritated, and mumbled groggily, "Honey, welcome back. I need sleep. Bother me in the morning, okay?" She softly blew me a kiss and turned away in an attempt to drift back into slumber land. But that was not going to happen.

I sat quietly for a few seconds, unsure of what to say, then I blurted out, "Hey, Gayle! How was your night with Danny?" All of a sudden, she bolted upward like a hard erection, and said "What? What are you talking about? Who's Danny?" I half smiled and replied "You know, Danny. The guy you fucked the other night."

As she continued, I thought this could be how stuttering began. "I, I, I don't know a, a, Da, Danny. Who, who, who t,t,t told you that?" She mentioned one of her roommates. "Was it Darlene? She's a fucking liar. You know she wants us to break up."

Gayle was not an actress, but she could have been, as tears began welling up in her eyes, but they didn't last long when I abruptly clicked on the tape so she could hear her incriminating voice. I did not enjoy the stunned look on her face, neither did I enjoy telling her to pack her stuff and get the fuck out of my house.... "NOW!" She did... and I never saw her again. This falling in love shit ain't easy.

I was once again distraught when Johnny Dark brought some fun into my life by introducing me to one of his new buddies, Taideusz Wladyslaw Konopka, otherwise known as Ted Knight, star of *The Mary Tyler Moore Show*. Johnny met Ted on *The Donny and Marie Show* on which he had become a regular, and they became good buddies. Soon after my disaster with Gayle, I was at lunch with Ted and Johnny, who recognizing the emotional pain I was experiencing, suggested we should go back to Maui. For me, my trips to Maui were always like an enema of the mind, flushing all the crap out of it.

Upon hearing of our plans, Ted immediately indicated he wanted to join us, saying he hadn't had a vacation in years. Even Ted's wife was thrilled that he was going with us, so we booked a flight and became the Three Musketeers, or rather the Three Stooges in Maui.

Even though Ted was worth millions and Johnny and I were worth hundreds, the three of us shared expenses equally, from our rent-a-car to our three-bedroom condo on the ocean. What I loved about Ted was though he was much more famous than Johnny or myself, he always made us feel like equals.

During the entire trip, we never stopped laughing, appreciating all that Maui had to offer from walks on the beach, body surfing, parasailing, and boating, but mostly we enjoyed the evenings when we would eat, drink, and toast the gorgeous weather and scenery, which included lovely ladies everywhere.

During our few rare serious conversations, I was surprised and jealous of Ted when he told us that he had never known heartbreak, having only been in love with his wife who was his high school sweetheart. I thought, what a lucky guy. Johnny and I were also lucky because Ted was so recognizable that we seldom had to wait for a table in just about any restaurant.

Much of Ted's humor hinged on farting, and he loved getting a laugh with a surprise fart. For instance, Ted would say "Hey, Murray, push in on my back, I have a really bad cramp." I of course unsuspectingly assisted him, then... "FRRRRAAAAATTTTTTTTTT," you'd hear a long, loud farting sound followed by Ted's hearty laugh.

Ted was a genius at setting up fart jokes, and almost always succeeded in surprising Johnny and I with one of them. However,

I did get him back one time when I awoke in the middle of the night, needing to take a leak. For fear of waking anyone, I didn't turn on the light and instead tip toed to the bathroom in the darkness.

At about the same time, I heard Ted get up and slowly make his way to the bathroom. Immediately, I sent a request from my brain to my stomach to squeeze as much gas as possible into the ready position. I then hid in the darkness against a wall and when Ted reached the bathroom, at the exact time that he flipped on the light switch, "BRAAAATTTTTT"... I squeezed out one of my proudest farts of all time.

It was timed perfectly, sounding as if it was connected to the switch. We laughed ourselves silly then went back to sleep. Later I was abruptly awakened from a dream of a large cannon exploding. When I opened my eyes, my face was inches from Ted's ass who was laughing so hard, he almost shit himself. I'm so glad he didn't.

When we returned from Maui, Connie got wind of my breakup with Gayle and stopped by. We made love, and again she hinted that we should get back together, but I knew it wasn't for the right reasons. I had to take a break from relationships and get back in that running stream, so I returned to finish writing my script *Night Patrol* with Bill Levey. Next, we had to sell it.

Some months later, I was having dinner at my friends Ruth and Kent's house, who had also invited Bill Osco, the producer of that awful film *The Being*, which I had been in the year before. During our conversation, I mentioned I had written a comedy film script for The Unknown Comic, and Osco was instantly interested.

My initial impression of Osco was that he was a conniving, shady kinda guy, and not very likeable, but because I was tired of performing gigs out of town, I was willing to accept just about any offer. Though he was ready to make a deal, when I explained I had a cowriter, Bill Levey, he expressed concern. Osco suggested we buy Levey out, but what he really meant was I needed to buy him out, otherwise Osco wasn't interested.

He said he was prepared to invest a lot of money into the project, and his wife Jackie, who had read the script, was eager to direct. Since I knew virtually nothing about film production, they sold me on their abilities to make a successful, funny film, and since I was excited about starring in my own movie, I agreed. I told Levey about my deal with Osco, and he didn't think much of it, but said he'd take $20,000 for his half of the script. After some astute negotiations on my part, we settled for $20,000. It was an investment in myself and a risk I felt worth taking, so I wrote him a check.

I felt better when Osco informed me that for my $20,000 investment I'd receive ten percent of the film's profits. He immediately opened an office, showing he meant business, and suddenly *Night Patrol* was a go, and I was going to star in my own movie. But first, he said we needed well-known names to boost the film's prospect of being picked up by a distributor

Months before, I had befriended former Presidential candidate and comedian extraordinaire, Pat Paulsen, whom I had met when we worked together in Vegas. Pat was well known from his appearances on *The Smothers Brothers Show* and even starred in his own TV series for a short time. Because we liked each other more than it's normal for two guys to like each other, I wanted him to become my best friend number five, after Ted, Freeman, Kent, and Jimmy— and he did.

I wanted Pat to costar with me in my film, *Night Patrol*, and because he was losing money in a "winery" he owned, he agreed. Pat admitted that money was tight for him and he could use a little extra cash, which was what he was going to get paid, along with the rest of us.

At about the same time, I had just finished a gig in Canada opening for Crystal Gayle, known for her hit song "Don't It Make My Brown Eyes Blue." In the show, we even worked out a bit where we impersonated Sonny and Cher. Crystal, known for her lengthy hair, stood stoic while I fell to my knees next to her playing Sonny Bono as we both sang "I Got You Babe." I then grabbed the bottom of Crystal's hair, and in Sonny's twangy voice said, "Cher, did you know that you have Kunta Kinte hair?" Crystal as Cher replied, "What makes you say that, Sonny?" Holding her hair, I responded "Because it's a long way back to its roots." It was corny but funny at the time, and the audience loved it.

At one point, I casually mentioned to Crystal about my impending movie, *Night Patrol*, and she joked "Is there a part in it for me?" Because she looked the part of the female lead, I told her that if she was serious, I would send her a script. Crystal replied that she was very serious, telling me that she'd been taking acting lessons.

When I returned to L.A., I had the script immediately sent to her, and then told Osco about it. However, Osco had learned about my friendship with Linda Blair and urged me to call her, believing her box office potential exceeded Crystal Gayle's.

At first I was hesitant, thinking Linda, not at all known for comedy, would surely say no. But I was wrong. Upon hearing my pitch and after reading the script, Linda jumped at the idea of doing something completely silly and out of her comfort zone.

I called Crystal, and before I could tell her our plans, she told me that after looking at our shooting schedule, she would have to cancel too many gigs, so she bowed out, allowing us to go full speed ahead with Linda. With Pat Paulsen and Linda Blair on board, I was sure our film would turn out great; I was further convinced when my friend Ruth Buzzi also joined the cast.

Night Patrol was set to be filmed in four weeks: two weeks of shooting, two weeks off, then two more weeks of shooting. The excitement built when we added some other friends of mine to our cast: Jack Riley of *The Bob Newhart Show*; Pat Morita, who was appearing on the series *Happy Days*; and famed little guy, Billy Barty. Added to this mix a quirky young comic I had just met, named Andrew "Dice" Clay. We actually tried to get another comic, Sam Kinison, but because his career was suddenly taking off, he politely declined.

Through the crew, we heard that another comedy cop movie was being made, called *Police Academy*. We were sure it was nothing like ours, but decided to rush production, hoping to get an earlier release date.

Bill Osco's wife Jackie Kong, our director, began rehearsals, and it didn't take long before I realized she was a frickin' megalomaniac. I hadn't noticed it on the set of *The Being*, but I only worked on that film one day. In front of my eyes, Jackie Kong acted more like King Kong, wanting to rule the set like a loony toon prima donna member of the Gestapo. Extras were told not to approach her, and she was prone to temper tantrums, yelling at the crew when she'd get upset. And all that in just the first hour! By the end of the day, Ruth Buzzi couldn't take it and quit. Perhaps all's well that ends well, but it was still a long way to the end of the shoot, and I was already committed.

With $20,000 invested, I couldn't walk away, so I called my friend from *The Gong Show*, Jaye P. Morgan, and pleaded with her to replace Ruth who I told her suddenly got sick. I just didn't say sick... of the director. Luckily Jaye P. agreed, rushed to the set, and we continued, but I was terribly afraid things could get worse.

I was grateful Linda Blair wasn't there that first day. I took Osco aside, telling him that Linda was our insurance for selling the film and had to be treated like a queen or she'd walk. Bill must have said something to his wife, because when Linda showed up, Jackie treated her lovingly and respectfully. Osco must have threatened her with no sex for a month, or perhaps it was the opposite. I also began to notice that Jackie slowly began treating me with respect, perhaps a little more than I deserved.

I've always had a distaste for people who belittle anyone, especially after my experience with Sonny Bono, and I did not like our director at all. I was bothered that she seemed to want to hang out in my dressing room, insisting we rehearse scenes privately. At first I thought it must be my imagination, but slowly I realized that Jackie was subtly coming on to me.

I knew she saw me flirting with girls on the set, especially now that I was single again, but no way, even if I liked her, would I engage in anything inappropriate with the producer's wife. In fact, no matter how sexy a woman is, if she's in a relationship with someone I know, in my mind they immediately became like a sister to me. I'm not saying I've never had sex with my sister, but... wait a second, I'm getting away from the point I was trying to make.

What I was trying to say was there was no way I would have sex with Jackie Kong, even if she paid me a million dollars. Okay, that's not true either. A million dollars is a lot of money, but seriously there was no way in hell, or here on earth, or even in Barstow, California, that I would have fucked Jackie Kong. But after a week, I was starting to feel that if I didn't respond to her in some way, she would seriously try to fuck me, but in a different way. What amazed me was that her husband Osco seemed oblivious to it all.

The end of the second week of filming arrived, and I was thrilled with the process. Though I was happy with the script as it was, Jackie insisted that during the break we should work together and make some improvements on it. However, I was convinced that she didn't have a funny bone in her body and she certainly wasn't going to have anything to do with mine. My funny bone, that is.

Coincidentally, Johnny Dark, who also had a part in the film, told me that Ted Knight had such a great time in Maui that he was ready to go back again. The timing was perfect. I told Jackie that I couldn't work with her because Ted, Johnny, and I had previously made plans for another trip to Maui.

I think she understood, but not completely. A few days later, I was standing at the airport counter with Ted and Johnny, and we were already laughing when I was suddenly shocked, hearing a familiar voice call out "Murray!" I turned and couldn't believe my eyes when I saw Jackie standing in front of me. She told me that at the last minute she booked a flight, and how great it was going to be that we'd be able to work on the script together in Maui. And to boot, her husband was too busy with more preproduction to join us.

Holy Shit! I thought to myself, *This can't be happening.* Luckily, she was in coach and we were in first class, so I didn't have her breathing down my pants—I mean neck. When we arrived in Maui, I reluctantly told Jackie where we were staying, and she said she would call after she checked into her hotel.

I was determined I wasn't going to let her spoil our fun in Maui and decided, no matter what the result, I was not going to spend one single moment with her. This was a vacation, and I wasn't going to jeopardize the good times I was looking forward to having with Ted and Johnny.

The following day when she called, I had Johnny answer the phone. We made up a story that I had met a girl the night before, spent the night at her place, and they had no idea how to reach me. The phone calls persisted, and each time either no one answered or the guys repeated the same story.

Aside from that major/minor annoyance, our week was once again fabulous. Johnny had taken up jogging, and every morning he ran from the condo to the Hyatt Regency Hotel. Ted and I would give him a thirty-minute start, then hop into the car, and meet him at the Hyatt where we would have breakfast. That routine continued every morning, then we would nap, spend the afternoons sightseeing, and then eat dinner at a new restaurant where the laughs would continue. Life was great for the Three Stooges.

One day, we drove across the island to Hana, where my buddy Bill Dana and his wife Evelyn were living. It's about an eighty-mile trip, which takes a minimum of two and a half hours, depending on how many stops you make. Aside from the many beaches, you're constantly surrounded by breathtaking views, majestic waterfalls, and lush, tropical landscape no matter which way you look. The rough part is that it has over 600 curves—many of them precarious—and more than fifty small bridges to cross. It was a hell of a drive, which I enjoyed immensely, but Johnny and Ted wished we'd brought along a barf bag. When we finally arrived at Bill Dana's house, we had a fabulous time enjoying a dinner they served us, and the laughs were plentiful. Overall, our entire week was a fun experience, except for the Jackie part. I never saw her again until we were back on set in Los Angeles.

Jackie apparently did not have fun in Maui and, feeling scorned, was intent on making the final two weeks of shooting miserable for me. She would purposely have me redo scenes, attempting to embarrass me in front of everyone, insinuating I was not a capable actor. But I really didn't care about this film anymore. At this point, my personal happiness was more important than any career happiness. My priorities had shifted slightly and for the better.

My deal with Osco was that I would be heavily involved in the editing process, but Jackie convinced him that I was no longer needed which was fine with me. The final product was, in my opinion, a pathetic, unfunny film, the context of which made no sense and barely resembled my vision. However, there must have been a hunger for bad comedies, because when New World Pictures released it in theatres, it became one of their highest grossing films of that year. Millions were made, but I never even recouped the $20,000 I paid for half of the script. The only money I ever received was through the union for my work as an actor.

One night, I was watching David Letterman with his guest Debra Winger, and I was pleasantly surprised when they mentioned my club "Show-Biz" where they used to hang out. It had been about ten years since I had last seen Debra, so I phoned her to say thank you for the nice mention. She was surprised to hear from me, and we chit chatted about her new love, the then-Governor of Nebraska, Bob Kerry, whom she met while filming *Terms of Endearment*. We also talked about the fact that she helped cast Freeman in the movie she had just begun shooting, *Mike's Murder*. Though Debra was a huge star, she still sounded like the sweet young thing who got me busted at my club years ago, when she was drinking underage.

Next, I called NBC in New York and asked for David Letterman, hoping to also thank him for the mention, and wondering if he would accept my call? He did, and we engaged in some lightweight conversation about the good old days and our mutual comic buddies. David then told me I should appear on his show again and suggested I call his producer, Robert Morton.

After hanging up, I felt David's words were genuine, but when I later talked to his producer, I sensed a different tone. His response was rather cool and he asked that I send a tape of some stand-up for him to look at. Perhaps I was oversensitive, but I assumed that Morton was giving me the brush-off at David's behest, and I never did send them a tape.

As the year came to a close, Paul Block, who had originally booked me on *The Tonight Show*, and the *Everyday* show, was now producing Alan Hamel's talk show in Canada. Paul called and asked if I'd like to guest host two of the episodes. I agreed immediately, but my anxiety shot through the roof when I showed up in Vancouver, unsure of whether hosting a talk show was something I would be good at.

I asked Paul if he could book my friends Ruth Buzzi and her husband Kent to be my first guests, and he thought it was a great idea. On the day of taping, Paul guided me through my duties, and once I was introduced and got my first laugh, I felt everything was going to be okay.

In addition to Ruth and Kent, my other guests included Levar Burton, comic Paul Provenza, and a well-known Canadian guitarist, Liona Boyd.

Once the shows were over, I arrived at the conclusion that hosting a talk show was probably something I could do, especially with a year or so of experience. Keep in mind: Johnny Carson hosted the tonight show for almost a year before he was relaxed enough to make hosting a talk show look easy. Now if I can only make writing these memoirs look easy.

My sister Annette with comics Skip Stephenson and Roger Behr.

Me with Ted Knight and Johnny Dark on the beach in Hawaii.

Me with Ted Knight and Johnny Dark visiting Bill Dana in Hawaii.

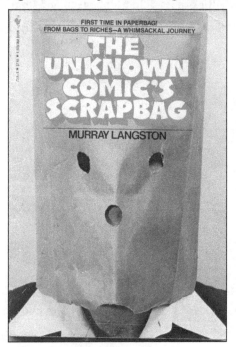

The Unknown Comic book.

1985

One night, I was at the Improv when I met Rodney Dangerfield, who was holding court with several comics around a table in the lounge area. I was invited to join them and noticed how everyone laughed at everything he said, which I believed was because he was a big comedy star. You could tell Rodney enjoyed being the center of attention, and from what I knew of his journey to the top, he deserved it.

I had met and worked with countless celebrities, but one I'd never encountered was Dolly Parton—who I loved. However, I was thrilled when she mentioned in a *People* magazine article that her husband would often put a bag over his head and pretend he was The Unknown Comic. Very cool.

Not so cool was Karen Hall, my ex-girlfriend's southern roommate who had surpassed her writing skills, branching into producing television shows such as *Moonlighting*. I found it rather disconcerting that she refused to help her two roommates Connie and Lou, never submitting them for any kind of a part when she could easily have done so.

Once making it to the top, Karen apparently felt she was above helping those who helped her. In my view, success really had a detrimental effect on her southern hospitality. I bumped into her at a shopping mall, wishing I had bumped a little harder, and asked if she was ever going to help out her ex-roomies. She responded with an uncaring, snobbish "I've just been too busy."

I had a two week gig in Lake Tahoe where I worked at with the Platters and after my first night, I received a call from Chris Bearde again. Gotta love that guy Chris. He wanted me to star in a pilot for a late night half hour sketch comedy show entitled, "Sunset Strip". Needless to say, I accepted the offer, but he needed me to shoot the following weekend however I told him I was committed to my gig in Tahoe and wouldn't be available. Chris replied, "Not a problem." He only needed me to shoot during the day, so he would lease a Lear Jet to take me back and forth from Los Angeles to Tahoe. Needless to say, I agreed again and we filmed a very funny pilot in which I performed sketches with an unknown sketch actor named Phil Hartman who two years later became one of the stars of *Saturday Nite Live*. A dozen years later, Phil died tragically, murdered by his wife. Also appearing with me on the show were Flo and Eddie, formerly known as The Turtles, who sprung to fame in the sixties with a huge number one hit, "Happy Together." Sadly, once again, the pilot did not sell and I began to wonder if I was destined to be "Unknown" with or without the bag.

After the pilot I was kept busy when I was asked to perform for the troops in Korea with my new best friend number five, Pat Paulsen. As a veteran I willingly accepted, recalling how seeing live entertainment from home was always such a welcome event. Though we weren't Bob Hope, many of the troops had heard of us, and our shows were extremely well received, making me proud.

The tour afforded Pat and I to get to know each other better and become closer friends. Driving around the outskirts of Korea, I was struck by how every inch of land was used in some capacity. In Korea, property was considered such a precious commodity; there was virtually no vacant land anywhere. Even the center dividers on the highways were used to plant either rice or vegetables.

When we returned, I was offered a small part playing a gay doctor named Ramon in a film called *Stitches*. It was a comedy about students in a medical school, starring Eddie Albert and Parker Stevenson. I was not given a script and had to ad-lib my scene, which turned out funny, but I wasn't looking forward to any Academy Awards.

Meanwhile, a local radio personality Rick Dees was hosting live comedy shows at Universal Studios, and he asked me to appear with a fellow Canadian, Howie Mandel. We had previously made appearances together on *Make Me Laugh* and in Canada on Alan Thicke's talk show. Besides being a funny standup, Howie was slowly gaining fame as one of the characters on the hit TV show *St. Elsewhere*. One night, I invited Howie to my home for a late-night spaghetti dinner after one of our performances, and my old friend Joe Battaglia cooked a spaghetti feast for us. Unlike Teri Garr, Howie loved it, and said he would know he's a success when he had his own Italian chef making pasta for his buddies.

Though the year had been mostly uneventful, I received a call from the producer of Jerry Lewis's Muscular Dystrophy telethon saying that Jerry wanted me to perform on it, and of course I agreed. When I was backstage preparing for Jerry to introduce me, I was a little anxious, knowing the large echoing auditorium was not the best setting for comics. However, I was more than pleasantly surprised when I rushed onstage after Jerry's introduction to see the entire audience, including the crew, with bags over their heads. It was a tribute to my bag character, which I really appreciated, and my performance was well received. Once again, my comic idol Jerry Lewis came through for me and I just couldn't help but feel love for the guy.

During this period, I also befriended a teen singing idol from my past, Frankie Avalon, along with his wife Kay and their eight children. I was invited to their home for dinner on many occasions and non-occasions. They were indeed wonderful people, and Frankie guested on a pilot for a talk show that I hosted, which unfortunately never sold.

Through Frankie, I became friendly with another teen idol, James Darren, and at one point, James and I were approached by a television producer to host our own variety show similar to Martin and Lewis. James would be the great looking singer and I, the comic foil. James Darren was incredibly good looking, which at times could be frustrating. At one of our meetings in an outdoor cafe, I recall the waitress swooning over him so much so that I doubt she even noticed that I was sitting at the same table opposite him.

Nevertheless, it was unbelievable and inconceivable that there was a possibility of starring in my own television variety show. James and I were brought to CBS studios where we met with the top executive in charge of programming. While the producer launched into his sales pitch, describing the great show he would produce for them, the executive seldom reacted and rarely smiled, and I was sure our shot at the big time was not looking good. At the end of the meeting, I thought I would give one final try at some levity before we left. When the executive extended his hand to shake, I slipped some money into it, folding his fingers over and said, "See what you can do."

The executive opened his hand and saw two crunched up one dollar bills. I immediately grabbed one of the bills from his hand and said, "Oops. I didn't mean to give you both of them." The executive finally chuckled, but it never led to our own show. So close yet so far. The story of my life. But, nonetheless, a great life.

Whenever I could, I still occasionally worked at The Comedy and Magic Club, where a new breed of comedians opened for me. One talented comic who impressed me with his originality was Robert Wuhl, who went on to costar in *Good Morning, Vietnam* with Robin Williams and *Batman* with Michael Keaton. I always loved watching new comics, never feeling jealousy, only awe, when it was someone I felt might be destined for stardom. Another young comic who opened for me was David Spade who was destined for fame as a regular on the late night show, *Saturday Night Live*. That same year I got to work in Las Vegas at the Sands Hotel with The Kingston Trio on the same stage where Frank Sinatra and the Rat Pack entertained audiences.

Me and my good friend Pat Paulsen with Steve Rossi.

The Kingston Trio and The Unknown Comic on the "Sands" billboard.

A brown-bagged audience awaits the arrival of The Unknown Comic, aka Murray Langston, yesterday as part of the Hubcap Comedy Festival at Moncton's Capitol Theatre. Langston, who came to fame on 1970s' TV show The Gong Show, is originally from Bathurst.

The audience with bags on their heads at Jerry Lewis's Telethon.

1986

O ne comic who I loved watching was Bobcat Goldwaithe, an eccentric personality, who gained fame with his rowdy appearances in the *Police Academy* films. I discovered he and his wife lived a few houses down the street from me. Even more coincidental, Bobcat told me that when he first moved to Los Angeles, he moved into the same small one-bedroom cottage in North Hollywood that I had lived in. He told me that the owners tried to impress him with the fact that The Unknown Comic had previously lived there.

Another comic I was impressed with, opened for me several times at a comedy club in Cleveland, Ohio. He had just been discharged from the Marines and his name was Drew Carey. After our shows, Drew and I would hang out and talk comedy, and I told him he needed to move to Los Angeles as soon as possible if he wanted to make it big. Drew also told me that for a while he lived in Las Vegas and used to hang out at the back of the lounge watching me when I worked at the Sahara.

I was surprised, meeting another Drew while having lunch at a small Mexican restaurant in Los Angeles. I was sitting alone when two women approached me and the older one said, "Hi Murray." I didn't recognize the woman who called me by my name, but I certainly knew who the other girl was. It was Drew Barrymore, who also said hello. The older woman then introduced herself as Jaid Barrymore, Drew's mom.

I was a bit embarrassed that I didn't recognize Jaid until she informed me that we had met years earlier when I was emceeing at the Comedy Store in Westwood, which she managed for Mitzi at the time. She also told me that on a few occasions when she would have to run errands, she would have me babysit a two year old Drew Barrymore. Who knew? Well, Jaid Barrymore did. When they left, I couldn't help but think that Jaid was very attractive, and I wished I had asked her for her phone number, which might have led to us getting married and me becoming Drew Barrymore's stepdad. It could have happened.

Though I was dating on a regular basis, I still longed to be in a relationship. Trolling for women was not something I really enjoyed, though I had become fairly good at it. But being good doesn't necessarily mean it was all good. At the Improv, I met a waitress named Melissa who was attractive and perky, and we struck up a friendship, which led to spending nights together over the course of several weeks. I had not given her any indication that we were heading toward a serious relationship but soon discovered her assumptions were substantially different from mine.

One night, after not having seen Melissa for a week, I entered The Improv and spotted her waitressing, thinking everything was fine. It was not. When she saw me, she angrily screamed at me because I hadn't called her in a few days and threatened to throw a bottle at me if I didn't get the fuck out immediately.

Not wanting to escalate the awkward situation, I got the fuck out and walked across the street to my other hangout, the Mustache Cafe. At the bar, I saw an old comic buddy, Allan Stephan, and when I told him what just occurred, he proceeded to tell me he also dated Melissa. He continued, telling me the bizarre ending to their short relationship, which occurred at his apartment. In a jealous rage, she began throwing many of his personal belongings against the wall, smashing them into pieces.

In the midst of her trashing his place, and in an effort to keep her from breaking more of his things, he finally suggested, "Can't we go over to your place and finish this argument?" Alan also explained that Melissa was a comic groupie who was obsessed with marrying someone successful so she could quit her waitressing job. All I could think of was you'd have to be crazy to marry this nutty screwball.

Even though I had now developed a fear of waitresses, on another night at The Mustache Cafe, I couldn't take my eyes, ears, nose, and throat off a new girl who looked like an angel. That devil in me couldn't resist this adorable creature, and I was overjoyed when I offered to take her out for coffee after work and she accepted. Her name was Shannon, and I took her to a well-known deli called "Cantors." On the drive there, we chatted, and I liked the fact that she had no idea what I did for a living. She said she accepted my invitation because she thought I was a nice guy who could be trusted. Well, I was a nice guy.

Once at the Deli, I spotted Rodney Dangerfield, again holding court at a large table. He saw me and called me over, offering me a job performing at his namesake club in New York. I accepted, and then moved to another booth with Shannon who asked me who he was. She had never heard of Rodney Dangerfield—and I liked that even better.

Shannon really surprised me when I discovered she was only nineteen: and I was forty-one which was almost twice her age. Okay, so you're better at math than I am. I also learned that she was from New Orleans, where she left an abusive relationship with her mom and had been on her own for two years. Granted she was young, but as I got to know her, I became impressed with her inquisitive mind. She was studying philosophy part time and seemed very intent on making a mark in the world.

I was also attracted to her because she showed little interest in getting into the entertainment business. Up to that point, most, if not all the women in my life, had been wannabe actresses. Nevertheless, Shannon was way too young for me, and I knew a serious relationship with her would end miserably. Two weeks later, Shannon moved in with me.

Timing is everything, especially for Shannon, when an agent buddy of mine, Marc Gurvitz, booked me to appear on the Bob Monkhouse show, a variety/talkshow in London, England. Marc also had a new girlfriend, so we decided to make this gig a fun vacation and take our ladies with us.

We had an amazing time sightseeing throughout London, plus a highlight was when we got to hang out with another of Marc's clients, Maurice Gibb of the Bee Gees. We were invited to his mansion, where he gave us a tour of his luxurious home and expansive property. Maurice was a charming host, even playing for us a batch of new songs that he'd recorded in his private studio.

Later, as we drank wine, he showed us several episodes of a British TV series, *Fawlty Towers*, that starred John Cleese. We all laughed ourselves silly, which for me is the only way to laugh.

When we returned home, I was happy to hear my Russian comic buddy—Yakov Smirnoff—got his own television series called *What a Country*. Ever since I gave him his first nightclub job in Las Vegas, we developed a fairly close relationship, and I was happy for his new found success. I could tell he looked up to me, when he bought a house in the hills just like I did, then installed electric gates like I did. He even bought a Rolls Royce as I had done. I was with a beautiful woman so it was just a matter of time before Yakov would also find a beautiful woman. Thankfully her name wasn't Shannon, it was Linda.

Sadly, I began to observe in Yakov a driven personality who was determined to be a success, not because of his passion for show business, but his passion to become wealthy. Yakov was rarely funny off-the-cuff or in public. To Yakov, comedy was a business to be taken seriously, and I wondered if his approach toward his goal would take a toll on his happiness. My happiness took a tumble when my Maui buddy Ted Knight died of colon cancer. His death was a shock even though I'd know about his illness. He told me he believed his cancer resulted from his battle with alcohol when he was younger, but he was grateful to have been in remission for years. His death was still hard to believe because in Maui he seemed so robust and full of life. Our fun vacations and the laughter we shared will always be indelible in my mind and in his memory, every once in a while, I'll let out a silent fart.

Alive and well was my ex-writing buddy Bill Levey, who offered me a small role of a bus driver in a film he was directing called *Lightening the White Stallion*. It starred Mickey Rooney, and I was sort of anxious to meet the first celebrity who I ever saw in person when I was a kid.

I could still vividly see myself at twelve years old, watching Mickey Rooney through a restaurant window, and now we were going to be working together on the same film. I wondered if he was still as intimidating and unapproachable as he was back then. I'd heard that he could be an asshole and he certainly proved it watching him on the set. I felt sorry for Bill, whose attempts at directing were constantly being usurped by the overpowering Mr. Rooney who refused to listen to him. Mickey Rooney was not shy about letting it be known that he knew more than anyone else about making movies and was a legend to be reckoned with. It was truly embarrassing watching this pitiful, self-absorbed, self-proclaimed icon.

There was nothing pitiful or embarrassing about being invited to an annual "Men Only" Republican Event called the Bohemian Grove Society. My lawyer, Tom Rowan, asked me if I would perform for free at this campground for the wealthy, located on 2,700 acres in Monte Rio, California. I later learned it was where some of the most powerful men in the world gathered for fun and frivolity. And there was little to no luxury involved. Everyone had to sleep in tents with virtually no modern conveniences available whatsoever.

Also invited, was my good friend Kent, a staunch republican, and though I was liberal, I was told this event was not about politics, only fun. We were picked up and driven to the airport, where Kent and I were escorted into a small private lear jet owned by billionaire Dave Packard cofounder of Hewlett-Packard. He welcomed us aboard, along with Tom and his dad—Dan Rowan—who brightened my day when he remembered my impression of a fork on his show, *Laugh-In*.

We were promised a weekend we'd never forget, and that turned out to be true. I enjoyed every minute of the drinking, laughing, and engaging in inebriated, intellectual conversation with so many successful people. It was also fascinating to see these rich folks gathered in the evening in front of their tents and peeing on trees. If I had owned a camera/phone in those days, I could have had a blast on YouTube.

I got to meet many highly recognizable dignitaries like Alex Haley (author of *Roots*) and Secretary of State, Henry Kissinger. However, of all the people I befriended during the three-day weekend, Dan Rowan was the best of the best. He took a liking to me, laughing at just about everything I said or did, and that made it easy to like him right back. We talked a lot about comedy, his divorce—which practically ruined him financially—his current wife, and his life living on a luxury barge in Europe, which he loved. Dan had a gentle and engaging personality, and I felt sure I had gained a new best friend

For years, health had been a priority in my life, so I was concerned when I watched Dan smoke one cigarette after another. I rarely expressed my views to anyone unless I genuinely cared about them, and within the first hours of knowing him, it was easy to care for Dan Rowan. Because my good friend Ted Zeigler was, to a large degree, responsible for me quitting cigarettes, I made an effort to convince Dan of the perils of smoking. He agreed that it was time for him to quit the nasty habit, and before our fun weekend was over, I felt helpful, believing I had a small impact on his decision. He also told me that he had already made plans to get a complete checkup as soon as we returned to Los Angeles before leaving for Europe. Days later, my newfound friendship with Dan was shattered, when his son Tom informed me that his dad would not be returning to Europe because he had been diagnosed with terminal cancer.

As the year came to an end, Shannon and I flew to my home town of Montreal where I was hired to tape another *Unknown Comedy Show* with my Ted Zeigler. It was produced by a friend of Ted's, James Shavick, and was taped at Club Soda, a popular nightclub in Montreal, with the intention of selling it to cable television. It was also one of the rare opportunities where many of my family and old friends could gather and see me perform.

The live show was a success; unfortunately, the producer was unable to sell it to cable, which again convinced me that The Unknown Comic's hour and fifteen minutes of fame had finally come to an end. It was time for me to head into a new direction and follow my philosophy that "Change is Growth." Now I just needed to figure out what the next significant change in my life would be.

Me and my girlfriend Shannon.

Me with Drew Carey, twenty years later.

1987

Out of the blue, though it could have been grey, Johnny Dark called and told me one of his comic buddies, Steve Oedekerk, was making a small film called *Smart Alex* and asked if I'd like a bit part in it. I agreed, even though nobody was getting paid, because it sounded like fun. Other comics who also agreed to work for free in the film were Lenny Clarke, Dom Irrera, and Thomas F. Wilson.

When I showed up, there was a tiny crew with Steve at the helm, and I became interested and curious, watching him direct this extremely low-budget movie. A few days later, Steve invited me to his small apartment where he had editing equipment set up, and again I was impressed with his knowledge of filmmaking. I wondered if this was the next direction I should head in. On *Night Patrol*, I had little interest in the production side of movies, but after watching Steve that was about to change.

But first, after working for free for Steve, I was again offered a paying job from the best ex-boss anyone could ever have, Chris Bearde. This time, it was the return of the game show, *Truth or Consequences*, which Chris was going to produce, and he wanted me to be the sidekick for the new host: a likeable guy named Larry Anderson.

It was a pleasure to be working in television again as the comic relief on the show. I loved that, within weeks, everyone became like a family, from the producers down to the crew and writers. It was a fun and fabulous environment to be working in. The show's two writers were: Milt Larsen, who founded a terrific restaurant in Hollywood featuring magicians called the Magic Castle; and Bob Logan, a novice comedy writer who quickly became my buddy because he laughed at everything I said, even though he knew I had no interest in dating him.

During production, I would have parties at my house, a perfect place for me to engage in more practical jokes. One fun joke was played on our model, Hillary Safire, the gorgeous young daughter of model Carol Merrill. Hillary was sweet, innocent, and you would never hear a curse word uttered from her childlike, naive mouth.

At one of my parties, unbeknownst to Hillary, I gave several of the guests extra swimming trunks, and told them to hide them inside their bathing suits. Later, when we were all sitting in the Jacuzzi, I suggested we all get naked. Everyone agreed, because they were in on the joke, except for Hillary who was completely against the idea. When everyone reached into the water and seemingly removed their bathing suits, throwing them aside, Hillary continued to refuse. However, as we taunted her relentlessly, she finally gave in, sliding completely under the water, removing her suit and then throwing it on the pile with the others.

After a few moments, everyone slowly exited the Jacuzzi, and Hillary was dumbfounded to see us all with bathing suits on. Appalled and embarrassed, she screamed some choice curse words at us until I threw her a bathing suit to put on. When she realized it was MY bathing suit, she screamed again, only louder. In the end, we all turned away so she could put her own suit back on and she eventually joined in the laughter, realizing that no harm was meant. She was a great sport.

My favorite practical joke of all time, was on the casting director of *Truth or Consequences*, whose name I sadly can't recall, so we'll call him Ed. It was hatched in my brain when Ed rushed over to me on the set, ecstatic that he had just booked Ruth Buzzi on the show. He was almost giddy telling me how much he loved Ruth, and then confused me when he said what a huge fan he was of my wife. What? Ruth Buzzi my wife? Ed had somehow heard through the wrong grapevine that Ruth and I were married, and I suspect it was because we had been great friends for years. However, once my wicked brain was able to process this misinformation, a brilliant practical joke was born, but I would need the help of both Ruth and my now young live-in girlfriend, Shannon. My plan was that at my next party, Ruth and I would play the married couple Ed had imagined, and Shannon would become Ruth's niece visiting from back east.

When Ed showed up at the party, everyone was already in on the joke as Ruth and I welcomed him, holding hands. We then introduced him to Ruth's supposed niece, Shannon, who told Ed how much she loved her Aunt Ruthie.

Next, I made sure Ed was seated around a table on the patio with Shannon on one side of me and Ruth on the other. With Ed sitting directly across from us in perfect view, I then turned to Ruth and said, "Ruthie, honey, would you please get me a beer?" Ruth jumped up and like a good wife, replied, "Of course, darling," and off to the kitchen she went.

Once Ruth was out of sight, I turned to Shannon, placed my hand on her lap and began whispering and flirting with her, all the while sensing Ed's eyes fixated on us. I continued whispering sweet nothings in Shannon's ear while caressing her thighs, knowing Ed was fuming at what he was witnessing. When Ruth returned, I quickly removed my hands from Shannon's lap and turned back to Ruth, smiling and thanking her for the beer. At the same time, I could see out of the corner of my eye a disgusted and angry look on Ed's face. The practical joke was on.

Later, as everyone meandered about, I made sure Ed was close by, and this time asked Ruth to get me a sandwich. The minute she was gone, I pushed Shannon against a wall and began nibbling at her neck, feeling Ed's glare as I got bolder. When Ruth returned, I again immediately separated from Shannon before she could catch us, fairly confident that Ed now hated me. Everyone, including myself, was having difficulty not laughing as it became obvious that Ed was furious, telling anyone within earshot what a fucking jerk I was.

The pièce de résistance occurred when Ruth excused herself to go to the bathroom, and once again making sure Ed was within viewing distance, I grabbed Shannon and kissed her hard on the mouth, our tongues going at it feverishly. However, Ed's tongue couldn't take anymore and he yelled out in my direction, "You are an asshole and I'm not staying here at your fucking party and watch you cheat on Ruth in front of everyone." That said, Ed stormed off toward his car.

Everyone finally broke up laughing, confusing Ed even more as I ran to him and tried to explain that Ruth and I were not married, that Shannon was actually my girlfriend, and that I was playing a practical joke on him. Apparently Ed didn't think it was funny as he blurted out, "Fuck you," got into his car and drove off. I felt bad that he took it so hard, but not bad enough where I wouldn't do it all over again. I saw Ed the next day, and all was forgiven, but sadly he never trusted anything I ever said again. I wonder why?

I never did play a practical joke on our host, Larry Anderson, but we became such good buddies that on a break from our production schedule, we took our girlfriends on a trip throughout Europe. Luckily for Shannon, this was her second trip overseas in a year with me, and the four of us had a great time driving through several countries and living the good life. Shannon and I were one lucky couple.

When we returned, I was saddened to hear about the loss of Dan Rowan, almost exactly a year from the day of his cancer diagnosis. Though I had only known him for one terrific long weekend, the effect on me was as if I'd lost a friend I had known for years.

Someone whom I hadn't seen in years was Jim Carrey, who I ran into at a coffee shop a few blocks from my house. He was with a woman, and upon seeing me gave me a big hug, and then introduced me to his fiancée. I doubt whether he noticed the stupefied look on my face as I replied, stuttering, "I, ah, er, already know her." It was Melissa, the crazed Improv waitress who had threatened me months before. She nodded, sharing a knowing smile, and after a little chat, I wished them both luck, knowing full well that Jim would need more than luck. Later, I learned that Melissa was pregnant at the time. I gave their relationship a year but I was wrong; it was seven years of bad luck for Jim Carrey.

However, it was lucky for Bob Saget, when he took my advice and moved to Hollywood where we became fast friends for a short time. Bob also proved to be a fun practical joker when, once on my old answering machine, he left a meandering message which lasted thirty minutes. Back then when we were hanging out, Saget invited me to his first marriage to his girlfriend Sherri, which was to be held in Philadelphia, but I couldn't go because I was planning an erection for that night. Bob had such a clean image with his successful shows, *America's Funniest Videos* and *Full House*, yet he could be so filthy and funny off the tube. My favorite line of Saget's is: "A definitive sign that you might be gay, is if you're sucking on a guy's dick... and you're thinking of another guy." Very filthy and funny.

Not so funny, was my girlfriend Shannon telling me that she wanted to go to Europe for a third time, but without me. She had developed a major yearning to go to Spain for a few months to study and learn the language. In my mind, I was still in love with her, and I feared this was a sign that our relationship had reached its conclusion. I knew I couldn't and shouldn't stop her, so off she went, and though she told me we would still continue our relationship while she was away and resume it when she returned, I knew in my heart, lungs, kidneys, liver, and every other part of me that the end was at hand, and on that hand, I was about to get the finger.

Me worried that one day Shannon might stab me in the back.

1988

Shannon had been living in Spain for months, when *Truth or Consequences* was cancelled, and I was out of work again. If the end of my relationship with Connie was painful, my sudden, but not unexpected, breakup with Shannon felt much worse. Even though I knew the odds of our relationship lasting were astronomical, the subsequent anxiety, wondering if Shannon would come back to me, was unyielding. My sense of loss seemed immeasurable—though I'm sure it was magnified out of proportion because of my own unbridled insecurity.

Deep down, I was sure Shannon loved me as much as someone her age could love anyone, but that was little consolation. I was single and alone again. Sure, I could get laid, I was in show business, but that meant little to me. It wasn't the sex which I craved, it was the intimacy and now that was gone. Sex and intimacy; the difference between having a hot dog or feasting on steak and lobster.

I had no desire to return to working comedy clubs and be stuck out of town away from my friends who at least provided me some measure of comfort. Freeman, Ted, Jimmy, Pat, Kent and Ruth, my five best friends were always there for me, and I took advantage of them whether we just hung out, had lunch, or simply talked on the phone. I grew to love every one of them.

Though I also loved my life, I was beginning to feel stagnated, and instinctively knew I had to get back in that running stream. I had to somehow occupy my mind with something, anything, that would replace my pathetic longing for Shannon.

So I decided to make a movie. That would surely force my thinking into a different direction. I was going to follow in Steve Oedekerk's film steps, but first I needed money. Steve made his movie on a shoestring, less than $20,000, but months later he still hadn't sold it, and so I decided to up my investment. I didn't have a lot of cash, so I took a loan on my house for $100,000, hoping I could make my movie for that amount.

Money was never a major factor in my life. Over the years, I had discovered that money was not responsible for making people happy, though it did possess the potential to add to someone's happiness. As far as I was concerned, if I could return to being happy and rid myself of the sad and morose state I felt trapped in, even if I lost a hundred grand it would be worth it.

But first I needed a script. I'm not sure why, but I was fascinated with the homeless, regularly handing them a few dollars, especially those who were handicapped. Typically, my reaction was more reluctant to give to those who appeared healthy, thinking that they were surely going to spend it on booze or drugs. I was truly ignorant about the reasons most people became homeless, and less sympathetic to many of them, wondering why they wouldn't clean themselves up and get a job. But it didn't take long for me to realize that though they were healthy of body, their minds were plenty handicapped.

I spoke with Bob Logan, my writer friend from *Truth or Consequences*, about wanting to make a film, and he told me it was his dream to be a director and that he had already completed several filmmaking courses. When I mentioned I wanted to make a film about the homeless, but with humor, he jumped at the chance of working with me, and together we began to write a script.

Wanting our script to have some degree of authenticity, we decided to spend a couple of nights on the streets of downtown Los Angeles, pretending we were homeless. We dressed appropriately, and because it was scary for a wimp such as myself, I kept a knife in my possession as we wandered through the back alleys of downtown L.A. In the news, there had been someone prowling the streets at night murdering homeless people, so we seized on that premise as the basis for our script.

We made up a story for anyone we met on the street that we were from Texas and new to the area, giving us a reason us to ask questions. It didn't take long before encountering plenty of different characters fending for themselves, from drug addicts, drunks, and bag ladies to a few deranged individuals who should have been institutionalized.

Within a week, we completed our script, which was similar to our own experiences. Our lead character was a female reporter, who disguises herself as a homeless person to write stories about the many characters she meets. I was to play the lead role of a man living on the streets who reluctantly helps out a young guy who had just become homeless.

We began rounding up a crew, as I called friends asking for their help, and at the same time, letting them know I couldn't pay anyone until I sold the film. My crew, however, would be paid, but a fraction of what they normally worked for, and I promised to pay an equal sum when and if I sold my movie.

I also enlisted the help of my comic buddies including Johnny Dark, Yakov Smirnoff, Tom Dreesen, Bob Zany, and Ruth Buzzi—who accepted the role of the Bag Lady.

Like *Night Patrol*, I knew if I could get Linda Blair to play the journalist, my odds of selling my film would be greatly increased. I was elated when Linda agreed to also work for nothing until my movie was sold and we set a start date. I couldn't believe I was about to produce my own full-length motion picture on a miniscule budget and on a two week shooting schedule.

Without a doubt, once I was entrenched in making my movie, my thoughts about Shannon were usurped by my constant attention to work. I became so busy, consumed with preproduction, I had no time to think about anything else. I was surging along that running stream.

Before shooting began, Ruth and Kent had a small party at their house, and Freeman brought along his neighbor, a beautiful, young blonde actress named Melissa—no relation to Jim Carrey's wife. My initial reaction was that she would be perfect to play Linda Blair's roommate. A few days later, I had her read for me and she was good enough to get the part. She also got my attention, but I was determined nothing was going to happen until I finished my film.

Once shooting started, my duties as producer included making coffee, picking and dropping off film at the laboratory to assisting Bob direct, all the while rehearsing and rewriting scenes. Sleep became a rare commodity. It was guerilla filmmaking: hiding from the police and stealing locations from all over the city.

Steve Oedekerk showed up on the first day of shooting to give me some advice, and then went on to make films grossing almost $2 billion: *Nothing to Lose, Bruce Almighty, Ace Ventura, Patch Adams, The Nutty Professor,* and *Jimmy Neutron,* were just a few of them. What a show off.

Once shooting was completed, it was time for another learning experience: post production, which included looping, sound effects, editing, and in my spare time, writing seven songs for the film. Unlike digital editing, which dominates today, I learned on 35 mm film in my guest house, where I assisted our editor, literally taking 20,000 feet of film and cutting it down to 9,000 feet. Every frame was analyzed, then cut and placed in an order which you hoped would result in a movie that made sense.

Being a novice film maker was an overwhelming task but one which I enjoyed immensely. I had poured myself into every minute of production, and when it was finished, we named it *Up Your Alley.* Next, I purposely rented a screening room to show the film at my old workplace, Universal Studios, one floor above where I labored as a computer operator. That was really kewl. After our one and only screening, we luckily landed a distributor, and my little film actually made it to the theaters.

I didn't become wealthy from my little movie and, true to my word, as soon as money came in and after my initial investment was recouped, I paid everyone the monies I had promised them. I was thrilled that I was able to pay my friends for working for free, especially Linda Blair and Ruth Buzzi, who both earned a nice chunk of money because I gave them percentages of my film. I then took a break and returned to Maui, where I purchased a McCaw and named it Alley. That's right. It was named, "Alley McCaw." That large bird soon became part of my family, even though at that time my family consisted of me, myself, and I.

I entered *Up Your Alley* in a film festival in Las Vegas, where I was approached by an actor I didn't recognize. He told me that he had just directed a small film called *976-EVIL,* and surprised me when he said he used to hang out at my club, Show-Biz. I felt bad because I couldn't remember his face or his name, Robert Englund, especially when I learned he'd been doing okay playing Freddy Krueger in the *Nightmare on Elm Street* horror films.

Because *Up your Alley* was a minor success, I hoped it might lead to another film. I also thought working with my partner Bob Logan might lead to another best friend, but once again my thinking didn't mean I was thinking right.

During filming, Bob told me he had another idea for a movie, and he asked if I would work with him on a script making fun of the movie *Exorcist*, to again star Linda Blair. He thought we were a great team, as did I, and asked if I would try to talk Linda into agreeing to add her name to the project, because she was reluctant to ridicule the *Exorcist*. At my urging she agreed, and during the ensuing weeks, I waited for Bob to call, but to my dismay, I learned that Logan decided to write the script without my help.

Then using our little film and Linda's name, he managed to land a deal to make the film *Repossessed* with a big studio and a multimillion dollar budget. When I called and asked why he changed his mind about writing the script with me, he blamed it on his agent wanting him to go out on his own. I knew it was bullshit and realized Bob was not destined to be one of my best friends.

My friendship with Linda Blair was solid, however, and when she found out what happened, even though she was being offered a huge paycheck to star in the film, she told me she wasn't going to do it because of Bob's actions toward me. I was grateful, but I wasn't going to stand in the way of Linda making money, so I talked her into continuing with the project. After seeing the finished film, it was obvious Bob could have used a writing partner very badly, which was how the movie turned out.

Back on the home front, I met an attractive new neighbor, Sue Shifrin, who lived six houses from me. We developed a friendship, and I would occasionally visit with her for coffee, hoping to get to know her better, but I could tell she had no interest in anything more than friendship with me. At first I thought she must be gay. Okay, I never really thought that, but the more I got to know her, the more I wanted to get to know her. I never saw her with a guy or even mention one in our conversations, and whenever I broached the subject, she would always change it.

Then one morning, I stopped by to say hello, and for the first time she had a man at her house. She introduced me to David Cassidy, the teen heart throb for so many millions of young girls in the sixties. They both informed me that David Cassidy was going to London to work in a show and that she'd be moving there with him. She sold her house and that was the last time I saw her. I was so confused. How could she pick David Cassidy over me? Then I caught a glance of myself in the mirror and the mystery was solved.

A few years later, a movie about David Cassidy's life aired on television and I was fascinated to learn how he had been infatuated with Sue ever since he first met her, before he became famous. For years, he sought a relationship with her, but she refused because she was ten years older than David and felt he wasn't mature enough. Years later, when his career sank into show business oblivion, losing everything, Sue reappeared and helped him to resurrect his life. I couldn't help but think what a terrific woman she was, not taking advantage of his earlier fame and wealth, but falling in love with him when he lost everything, including his youth. It was nice knowing that this romantic fairy tale story occurred right down the street from me. Like I've said, Hollywood is a very small town.

About this same time, I was developing a more intimate relationship with Melissa, the actress from my film who Freeman had introduced me to. This time, I was smart enough to not have her live with me after only a couple of weeks. It would be almost a month before she moved in with me. Though I was attracted to her, my one lingering fear was that I was still on a rebound from my relationship with Shannon, but I hoped that Melissa would help me to reach a full recovery.

On the club circuit, I heard that the Comedy & Magic club in Hermosa Beach was celebrating their tenth anniversary with a television special, and most of the popular comics of the time were set to appear on it. I was disappointed when, after all the help I had given Mike Lacey to keep his club afloat, I was not invited because the popularity of my Unknown Comic character had somewhat faded. Thank you Mike for another showbiz knife in the back.

Another possible knife in the back was imminent when I noticed that my friendship with Yakov Smirnoff, with his newfound success, was slowly deteriorating. When I stopped by his house to say hello, I felt snubbed when he told me he was too busy working on his television show to talk with me.

It wasn't what he said, I can certainly appreciate anyone being too busy, but it was how he said it, using words which you knew underneath really meant, "Fuck off"—of course in a Russian accent. I began to suspect that the light at the end of the tunnel was slowly dimming on our friendship.

Karma is a funny thing, but not really. What goes around comes around, and out of the blue, my phone rings, and when I ask who it is, the person on the other end replies, "Mickey Rooney." Shocked, I nevertheless recognized his voice as he proceeded to tell me that he had just watched my film *Up Your Alley*. He continued to tell me that his agent gave him a copy and informed him that I had made it for $100,000. He then asked if I'd meet with him to discuss a script he had, and if I would give him guidance on how to make a low-budget movie.

During our one-sided conversation, I was first struck with how the word "fuck" punctuated almost every sentence. "I've got this great fucking script," or "The fucking people in this town are fucking assholes," made it somewhat surreal that this was the legendary Mickey Rooney on the phone with me. Once again, my mind reeled back to when I was a kid, watching Mickey Rooney eating in a "fucking" restaurant. At this stage of my life, recalling how Mickey Rooney treated people on the set, I decided he would not be a fun person to work with. Though he gave me his phone number and asked that I call him back, I simply decided, "Fuck him," and I never did. He wasn't going to change. I had come to the conclusion that the reason so many people act like assholes is because it's so easy.

A huge change was about to take place in my life, which was going to dramatically have a major effect on me and my future. Melissa told me that she was pregnant. Wow! I was going to be a father. My philosophy that change is growth was about to have the most significant impact on my life to date.

I had never been married, but I wanted this relationship to work and our baby to have parents, so even though we'd only known each other a short time, I decided to give it a shot... and hope I wasn't shooting myself in the foot, or groin... or head. I wasn't completely convinced I was in love with Melissa, but in my mind, the most important factor was this new baby coming into my life, and I was determined to make it right, even if I was wrong.

My friends Jimmy and Judy offered to let us get married in their beautiful Las Vegas home, and we turned it into a fun event with everyone, including the preacher, wearing bags over their heads. The lead singer for the Temptations showed up, and invited us to their show at the Hilton to celebrate. At their performance they introduced us, and then invited me on stage, where I got to sing one of my favorite songs along with them, "My Girl". The audience laughed as I attempted to follow their perfectly choreographed steps, massacring them in the process. Laughter was a terrific way to end a wedding day... and to end the year. I just hoped the laughter would continue now that I was a married man.

Me carrying Linda Blair, while working on *Up Your Alley*.

Me and Bob Zany in a scene from *Up Your Alley.*

Ruth Buzzi as a bag lady with her husband Kent on the set of *Up Your Alley.*

My girlfriend Melissa and Linda Blair in *Up Your Alley.*

Poster for my little film *Up Your Alley.*

Jimmy and me preparing for wedding.

My Unknown Wedding Picture.

1989

At one of the film festivals I attended, I met a man named Tom Broadridge, who owned a small film-distribution company. When he found out I made *Up Your Alley* for so little money, he offered to invest in another film if I could come up with a good script.

I jumped at the opportunity, and enlisted a writer/friend of mine, Steve Finley, to write a script with me. From his idea about a man who acquires a notebook on which anything he writes comes true, we completed a romantic comedy called *Wishful Thinking*. When we gave it to Tom he loved it and was prepared to invest.

Because this film was NOT going to be shot guerrilla-style and the actors and crew would need to be paid union wages, I drew up a budget of $500,000 including a $20,000 salary for myself as producer/writer/actor.

However, I was disappointed when Tom told me that he was only prepared to invest $200,000, plus he had a director friend whose salary he would pay separately. Not feeling I was in a bargaining position, I accepted his offer, and once again, with this low budget, I was probably going to have to make coffee for everyone.

I met with the director Tom recommended, and he seemed quite capable. So capable that Tom called me a few days later and said, "He wanted too much money" and followed with, "Why don't you direct it?" At first I thought it would be too much to handle, but when I thought about how much I would learn from directing my own movie, I agreed.

So, into production we went, and once again my old friends Kent and Ruth came onboard, along with Johnny Dark, Vic Dunlop, and my new friends Charlie Brill, Billy Barty, and boxer Ray "Boom Boom" Mancini, who I had met at a celebrity event. My wife Melissa wanted the lead female role, since she'd been sleeping with the director, but being five months pregnant that was out of the question.

So, I held open auditions at my house on my couch, where my pregnant wife frequently sat presiding over the auditions. A gorgeous, talented actress named Michelle Johnson walked in, and when I learned she had costarred in a movie with Michael Caine and Demi Moore called *Blame it on Rio*, she got the part.

We filmed for a month, and though it was still fun, having to direct made it much more difficult. Though *Wishful Thinking* failed to make it to the theaters, it still earned a substantial profit for the distributor on video, and I got to direct.

Months later, I also got to direct the video of my first child being born. We already knew she was going to be a girl and named her Myah Marie. It was very early on the morning of March 24, when chaos erupted in my house after Melissa's water broke. Because I couldn't reach a plumber, we went directly to the hospital, where I continued to be in a frenzied state, though I tried to act calm. I called Ruth and Kent who had already been designated as godparents, and they rushed to the hospital to join us.

Melissa was determined to deliver naturally, without taking drugs for pain, however, within seconds of her first contraction, she pleaded for an epidural. With camera in hand, I was prepared to record the awesome event I was about to witness, but once I saw my baby's head preparing to exit Melissa's loins, overwhelmed with emotion, I quickly handed the camera to Kent, who continued to videotape.

Once Myah was born, the Doctor handed me scissors with which I clipped the umbilical cord, and after I regained consciousness, he then placed Myah onto Melissa's chest. As the doctor swabbed her face, her eyes suddenly opened and saw my face only inches away. Myah immediately burst into tears, crying loudly and letting everyone know that she was going to be okay, and that she considered me to be very scary.

We cracked a bottle of champagne and toasted her birth. It was unreal and surreal at the same time, and I knew my life was about to take a dramatic plunge into the unknown—an unknown I felt excited about. I thanked a tired Ruth and Kent for sharing the birth experience of our new baby, and soon after, they left to get some badly needed sleep.

Unfortunately, after they left, shit happened. Prior to coming to the hospital, I had noticed little bumps on my arm, which I would occasionally scratch. When the attending nurse observed this, she looked at my arm and immediately suspected chickenpox. She called the head nurse who upon her examination concurred with the first nurse. They then called for an infectious disease specialist, who asked if I had ever had chickenpox. When I replied I didn't know, he also diagnosed the small bumps as possible chickenpox. We were then told we would not be permitted back into the maternity ward because chickenpox was considered contagious and dangerous to the other infants.

We were then ushered into a hallway corridor where Melissa and Myah were left on a gurney. I was also told that when we left the hospital, we would not be permitted to use the regular elevator, but would have to use the freight elevator. By that time I was extremely agitated, and rather than have Melissa and Myah be forced to stay in a hidden hallway area, I made the decision to pack up our things and get the hell out of there immediately.

Back at home, with Melissa and Myah comfortably settled in our bed, I rushed to the phone and called my mom, telling her what happened. She was quick to inform me that I DID have chickenpox as a child, which gave me some relief knowing Myah was not infected. The next day, I went to a skin specialist who recognized the little bumps as mite bites, which I had probably received from my macaw. I was incensed that three supposedly competent medical professionals had misdiagnosed me and, to a great degree, ruined the birth experience of my daughter. I sent them a stern letter refusing to pay the hospital portion of the bill and never did hear back from them.

Nevertheless, I was so excited about having this baby; I couldn't wait to show her off. Even though she was only hours old, and while Melissa was still in a drug-addled state, I took Myah to my local breakfast hangout, Good Neighbors. Everybody ooo'd and aah'd at this gorgeous little girl that just fit into the palm of my hand, and as I looked down at this beautiful creature, I really had a sense of what love was all about. I knew this was going to be unconditional love, and I also knew I was one lucky guy.

Not so lucky was Linda Blair, who was undergoing some serious financial problems, so I suggested she move in with me, Melissa, and Myah until she was able to reorganize her life. For a while we were all one happy family, and I was glad that I was given the opportunity to repay Linda for helping me out by appearing in my little films.

This was also the first year I received an invitation to the American Comedy Awards, which were televised on ABC. Its goal was to honor all forms of comedy, and it became an annual event that I thoroughly enjoyed for the next several years. I got to dress up in a tux and party with all my contemporaries along with the top comedy stars of that era. One of my favorites was Albert Brooks, who always greeted me with a smile and a promise that one day we would work together, but alas, we never did. I still think he's a genius.

Another major change was about to take place in my personal life, but it was of my doing. Now that I had a baby, I was worried about her health and well-being, and didn't want to raise her in smog-infested Los Angeles. At the same time, I was concerned about my own health and was growing disgusted with traffic and big city life. I had always lived in a large metropolitan area, and now I dreamed of living somewhere in the mountains, where I was sure the pressures of show business would be lessened. I yearned for a more peaceful existence now that I had a family.

I placed my house on Lankershim for sale at a whopping price of $900,000. I had paid $210,000 for it and invested another $150,000, so according to my calculations, my profit would have been more money than I had made in my previous twenty years in show business. Why didn't I go into real estate in the first place?

One day, my realtor called and informed me that she had someone interested in a little hideaway such as my house provided. When they showed up, I was introduced to an attractive young lady in a t-shirt and tight jeans, who seemed to immediately find my house to be exactly what she wanted. She was a touch aloof, but friendly, and was introduced to me as Stephanie. Immediately, I recognized her as Princess Stephanie of Monaco.

Meeting royalty is not a common occurrence for most people, though Princess Stephanie would probably be classified as more of a tabloid personality. She returned to my home several times, once with her attorney, another time with her brother, and both liked my place. However, the last time she showed up was with her boyfriend, a musician whose name escapes me, and rightfully so because he didn't like my house and cost me a sizeable sale. Fortunately, it sold a month later but at a lower price, and then I became consumed with finding a new house away from home.

I searched east toward Palm Springs: too hot and too much traffic. I searched west toward Santa Barbara: too expensive and too much traffic. I searched south toward San Diego: too much traffic and too much traffic. I searched north toward a little town called Tehachapi: Bingo! Hardly any traffic and reasonably priced property.

I bought twenty-six acres, and when Ruth and Kent came out to check the area, they also bought several acres up the street from me. We decided to design our own houses, and we enlisted the help of a mutual friend to build them. My new Spanish-styled home, which I was going to name "Casa de Ha Ha" was going to take approximately four to six months to build, and my plan was to pay cash and own it outright so I would no longer have a mortgage.

Having made a nice chunk of money off the sale of my house, I also purchased a small beach house in New Brunswick, Canada, where my parents lived. My plan was to bring my daughter Myah to the beach house every summer, so she could visit with all my relatives, since I was the only one in my family living in the U.S. In Canada, Myah would have contact with my entire family who were now grown up.

The changes in my life continued when my best friend number five Pat Paulsen told me he was part-owner of a legit theatre in Traverse City, Michigan, and asked me if I would costar with him in a play called *Run For Your Wife*. It was a hysterically funny British play about a cab driver who is married to two women. I was to play the cab driver, Pat would be my next-door neighbor, and I convinced Pat to give the part of one of my wives to my real wife Melissa. I was very happy knowing that I could bring along my new family, and I'm sure Pat knew I would have turned down the part otherwise. I hadn't acted in a play in over twenty years, and that was in a small fifty-seat theater, so when Pat told me the size of his venue I felt like I was going to Broadway.

I was so excited; I had my entire part memorized before we left Los Angeles. We spent a week in Traverse City rehearsing, which I found exhilarating, and I couldn't wait for the play to open. I was amazed when I noticed that as we got closer to opening night, everyone in the cast, including Pat, seemed extremely anxious, yet I didn't feel one iota of nervousness.

My reasoning for my lack of nervousness was: when I performed stand-up, I always experienced some measure of anxiety because it was just me against the audience, but now I was in a group and felt much safer, so I saw no reason to be worried. Plus, if there were any problems, I could always blame it on someone else. The play ran for two weeks and was a huge hit, selling out every night. I loved it and felt sad when it came to an end.

When we returned to L.A., once again I was offered another job hosting a local TV show called *Comic Strip Live*. In it, I introduced new and seasoned comedians, and I interviewed comedy legends such as Henny Youngman, Louis Nye, and the renowned and later crowned Las Vegas legend, George Wallace—a super duper nice guy. Life was not only good, it was great. I even wrote a song called, "It Don't Get Much Better Than This."

A rare group family picture.

Linda Blair changing Myah (aged two months.)

Myah with her Godmother, Ruth Buzzi.

Me and Myah on a train to our beach house in Canada.

Mom and baby Myah.

Me and Myah with Linda Blair and painter Wyland in Hawaii.

Me and Myah at nine months.

Poster for my little film *Wishful Thinking.*

Me with one of my best friends, Pat Paulsen.

1990

After hosting forty episodes of *Comic Strip Live*, it was cancelled, and again for the thirtieth or fortieth time I was out of a job... and you think you want to be in show business??? But, before its demise, I brought my baby Myah on the show, at nine months old, and showed the audience that she could stand by herself.

My house in Tehachapi was still months away from completion, so I had time to kill. Because I had so much fun acting in my first major theatrical play, I wanted to reprise *Run For Your Wife*. However, I wanted to Americanize it, and I sought permission from the author, Ray Cooney, to rewrite his play, which he granted. I also wanted to direct the play, feeling capable since I had now directed a film. Pat Paulsen had a producer friend who was willing and able to mount it at a theatre in San Francisco, so off we went to the city by the bay.

Once again, Pat played my neighbor and Melissa played one of my wives, while my old friend Linda Blair played the other wife. The play ran for a few months and once again was truly a joyful experience. I was sad to see it end yet happy to hear that my new house in Tehachapi was ready for us to move into.

Without warning, Yakov Smirnoff called me because he heard about my move to Tehachapi and wanted to see my new house. While there, we looked at some land, and he showcased his newly acquired pretentiousness, telling me he might make an offer on a 300 acre plot of land, but first he wanted to investigate the purchase of a helicopter to go back and forth to Los Angeles. I was very impressed... NOT!

Yakov was now engaged to his girlfriend Linda, and I wondered if his obsession with money and success would have a negative effect on their upcoming marriage. Privately, Yakov asked me if I thought Linda loved him for himself or his sudden fame and money. My response was probably all three. "Of course," I said, "there's a good chance if you hadn't reached the level you're at, that she wouldn't be interested in you. So what!" I told him. "The fame and money are who you are. Just enjoy the fruits of your labor." When they married, he asked Melissa and I to join them in Hawaii to share their wedding experience, which we did at my expense of course. I joined them, not to please Yakov, but to please Melissa, Myah and Me.

Meanwhile, I was offered a small roll in a movie called *Digging up Business*, where I worked alongside my friend from the "Laugh-In" days, Gary Owens, and my little buddy Billy Barty. Billy and I played two workers in a crematorium. It wasn't much of a movie but it was much fun, which is my criteria when offered anything. As mentioned, becoming wealthy was never an issue when making major decisions. Being happy and content was always at the top of my list.

I'm not sure if having a baby was the reason, but at this stage in my life, I felt I no longer possessed the need for applause. My newly found passion was my baby and staying healthy, both physically and mentally. In my mind the only thing that could infringe on my current state of happiness would be a problem with the health of my baby or myself.

In my new home of Tehachapi, I learned that there were two celebrities who had resided there for years, Jack Palance and Chuck Connors. I bumped into Chuck Connors, looking every bit the star with long flowing gray hair, at the local store, and I reminded him of us working together on *The Sonny and Cher Show*. He invited me to his home, and he was absolutely charming and friendly, with his boisterous personality offering one drink after another. An interesting part of his home was that his guesthouse was an exact replica of the little house he lived in on the *The Rifleman* TV series.

I talked my loveable friend Pat Paulsen into performing his act with me in the clubhouse of my new community, and he agreed. We packed the place, attracting Jack Palance and his wife to our show. Jack seemed pleasant enough, hanging out with Pat and I for hours after our show, but many people in the community told me that when he was approached for autographs, he had a tendency to be rude.

Though I rarely performed anymore, I accepted an invitation to a question and answer seminar by college students at UCLA in Los Angeles. It was a seminar on comedy, and when I was told my fellow speakers would be Richard Lewis, Harvey Korman, and Dudley Moore, I immediately accepted.

The questions were thrown fast and furious, and we all answered them quite handily. Prior to the event, I thoroughly enjoyed spending an hour with everyone, especially Dudley Moore who I met for the first time. I was never sure if he was keeping in his "ARTHUR" character by pretending to be inebriated or if he really was, but he was certainly friendly, funny, and entertaining.

Richard Lewis, who was always original, and Harvey Korman, who was one of the geniuses of comedy acting, made it an evening to remember. My favorite response to a question was when I was asked, "How did you come up with the idea to do comedy with a bag over your head?" My reply was, "It came to me the first time I saw Harvey Korman performing comedy. And I said to myself, "shit, I could do that with a bag over my head." Harvey laughed the loudest, and I felt very honored that he considered me a friend.

Another talented guy I had developed a sporadic friendship with was Jerry Van Dyke, who I had met years before when we both worked the lounge in Vegas. Jerry and his totally adorable wife Shirley loved tennis, and we often played together whenever we were hanging out. Our main hangout was Jerry's Deli, where we frequently met for breakfast—by the way, Jerry's Deli was not named after him. After years of struggling under the shadow of his brother Dick Van Dyke, Jerry had finally made it, starring in a new hit television series *Coach* along with one of the alumni of the early days of the Comedy Store, Craig T. Nelson.

Trouble was brewing in my personal life because Melissa was not crazy about living in Tehachapi. In fact, as much as I loved it, she hated it. She wanted to spend more time in Los Angeles pursuing her acting career, and I could see the handwriting on the wall, even without my glasses. I was convinced much of the problem was our age difference of eighteen years, three months and two days, give or take an hour.

I still wanted our relationship to work, especially for Myah's sake, and realizing how important it was for Melissa to spend more time in Los Angeles, I wholeheartedly accepted her desire to get a part-time job at Jerry's Deli as a waitress. She said she needed the extra money for pictures and, as the weeks passed by, she began spending more time in Los Angeles, staying over at her girlfriend's apartment. I slowly noticed that the handwriting on that damned wall was growing larger by the minute. I had a pretty good hunch that this was not going to end well. It was the end of 1990. Was it also the end of our marriage?

Cover of magazine for the play I directed, *Run for your Wife.*

Me with Linda Blair performing in the play, *Run for your Wife*.

I designed my house in Tehachapi.

Me with one of my new neighbors in Tehachapi, Rifleman Chuck Connors.

Me and Myah with Russian Comic Yakov Smirnoff.

Me and Melissa with Yakov Smirnoff and his new bride Linda in Hawaii.

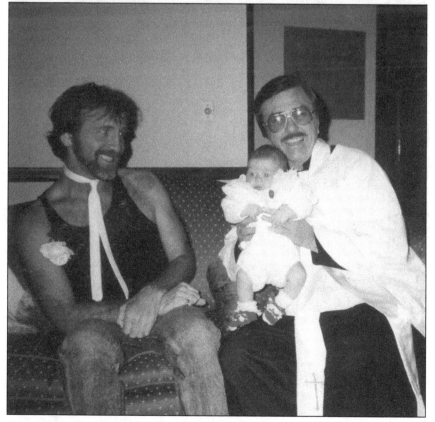

Me and Myah with the lovable Gary Owens.

A poster for the film *Digging up Business.*

1991

My thinking, which often got me in trouble, was that Melissa needed more time for herself and her career. After all, just because I was enjoying my semi-retirement shouldn't mean that Melissa should be forced to go along with it. There was no doubt that we had differing views on what was important to us, nevertheless, I was still determined to make our marriage work. Consequently, I rented a small apartment only blocks from Jerry's Deli so Melissa and I could spend more time together. I was also intent on making sure that Myah would see her mom on a regular basis.

I soon realized that I had a major feminine side seeping out, because I loved every minute raising Myah, often by myself. This major adjustment in my life, involving changing diapers, giving baths, feeding, and playing with Myah were simple pleasures I embraced. The trials and tribulations supposedly associated with caring for a baby were not at all evident to me, and to this day, it's still a mystery why being a hands-on father was so important to me, but it was.

Even though I now lived in Tehachapi, I did appreciate our small apartment in Los Angeles because to a certain extent, I did miss bullshitting with my buddies at Jerry's Deli. And though I was semi-retired, it was mostly from travelling and performing in clubs, which would keep me away from Myah and that wasn't going to happen.

I wasn't resistant to film or television work which having a place in L.A. allowed me to participate in. My comedy buddy Vic Dunlop called and offered me a small part in a little film he wrote called *Breakfast with Aliens*. Again, there was no pay unless he sold it, but Vic worked in my film *Up Your Alley*, so I of course reciprocated.

However, another payday happily arrived when I was asked to work in a new version of the *Candid Camera* show, starring Dom DeLuise. I made a deal to not only perform but also write many of the bits. One of my favorites was when I played a pregnant man in a gynecologist's waiting room, and I amazed myself when I convinced every woman who sat next to me that I was indeed a pregnant man. I even had one lady place her hand on my fake protruding tummy and tell me she could feel the baby kicking.

The show lasted six months before being cancelled, and its creator Allen Funt, who authorized this version, stated in his biography "Candidly" (1994) that he regretted his decision, made for financial reasons, because he felt the segments were weak, uninteresting, and too preoccupied with incorporating the show's sponsor, "Pizza Hut" into the bits.

My belief was that though the bits were well executed, they were often ruined in the editing process. Because it was a daily show, the editing was rushed, and the editors did not have a full understanding of how the bits should be cut. In the original *Candid Camera* series, Allen Funt oversaw all the editing, knowing exactly how to make them work but, regardless, I had a great time working on the show, especially with his daughter, Juliet Funt.

Also on the series, was another celebrity offspring who directed most of the pieces I worked in. He was a young guy name Rac Clark, son of Dick Clark. Rac was quite candid, telling me how he wished he'd had a closer bond with his famous dad when he was a kid, but was quick to interject that their relationship grew very close when he reached adulthood and moved from back east to Los Angeles.

With another show cancelled, I was again out of work and sitting in Jerry's Deli while Melissa was waiting on me. She pointed out Jon Voight sitting by himself and said she'd been waiting on him all week and that he seemed like a nice guy. I wondered if he remembered when we worked together on a political campaign when I was on the *Sonny and Cher Show*, and so I stopped by his table to say hi. He recalled the event, but it was obvious he didn't recall any particulars, especially me.

Nevertheless, he invited me to join him, and within minutes, we were immersed in intellectual conversation, mostly about politics and religion. Voight seemed fascinated with my views on life, and in the ensuing weeks we met for breakfast several times, engaging in fun, stimulating dialogue, exchanging ideas and philosophies. We never once talked about show business, which I think he appreciated.

Though I assumed Jon Voight found me to be a fascinating and interesting individual—which on a good day, I am—I assumed wrong. I soon learned that the real reason he was frequenting Jerry's Deli was my wife Melissa. Apparently Jon did not know I was married to Melissa when he slyly handed her his phone number and asked her to call him. Perhaps my new assumption that Jon was hitting on my wife was incorrect, and he really just wanted to be phone pals with her. However, when Melissa informed him that she was married to me, he suddenly stopped showing up. You do the math.

In the news, I was saddened to hear my old mentor Redd Foxx died on the set of his new series, *The Royal Family*. He suffered a massive heart attack during rehearsals as his costar Della Reese bent over him pleading, "Don't die Redd, don't die," but he did. I'm so grateful that, to this day, anytime I think of Redd, a smile automatically crosses my face. I considered Redd Foxx a special and uniquely very funny man whose memories I will always cherish. I think it might be time for Jamie Foxx to play Redd Foxx in a film about his life.

I received more upsetting news while sitting in Jerry's Deli waiting for Jerry Van Dyke to join me for breakfast. I received a call from Melissa, telling me that Jerry called our apartment and told her he wouldn't be meeting me because he had just received news that his daughter had committed suicide. I seriously couldn't help but wonder why on earth he would take the time to call and let me know he wouldn't be able to meet me after receiving such horrendous news.

Myah is just too cute.

Myah at age three with Ruth Buzzi.

1992

One of the worst things about getting old is losing so many people along the way. Even at the not yet ripe old age of forty-eight, hearing of the passing of those you've grown to know personally really smacks you in the face. 1992 was the year my neighbor Chuck Connors died of lung cancer. Not really much of a surprise because of his passion for drinking and smoking, but still sad.

I was oddly tied to another sad day when I received an urgent call from my agent George, who asked if I could put a comedy show together for the Riverside Hotel in Laughlin, Nevada. Comedian David Brenner had cancelled an upcoming weekend and they needed a replacement show a.s.a.p. I told him to give me twenty-four hours and I would put a show together. The next day when I called, George apologized and told me that the hotel had informed him that they had just replaced David Brenner with comic extraordinaire, Sam Kinison.

Tragically, on the weekend Kinison was to appear in Laughlin, his car collided head-on with a pickup truck. After the impact, the other driver, a drunken seventeen-year-old boy, reportedly exclaimed, "Look at my truck!" Kinison stumbled from his car and collapsed, asking God why he had to die, why now. "Okay," he finally whispered. "Okay... okay." He then stopped breathing and died at the unfunny age of thirty-eight.

I didn't know Sam well because, again, I was not into drugs and Kinison had a highly publicized addiction problem. Nevertheless, I was a huge fan, and the times when we frequented the same places, he was always genuinely warm and friendly. He was without a doubt one of America's most distinctive and original comedians with a huge comedic career ahead of him, which was not to happen. I've often wondered if David Brenner was ever aware that had he not cancelled his gig, Kinison might still be alive today.

I considered myself fortunate that I had yet to experience the loss of a family member or one of my best friends. Still, losing comic buddies and acquaintances along the highway of life is like losing pieces of a puzzle; you wish you could put them back in place and be whole again, but that's not going to happen. All the more reason to cherish all those who add love and laughter to your life.

One such person, who I worked with on the Hudson Brothers kid show, was the wild and crazy Rod Hull, who became famous with his puppet bird, Emu. Emu would attack anything and anyone for no apparent reason, and even Johnny Carson was a victim when they guested on *The Tonight Show*.

I was booked in London for *An Evening at the Improv*, and while there, Rod invited me to visit with him and his family. Rod lived in a huge English estate known as "Restoration House" about an hour outside London. Rod had purchased this historic site where King Charles II spent the night on the eve of his restoration to power after being ousted by the military.

I took the train to his home in the quaint town of Rochester, Kent, England, where I spent an extremely pleasurable weekend with Rod and his family. Rod guided me along the ancient cobblestone walkways to meet his English buddies at the various pubs he frequented, and I enjoyed every moment. Rod's large home was separated into two sections; one for his family and one that was roped off for tourists who frequented this Elizabethan mansion. Because the tourist season had not yet begun, I was given the bedroom King Charles II had slept in. It was awesome sleeping in a truly, original King-size bed. Rod Hull was truly a charming, humorous host, and he provided me with historic memories, which I will never forget.

Back at home in Tehachapi, I developed a new friendship with a local police officer named Dave Watts. Dave was a combination cop/musician who was a sergeant in the relatively small Tehachapi police force. Along with his wife Darlene, we began spending a lot of time together, and I would often take Dave with me to play piano when I occasionally performed one-nighters. Sometimes, when we were on the road, I would pay him twenty bucks to frisk me for ten minutes, often with a happy ending. All right, I was kidding. I paid him fifty bucks.

Christmases in Tehachapi were a beautiful thing to behold because of all that white stuff which would cover the ground around that time of year. I believe it's called "snow." Though there has been little mention in the past several chapters of the mentally challenged boy I shared time with, Alan Cook, he continued to be a part of my life, sharing holidays with me, especially Christmas. Alan, though still slow, matured into a young man and became a valuable asset to the retirement home he resided in as a skilled handyman.

On this Christmas, along with Alan, Pat Paulsen—who would have been alone—joined us for the holiday festivities. I loved Pat, who could always make me laugh, especially when he brought a gift for my little four year old girl, Myah.

On Christmas morning, when she opened her gift from Pat, she was surprised and confused upon seeing a large toy Army tank. At first, Pat played it straight when I asked why he would give such a ridiculous gift replying, "What's the problem? She can paint it pink and it's a Barbie tank." It was a joke, and of course he presented other gifts to her, most notably, a can of pink paint. I loved my pal Pat.

My best friend Jimmy with Myah.

My little Myah is growing up.

Me, Melissa, and agent George with Steve Garvey at a celebrity event.

My new buddy, Dave the Cop.

The historical mansion owned by Rod Hull, where I slept in a king's bed.

1993

My friend Kent, who was interested in buying another classic car, took me to Pat Boone's home as he was selling his Rolls Royce. I reminded Pat that we had worked together on the short-lived *Pat and Debby Boone Show* on which I had appeared back in the 80s. I had heard Pat was religious but was still taken aback when he gave me a book he wrote, suggesting I should read it.

Always curious about what makes religious people tick and tock the way do, when I returned home, I checked it out. As I read through it, I'm sure Pat Boone meant well and was serious about his faith, but I couldn't help but chuckle at a passage where he spoke about how he came to believe in God.

He wrote that when he was a kid, he took an autographed baseball— a prized possession of his dad's—outside to play with. While having fun, he accidently threw the ball into an area where he couldn't find it at the same time his mother called for him to return to the house to eat. He further recounted how he was terrified how his dad would react if the ball was lost, so ignoring his mother's plea and desperate, he continued to frantically search for it.

With his mother repeatedly calling for him, he decided to ask for God's help, so he stopped, looked up and pleaded with the Lord to point him toward the ball. As he thrashed about the tall grass, he looked down and lo and behold, there was the ball on the ground right before his eyes. He further wrote that he knew then and there that there had to be a God. A God who would always help when it was needed. I couldn't read any more.

So, I thought about God and why he couldn't help all the kids dying of starvation in the world every few minutes but yet found time to help Pat Boone find his dad's baseball. The answers might be floating somewhere in the universe but they certainly weren't to be found anywhere in my brain. Religious belief had over the years become something beyond my comprehension. My personal views had evolved far from traditional faith in religion and more toward analysis of myself and the world around me.

Being reliant on some dubious supreme being in the sky didn't seem very logical to me. I used to tell a joke where I said, "I used to be an atheist... until I found out I was God." It usually got a laugh, and still does, but that joke became the basis for my belief system. Believing in yourself and having faith in your own abilities to better yourself just made more sense to me. Whenever I discuss religion, I never get angry because I always preface any conversation with whomever I might be exchanging views with that I could be wrong and they could be right... or vice versa. Neither one of our views is fact which can be proven... They're just opinions.

Perhaps if I had more religion in my life, my marriage might not have ended this year. Not that it was unexpected. It was obvious Melissa and I were growing apart, due largely to the fact I enjoyed my life in the mountains and Melissa enjoyed her life away from the mountains. When it was again time to revisit our beach house in Canada, and Melissa told me that she preferred that we go without her, I saw the handwriting on that damned wall again. But this time, the lettering had grown quite large.

After a few days at the beach house, I received a call from Melissa telling me she was not happy in our relationship and perhaps we should have a trial separation. My initial reaction was what took so long? I'm not stupid and figured she must be interested in someone else because most people don't generally leave a relationship unless there's someone waiting in the wings. I wondered if it was Jon Voight, but not really.

I really couldn't blame Melissa, and even though I felt our relationship had been doomed from the beginning, I still felt a sense of loss and failure. My only hope was that we could handle a divorce in a civilized manner so our daughter Myah wouldn't be subjected to any serious sadness.

When I returned to Los Angeles, Melissa had already removed most of her belongings from my home in Tehachapi and moved in with her mother. Even though our marriage lasted less than four years, I agreed to pay off her credit cards—which were substantial—and assist her financially in purchasing a condo in the Pacific Palisades, an affluent area near the beach. I was happy that our daughter Myah was not an issue, because Melissa felt she needed time for herself, to figure out what she was going to do next. Besides, I felt I was more secure and able to provide Myah with a stable environment in Tehachapi rather than the confusing life I suspected she would have with Melissa. A few months later, the divorce was official and I was single again.

As I had guessed, it didn't take long before Melissa was in a relationship with a personal trainer named Jeff. It also didn't take long to realize I was enjoying my life as a single dad. Myah had become quite precocious, and at times we were like a comedy team, developing bits together. At the age of two, whenever we were at dinner with friends, I would let her take a sip of my wine, to which she would always respond, "Mmmm...nice bouquet."

Another fun bit was, I taught her to give specific answers to political questions, so if we were sitting in a restaurant next to patrons who could overhear, the fun would begin. I would loudly ask her if she thought Clinton was doing a better job than Bush and she would reply, "Yes, because Bush was getting too old, like Reagan." or I would ask her, "Do you like our Vice President?" and she would reply with her rehearsed answer, "Yes I like Al Gore and I think he's smarter than he looks." People would actually think I was having a political discussion with my four-year-old daughter.

One funny incident occurred when we were sitting in Jerry's Deli with friends and another of my buddies, comic John Mendoza. John, who knew Myah was four, was joking with her saying he could tell her exactly how old she was. Lovable Myah shook her head and said, "No, you can't." John reiterated, "Yes, I can." Myah repeated, "No, you can't."

So John jokingly said to her, "You're nine years old." Myah chuckled and replied, "No, I'm not." John then said, "You're two years old." Again Myah laughed and said, "No, I'm not." John continued with, "Then, you're six years old." Myah again repeated, "No, I'm not." John tried again, "You're three years old." Again, Myah replied, "No, I'm not." Finally, John knowingly said, "You're four years old." Myah's eyes suddenly widened as she replied ever so slowly, "How-Did-You-Do-That...?" Her innocent, bewildered response caused everyone at the table to laugh hysterically. Myah had no idea why everyone was laughing, but you could tell she enjoyed it.

One evening in Tehachapi, I took Myah to a local community hall for a parent and kid bingo game. We were seated opposite a very attractive woman who was with her five-year-old daughter. Besides looks, she had a terrific sense of humor, responding to my foolish questions with even more foolish answers. By the end of the evening, this Hungarian beauty, Margit Dornay, and I planned a date. It didn't take long before we knew we enjoyed each other's company and began seeing each other on a regular basis.

Life was nice until my ex-wife Melissa called and told me she wanted more furniture out of my house, which I was not prepared to give her. I felt I had been overly generous after our break up and told her if she wanted anything else from me she should take me to court. Rather than go through all that court nonsense, she decided to show up at my house unannounced with a male friend of hers. I immediately recognized him. He was an ex-boxer named Randy Shields who had fought champions Thomas Hearns and Sugar Ray Leonard. I had met Randy a few times at Jerry's Deli, and he too was fond of Melissa, and whether they ever took it beyond the fondling stage I didn't know and didn't care. But what I did care about was not allowing Melissa to ransack my home.

The most troubling part of this scenario was that Melissa had our four-year-old daughter for the weekend and was returning her to me. To this day, Myah recalls feeling terribly uneasy spotting a gun inside Randy Shield's jacket. I had known that Randy worked as a part-time bodyguard and had a permit to carry a gun. Coincidentally, only months before he was in the news for shooting two guys as they ran from a restaurant after robbing it.

I was standing outside when I saw them drive up, and I quickly locked my front door behind me. They exited the car, leaving Myah inside, and Randy did not hide the fact that his gun was protruding from his jacket while Melissa stormed toward my front door, demanding I open it.

When I refused, she picked up a large rock and threatened to throw it through the window if I didn't open the door. Call it stupidity but I was not about to let her throw that rock, so I yanked it out of her hands and tossed it to the ground. She screamed and I guess that was Randy's cue. He immediately attacked me throwing a barrage of punches to my head, face, and body. My instinct was purely defensive, as I held my arms and hands in front of and around my head, trying to keep from getting knocked out.

Even if I thought I could fight back, what chance did I have against a gun? As bruises and welts began to explode on my face and body, Randy kicked open the door and inside they went. As they began removing stuff, I slowly made my way to the phone, dialing 911 and informed the local police I was being robbed and warned them that they had a gun.

Minutes later, two patrol cars showed up, and the police, with guns drawn, arrested and handcuffed Randy, then took him and Melissa to the station. For all Melissa's effort, nothing was taken from my home. Myah remained with me, and to this day it pisses me off that Melissa allowed such an incident to occur without any consideration for how it would affect our daughter.

I was prepared to take Randy to court on assault charges, but it became a "he said, she said" scenario when they told the police Randy came to Melissa's defense because I was strangling her. To protect themselves, Melissa later applied makeup to her neck to look like a bruise, took a picture, and sent it to the police station. It's unfortunate that the police didn't take pictures of her neck at the scene which would have proven their allegations to be false.

In the end, I let it all go, not wanting to go through a court scene myself. Personally, I believe Melissa's intention from the beginning was to have Randy physically assault me. I think, subconsciously, she felt I never loved her enough emotionally or financially and this was her way of getting even. I have to say, for several days after, I learned that love really does hurt.

Some weeks later, I related this story to my boxer buddy Ray Mancini. He was furious, and offered to find Randy and kick his ass for me, but I told him thanks but no thanks. As far as I was concerned my life was wonderful, and I was happier than Randy or Melissa combined. Contributing to my joyful state was the new woman in my life, who had been nursing me through this minor crisis: Margit, or as she preferred to be called, Gita.

My parents fiftieth anniversary took place this year and we decided to set up a cute practical joke on them. As far as my mom and dad knew, only my sister Suzanne would be able to join them because the rest of us made up stories that we could not make it for either personal or logistical reasons. So it was set that my sister Suzanne would take them out for dinner at a restaurant.

Unbeknownst to my parents, Suzanne planned ahead of time that a back room at that restaurant would be set up to accommodate a large crowd of their friends and relatives to show up and surprise them including we five kids. No doubt that my parents were upset hearing that everyone except Suzanne couldn't get away from their daily lives to show up and share their fiftieth anniversary. But show up we all did, and after they arrived at the restaurant and were seated alone at a table with my sister, I was the first to sneak up and surprise them, then escort them to where everyone was awaiting their presence. My parents were truly shocked to tears and their fiftieth turned out to be an exhilarating experience which was pure happiness for my mom and dad and for me too.

The year ended on another happy note when I received a call from an old friend, Claudia, who told me she was working as a wardrobe mistress with Bette Midler on a TV movie called *Gypsy*. I was a huge fan of Bette Midler, an incredible performer in so many areas of show business.

Claudia told me that my name was brought up in the midst of a conversation about comedy, and upon finding out she was a friend of mine, Bette Midler told her she would love to meet me and to invite me to the studio. I, of course, accepted the invitation and a date was set.

Myah, who at the time was almost five, was already acquainted with her work, having seen the movie *Beaches* several times. When I mentioned I was going to meet Bette Midler, she jumped for joy and pleaded for me to take her along.

When we arrived at the studio, Claudia guided us onto the set where Bette was in the middle of shooting a scene. She immediately noticed us, waved, and told Claudia to have us seated until she was finished. As I watched her, it was obvious, witnessing take after take, that Bette was a perfectionist. She didn't settle for mediocrity, letting the director know when she felt a scene was done to her satisfaction.

She truly looked the part of a star, softly commanding in her demands yet overtly gracious when they were met.

After about thirty minutes we were introduced, and she couldn't have been friendlier. She invited us to join her for lunch in her trailer where she told me how much she enjoyed The Unknown Comic. I didn't hesitate to return the compliments, which I meant wholeheartedly. We chatted, joked, and she couldn't have been sweeter to Myah, who was swept up by her glowing, outgoing personality. When it was time for her to go back to work, she thanked us for visiting and I thanked her for letting us share a slice of a day with the Divine Miss "M".

Me and my sister Suzanne, surprising Mom and Dad at their fiftieth anniversary.

Me saying a few words at my parents' fiftieth anniversary surprise party.

Myah celebrating her fifth birthday.

Me and my new love, Gita.

1994

I was truly amazed at what a fiercely devoted father I had become. Any selfishness that I previously possessed was gone. My life was now all about raising my little girl Myah. I considered myself very fortunate, having reached a point in my life where I could remain semi-retired, enjoying a lifestyle in a comfortable country setting, where horses and deer were plentiful.

However, more drama was right around the corner when Melissa married her boyfriend Jeff and decided to take me to court in an attempt to get legal custody of Myah. Fortunately, because Myah had been living in my home in Tehachapi for almost five years, the judge saw no reason for her to be moved to Melissa's condo in the Pacific Palisades. The Judge ruled that I was to be given primary custody of Myah, with Melissa being granted occasional weekends and holidays.

My relationship with the new lady in my life, Gita, was growing, and there were signs we might take it to another level, but until then, we were content seeing each other sporadically. The fact that she had a daughter about the same age as Myah gave us both extra reason to connect sooner or later.

On the professional side, I refused any gigs that would take me away from Myah. However, when she was with her mom, I accepted weekend jobs giving me extra spending money.

My agent George knew of my friendship with Jerry Van Dyke, whose TV show *Coach* was now an unqualified hit. He asked me if I could convince him to appear at the Riverside Hotel in Laughlin, Nevada, with me as the opening act. A price was quoted, Jerry accepted, and on opening night we had a packed house.

In the past, I would usually announce the show on a microphone backstage, then introduce The Unknown Comic, put the bag on my head and run onstage. However, this time things did not go as planned.

With Jerry standing by my side and a packed house waiting, the sound booth cued me to begin the show. I grabbed the backstage microphone and began, "Good evening, ladies and gentlemen, the rest of you know who you are. Welcome to the Riverside Hotel starring that guy you love to laugh at from the TV series COACH, Mister Jeerrry Vaaannn Dyyykkke."

The audience applauded as I continued "But first, to open the show, here comes that crazy man with the bag over his head. He's the Prince of Puns, he's the Merlin of Mirth, put your hands together and welcome..." I suddenly stopped and looked for my bag, which was always right next to me. My head swung around in every direction searching for it and within seconds the realization set in that my BAG was NOT there...but still sitting in my hotel room. This had never happened before, ever. I stuttered as I continued speaking into the mike... "Ah... ah... ladies and gentlemen... please hold on a minute... uh, don't go anywhere... I'll be right back...."

Jerry, who was standing next to me, curious as to what happened, quickly asked, "What's going on?"

"I can't believe it." I replied. "I forgot my bag. It's in my room."

"WHAT! You forgot your bag in your room?" Jerry responded, chuckling, then quipping. "That's like a hooker showing up and saying... I left my pussy at home..." A very funny remark... from a funny mind.

He continued laughing as I ran to my room, retrieved my bag and returned, breathing heavily, then reintroduced myself and began my set. After the show, Jerry was relentless in his continued harassment, telling everyone in sight what happened. Despite this minor faux pas, all the shows went great, and it was a week filled with fun, tennis, and lots of laughs.

Jerry and his wife Shirley got to know my little girl Myah because I often brought her with me when we met for breakfast or dinner. One night, as Myah and I were at home watching Jerry on his TV series *Coach*, at the end of the show, my little girl, confused, asked,

"Where's Shirley?" She was still too young to understand that television wasn't real life.

Unlike Jerry, it had been years since I appeared on television when I was invited to appear on a new talk show hosted by Vicki Lawrence. I thought it would be fun to bring along my cop friend Dave and his wife Darlene to the NBC studios where "Vicki" was being taped.

I was one of three comedians invited on an episode to play a comedic version of the *The Dating Game*, in which we would each be given a choice of three girls. Coincidentally, the other two comics on the show had both opened for me years before. Drew Carey, who was on the verge of getting his own show named after him, opened for me in Ohio, and Paul Provenza, who had opened for me in Tucson, was a regular on a new TV series, *Northern Exposure*.

I was actually invited to be on the show because of Vicki Lawrence's husband Al Schultz, who had been a makeup man at CBS when I was appearing on the *The Sonny and Cher Show*. He was one of the coproducers of his wife's show, and when one of the writers, Monte Aidem, mentioned he was a friend of mine, Al had him call me and invite me to be on the show.

I always liked Al, a large figure of a man, with a friendly face and likeable demeanor, unlike his wife Vicki, who from my perspective always appeared distant and unfriendly. Vicki still surprised me at what a good actress she could be. Prior to the show, as I expected, Vicki was again aloof, barely acknowledging me when Al reintroduced us. Yet the moment the show started and I ran onto the set, Vicki acted like we had been friends all our lives.

One memorable moment, which occurred prior to taping, happened when I was standing in the hallway with my cop buddy Dave and his wife Darlene prior to the show. Suddenly, Darlene squealed with delight upon seeing actor James Garner heading down the hallway in our direction. He was appearing on the *Tonight Show*, which was being taped directly across the hall from us.

Having never met him, I was also impressed, seeing James Garner strut his movie star good looks and larger-than-life smile toward us. As he got closer, Darlene continued to swoon, and for a second I couldn't help but notice that he was staring directly at me.

I began looking around, thinking he must be looking at someone else, but as he approached, he suddenly reached out his hand and grabbed mine. He shook it and said, "I just have to tell you that I really enjoy your work." I was completely surprised and responded with a meek "Uh, Thank you." I couldn't help but think that this was ass backwards. I was the one who should be telling James Garner how much I admired his huge body of work.

Once he left, Dave and his wife turned to me with eyes wide open and said, "You know, we were never really impressed with you before... but we are now." Even though I had gained a small amount of recognition in show business, having someone the caliber of James Garner compliment me gave me a tremendous amount of personal satisfaction. Now, I could die happy.

Jerry Van Dyke appearing with The Unknown Comic in Laughlin, Nevada.

1995

I'm fifty-one years old and my daughter Myah is now six. There's no doubt that life moves a little faster as you age, but I had no complaints. I was lovin' my life.

In our little mountain community, along with Ruth and Kent, we were all one happy family. Gita and I decided to try living together, so she rented out her house and moved in with me. We had a passionate relationship that seemed to be the glue binding us together. Not a bad way to go.

However, small problems existed, and my hope was that they wouldn't get any larger. We both had kids, which was good, but we disagreed on the methods of raising them, which was bad. We were both raised Catholic, but she was still devoted to the church and I thought religion was bullshit, which was a problem for her. I was very liberal in my views, which for me was good, and she was a conservative, which for her was good... but not so good for the two of us.

Looking back, there's no doubt that I had a tendency to spoil Myah, but I didn't really notice it. How could I? Love is blind and I loved my daughter. One interesting anecdote related to Myah and Religion occurred when we visited Gita's parents in San Diego. Gita's dad, an extremely devout Catholic who attended church daily, insisted we join him at Sunday services. I was okay with it because at that point I had raised Myah to have an open mind about all things religious.

Though Myah knew I didn't think much of organized religion, I would tell her that she shouldn't believe what I believed just because I was her dad. I tried to explain that she should develop her own beliefs as she got older and had a better understanding of what religion was all about. I was against any kind of brainwashing of my daughter.

That said, we sat through mass, listening to the priests repeat over and over how we needed to adore and worship the Lord. The theme of worshiping God seemed to be hammered at the congregation throughout most of the service.

When Mass ended, while Gita and her family gathered together, Myah and I wandered off admiring the beautiful courtyards. As we strolled about, Myah, who was only six, seemed a bit confused and said, "Dad, isn't God supposed to be better than us?"

Not sure what she was getting at, I replied, "Well, yes that's what religions teach." "But Dad," she continued, "God must have a big ego if he wants us all to worship Him." I was momentarily stunned at what she was saying as she followed with, "Because if I was God, I wouldn't want people to be worshiping me."

It was a pure example of an "out of the mouths of babes" revelation. I had never read or heard anyone ever utter anything so profound regarding religion and the worshiping of God. What an ego God must have to want us all to scurry to the countless churches around the globe and adore and worship Him. My little girl had further enhanced my understanding of why religion didn't make a whole lot of sense to me.

On July 23 of this year, I received a call from my sister Suzanne, barely able to talk, giving me the jolting news that my father had died. It was a monumental shock because my dad was the first really close person to die who I loved. I reacted as expected, immediately choking up, with tears streaming down my face as Suzanne fed me the details. He had passed away in his sleep with no sign leading up to his death.

Except for one significant hint my dad shared with me the last few times we were together. Because his injuries had made him practically immobile, coupled with the fact he was in constant pain, he felt he was no longer enjoying life. In his words, he was merely existing, and expressed to me a desire to die. And so, his wish finally came true at the still young age of seventy-four.

I flew to Canada for the funeral, which was at first overwhelmingly sad then oddly gratifying. I'll never forget entering the funeral home and approaching the entrance to the room where I saw my dad in the distance, laid out in an open coffin. I stood motionless for a long time before I was able to gather the emotional strength to get a closer look at my deceased father. Tears overflowed as I moved slowly toward the coffin, transfixed on my dad's appearance. The initial shock gradually transformed into a more serene sensation as I gazed at the peaceful and pain-free look on his face. My dad appeared handsome, with a tiny smile on his lips, and he looked twenty years younger.

It was all so surreal. As the hours passed, throngs of people showed up, most sharing their grief while others told stories about my dad. Before long, bits of laughter could be heard among the crowd when humorous anecdotes concerning my dad were passed around.

One story I had never heard was how my dad had bravely rescued a woman and her baby from the second story of a burning building when he was only twenty years old. A friend of the family gave me a newspaper account of the incident along with the thank you note that the woman's mother had sent my dad, thanking him for saving her and daughter's life.

Why did I never hear this story from my dad? I knew he was fairly modest and certainly not a braggart, but he was a hero and never said anything to anybody about it. What a great guy he was, which was why I loved him so much and always will.

When we cleaned out his room, gathering my dad's belongings, we found a small bottle of brandy under his mattress. My mom told me she would sneak brandy into his room on a regular basis because it helped with his pain, and he would indulge with a couple of shots every night. I decided, along with my brothers and sisters, that before he was to be buried, we would toast him with shots from the bottle of brandy we found.

On the final day of viewing, before being placed into the hearse for the funeral procession, we five kids were left alone with my dad. I lined up five shot glasses along the side of the coffin and filled each with brandy. We then lifted them to our mouths and toasted our dad as we expressed our appreciation and love for him. At the same time, I tilted the bottle to my dad's mouth and trickled a small amount of brandy onto his lips. I then said, "We'll know he's gone for sure if he doesn't lick his lips." He didn't, but we all chuckled anyway, and then continued on to the graveyard where he was buried.

The rest of our family enjoyed a nice reunion, and before I left, I told my siblings that I planned on returning to Canada to attend six more funerals. That's right, I was going to outlive them all, but of course I was joking, but deep down, maybe not.

Within weeks after my return to Los Angeles, Gita and I broke up after having lived together for a little more than four months. Our relationship seemed laden with problems associated with not only religion but also with the fact we clearly both wanted to be in control.

I admit I prefer having some control in a relationship, but I'm also willing to compromise on issues. Gita, in my view, lived by a saying on a t-shirt she wore when I first met her which read "It's my way or the highway." With her, there was little room for compromise and we were becoming a lot like Congress. The fact that she was a conservative and I was a liberal only led to more futile arguments. It was a shame, because when things were good between us they were very good but when they were bad it was hell—and Gita believed in hell.

Once again I was single and once again I was afforded another opportunity to pull off another practical joke. My pal, Pat Paulsen got married to a wonderful new woman in his life, Noma, and he wanted me to join them in Vegas at the home of our friends Jimmy and Judy. Jimmy's house had two guest rooms separated by a bathroom so Pat and his bride stayed in the larger one and I slept in the other.

At the end of our first night together laughing and drinking, we all retired to our respective bedrooms and went to sleep. I awoke at about two in the morning to go to the bathroom, and as I prepared to step out of my room, I heard a noise. I peeked into the hallway and saw Pat Paulsen heading to the bathroom.

Once Pat was inside the bathroom, I tiptoed over to his bedroom and quietly tapped on the door. His new bride answered and I asked if she would help me play a practical joke on Pat. When she agreed, I told her to go into the closet while I crawled into the bed and waited for Pat to return. It was very dark, and when he came back and crawled into bed, I quickly clasped his hand in mine as he lovingly whispered, "I missed you so much. Did you miss me?"

Instead of answering, I kissed his fingers as he attempted to pull them away to seek further adventures. All the while, my insides were killing me trying to suppress the laughter. As Pat tried to snuggle closer, whispering sexy things he wanted to do to me, I decided it was time to bring this episode to an end before he brought his episode to my end. I let his hand go and he immediately reached for one of Noma's breasts, his fingers instead finding my hairy chest.

Less than a fraction of a second passed before Pat screamed, jumped out of bed, and turned on the light. Upon seeing me laughing uncontrollably, Pat quickly responded with a barrage of curse words before seeing his new wife in hysterics exit the closet. It took a while before Pat calmed down and realized I had pulled off another practical joke of a lifetime. Of course, I was unable to sleep the rest of the night for fear of retaliation from the mighty Pat Paulsen.

Myah with a bird on her head at age six.

My great friend Pat Paulsen with his new wife, Noma.

1996

As the new year began, it was good news and bad news. The good news was I was offered a lucrative job in Las Vegas. The bad news was Melissa wanted to take me to court again. She was remarried and believed having custody of Myah would complete her new family. However, I was still convinced Myah was better off with me, so even though I knew it was going to cost another chunk of my savings, I again attained an attorney and off to court we went.

Once again, the judge saw no reason to change Myah's living situation. However, he added that Myah's feminine side might be better served if she spent more time with her mom but left that decision up to me. That decision, along with the fact my savings were fast depleting, became a motivating factor in accepting the job offer in Las Vegas.

The Boardwalk Hotel and Casino, located on the strip, was being renovated, and I was offered to design my own showroom to perform my act in. The owner was an amiable older mafia-type who liked me, and we signed a contract which necessitated me finding a place to live in Vegas. An ad of our contract was placed in the papers for publicity indicating it was a "million dollar deal" in which I would receive $10,000 a year for the next hundred years.

The truth was I would receive the full amount of whatever ticket price I charged per person to see my show, plus fifty percent of the drink revenue. Such a deal was unheard of in Vegas, and my plan was to start by only charging $5 per person.

I discussed my plans with Melissa, proposing that I'd take Myah to Las Vegas where she would go to school and let her fly to her mom's on weekends and holidays. The following year, in the wake of the judge's recommendation, we would reverse the situation where

Myah would live with her mom and would spend weekends and holidays with me. My thinking was that during those alternate years when Myah was living with her mom, they would be able to share all those girlish activities I was not able to provide, at least not in public.

I purchased a condo in Vegas, a block from my good friends Jimmy and Judy, moved in, then found a school for Myah. Working in my new petite showroom proved to be more demanding than I anticipated. Though I only spent an hour performing each night, the rest of my time was consumed with getting people into my showroom. Besides appearing on all of the local TV shows, I would literally stand in front of the hotel for hours, handing out coupons to people walking by, often right up to showtime. Slowly but surely, small crowds began showing up on a regular basis, and before long I was soon earning a nice living. My time with Myah was still plentiful, except for my hour on stage in the evenings, when I hired a babysitter.

Despite our differences, Gita and I resurrected our relationship largely because sex was still a dominant factor. Eventually she quit her job in Tehachapi, moved in with me, and assisted with the operation of my little showroom. Once again, life was great. Besides Gita, I had: my daughter; my mom; my siblings; and my best friends—Ted, Pat, Freeman, Ruth, Kent, Jimmy, and Judy. Not so great was my relationship with Yakov Smirnoff, which was fading fast. From my perspective, Yakov was a user whose friendship was predicated, not on the kind of person you were, but on what you could do for him, and there wasn't much I could do for his career anymore.

One friend who seemed constant was Lucie Arnaz, who called me when she was coheadlining with the Smothers Brothers at the Desert Inn Hotel. After our shows, I would meet with Lucie and Tommy Smothers for late breakfasts and we talked and joked about the old days, the current days, and the days of wine and roses. Lucie was still as charming and attractive as ever and I was grateful for our continuing friendship.

For extra money, I had t-shirts made, and one night, I was pleasantly surprised when famed sports commentator John Madden saw my show with his sons and bought several of them.

Sadly, bad news reared its ugly head again, when Pat Paulsen informed me that he had cancer. His wife Noma was determined to find a cure, while Pat showed such strength of character, never displaying even a hint of anger or fear. I desperately didn't want him to die. I considered him one of my best friends and I wanted to continue sharing laughs with him.

I wasn't laughing when I began to notice I was having difficulty with my breathing. For some unknown reason, while performing, I would occasionally run out of air and struggle to finish a joke. My initial self-analysis was that it might have something to do with my years of breathing with a bag over my head.

Sensing something serious, I went to a doctor who diagnosed me with having excessive anxiety related to either my performing or my erratic relationship with Gita. He gave me a prescription to ease my angst, and though I was fervently against drugs of any kind, I felt compelled to take them to ensure I could perform. Unfortunately, several weeks later, my breathing problem seemed to worsen. Nevertheless, I felt I had no choice but to continue performing.

When fall arrived, I kept my promise and turned Myah over to Melissa. It was a bit disconcerting knowing that, for the first time, custody would be reversed, and Myah would live with her mom. Over the years, whenever Myah asked me questions about her mother, I would never say negative things about her. My response was always that her mom loved her and wanted the best for her. It's tough enough for kids to grow up with separated parents without them trashing each other. When Myah would try to dig deeper about the reasons for our divorce, my customary response would always be, "I'll explain it to you when you turn eighteen."

Long-term contract for my appearance at the Boardwalk Casino in Vegas.

1997

I revisited the annual Comedy Awards with Gita, and once again, the entire event was filled with laughs, fun, and seeing old comic friends. Jim Carrey was being honored, and we hung out for a while. Interestingly enough, I learned that neither of us had ever seen the show we did together, *The Sex and Violence Family Hour*. I wondered if Playboy, which produced the show, had any idea it owned Jim Carrey's very first television appearance.

My relationship with Gita was back on track after a few bumps in the road, when out of the blue, she proposed that we should get married. Well, proposed might not be the right word, more like recommended, advised, or threatened. I was reluctant, knowing we had issues, but she believed that marriage would solidify our feelings for each other.

Gita could be persuasive, and regardless of the problems that existed, I was convinced I was in love with her. If not, why did I miss her so much when we were apart? If marriage would make her happy and keep us together, I agreed, and we set a date. Because we were both extremely busy with running our showroom, we decided on a "quickie" wedding at one of the Elvis wedding chapels in Vegas.

It turned out to be a quickie wedding in more ways than one. Three weeks after our marriage, we had an argument, of which I recall nothing. She packed up, left Vegas, and headed back to Tehachapi. WTF? I really began to consider that the doctor might have been correct about my breathing problems being related to anxiety. I certainly had more than the required amount in my relationship with Gita.

After she left, my difficulties breathing intensified, often making it almost impossible to get through my act. I frequently found myself gasping for air in the middle of a joke, unable to finish the punch line, which is not good for a comedian.

I sought the advice of another doctor, who suggested I keep an oxygen tank backstage and use it before and after my shows. I tried it, and at the same time I continued taking various drugs hoping one of them would be effective in curing this curious hardship I was experiencing.

Though I tried not to show it, my breakup with Gita was very painful emotionally, but logically I knew we had been headed toward a dead end and after a few months, I filed for divorce. Was I destined to be single? It sure seemed that way after two failed marriages.

To make matters worse, I received the horrible news that my dear friend Pat Paulsen succumbed to cancer and died on April 24. I had rarely met a grown man whose personality exuded such simplicity and pure innocence. He always had a ready smile, loved laughing with his friends, and I felt grateful to have been considered one of them.

Like myself, Pat was not a religious man, somewhere between agnostic and an atheist. Toward the end, I asked if his beliefs had changed, and he replied that they hadn't and that he was very content with the life he had been gifted with.

At the memorial service attended by hundreds, I had never before seen such love and respect shown to an entertainer. There was a mixture of laughter and tears as everyone recalled the cherished memories of such a beautiful human being. When it was my turn to speak, I managed to get a few funny lines in related to Pat's love of crossword puzzles. "Pat was a crossword puzzle fanatic. So much so that he requested that he be buried six down and three across." But halfway through, I broke into tears. I had just lost one of my five best guy friends and now had only four left: Ted Zeigler, Freeman King, Jimmy Delisse, and Kent Perkins.

A year had gone by since Myah moved in with her mom, and my plan to have her return to living with me in Vegas for the new school year did not materialize. Myah told me that she wanted to stay with her mom because she had developed new friends and didn't want to be separated from them. I didn't see that coming, but I understood her feelings and reluctantly gave in to her wishes. I only hoped for her sake that I was making the right decision.

My dear friend Pat Paulsen—sadly departed—with Johnny, George, and me.

1998

This year began with news that Sonny Bono died after skiing into a tree. Though I was not a fan of his, I was nevertheless saddened when I heard that he died in such a tragic manner, long before his time. Only a week earlier, one of the Kennedys, Michael Kennedy, also died after injuries sustained from hitting a tree in a skiing accident, which led me to joke, "There'll probably be another famous person who will die the same way because as everyone knows, celebrities always die in 'trees.'"

I was amazed at the amount of news coverage associated with Sonny's death, having no idea he had made such an impact on America, but apparently I was wrong. Because of my association with *The Sonny and Cher Show*, a local news station requested an interview, which I agreed to.

I was somewhat conflicted about what to say when asked, "So what kind of man was Sonny to work with?" I didn't really like him, yet I responded, "He was a lot of fun to work with." Then added, "Working on *The Sonny and Cher Show* was like going to a party every day." And for me it was, but Sonny was not the reason. My recollection of Sonny was still that he treated those of us who were not at his level like inferiors.

After the interview, I felt I had lied and for the wrong reasons. Weeks later, I was again approached by a cable outlet asking if they could interview me for a biography about Sonny. I again agreed, but this time I was determined not to lie or sugar coat the truth. When questioned about Sonny Bono, I stated that he treated the regulars on the show with little respect and a lot of arrogance. I wasn't angry at Sonny, simply hurt that he made our experience working with him less enjoyable than it could have or should have been.

I'm not positive, but I believe my honesty ruined the less-than-close relationship I had with Cher. Prior to his death, Cher would usually respond when I called her if we were in Vegas at the same time, but any future communication between us suddenly ended. I had heard through mutual acquaintances that she was not happy with my candid description of Sonny, but I could be wrong. Whatever the case, I'm glad I told the truth.

While working in Vegas, I was asked to appear in a small movie being produced by a young man named Chris Owens. I played a bartender in the film about two guys travelling from the border of Canada to the Border of Mexico called *Border to Border*... very clever title.

I was introduced to Chris through his father, Gary Owens, who I met on my first television appearance when he was the announcer on *Laugh-In*. All through the years, Gary and I maintained a mutual admiration for each other's humor, and though Gary and I were not as close as I was to Pat Paulsen, similarly, he also radiated a gentle personality and a love of laughter.

My gig at the Boardwalk came to an end after the owner died and the new regime wanted to replace me with a novel idea in Vegas: an Elvis impersonator. In truth, I had grown tired of the daily grind, especially with my ongoing breathing problems, and I looked forward to returning to a more casual life of semi-retirement. I also missed being with my daughter Myah on a regular basis, and wondered if after I moved back to Tehachapi, she would want to live with me again.

I sold my condo, packed up, and weeks later, I was back to being semi-retired at my home in Tehachapi. Myah was still in the middle of her school year so deciding where she should live would have to wait until school was out. Within a month, I was offered another film, but this time they want me to star in it.

The producers had already talked to my comic buddy, John Byner, about taking the lead role, but after reading the script, he suggested that I would be better suited for the part. It was called *Insanity* and centered around a whacky, off-the-wall character who lived in an insane asylum. My initial reaction was that it could be another *One Flew Over the Cuckoo's Nest*, but after reading the script and finding out the budget, I figured at best it would most likely turn out to be *One flew into the Cuckoo's Crap*.

However, because I was out of work and they offered me a sizeable chunk of upfront money—we're talking in the hundreds—I felt I had nothing to lose except my dignity, which I had given up years before when I went on my first audition. And with my ego intact, I really believed my contribution would somehow lift this project to a level of mediocrity that at least wouldn't embarrass me. So into production we went.

The producers were a couple of likeable guys, and for the most part, I enjoyed making the movie. Unfortunately, the end result was a film which was disconnected and erratic, making no sense to the viewer. There were intermittent bits which were funny but not enough to salvage this mess, which in my view was ruined by a young foreign director who had absolutely no sense of how to film comedy. Consequently, it was never released, and a copy of *Insanity* remains on my shelf, if anyone's interested.

Insanity must have rubbed off on me in more ways than one, because I began seeing Gita again. Back in Tehachapi, we bumped into each other at a local store, and a short time later, we continued to bump into each other throughout the night. I have no idea what I was thinking, or even if I was thinking, but I was suddenly back on that crazy Gita merry-go-round, which was so hard to get off.

Nevertheless, and forever more, in an effort to rekindle our spark, Gita and I decided to rent an RV and travel cross-country with our two girls, Gillian and Myah. We drove the southern route through Texas and headed to my beach house on the far east coast of Canada. On the way back, our plan was to return using the northern route through Chicago and Denver.

During our trip, we found ourselves in Missouri, where we spotted a large billboard advertising Yakov Smirnoff who was now a big star in Branson. I decided to stop by and see if there were any remnants still left of our friendship, and I wondered if his distant attitude would prevail, and sure enough it did.

I called him on the phone, and rather than invite us to his home, Yakov suggested we meet at a coffee shop. We met with him and his wife and managed to muddle through some inane dialogue about his career and success, and after we left, I knew I would never call Yakov again.

As we traversed the country, most of our trip was fun, sharing all the sights with our two daughters, but Gita and I still managed to have a few irrational spats over nonsensical issues. Once again, our relationship was frustrating me.

When we returned from Canada, I received a message to call James Marcel, the amazing juggler I used in my Vegas show years before. When I dialed his number, I was surprised when a female voice answered, which was not unusual since James was good looking and had a reputation for allowing women to touch him inappropriately.

James Marcel had no problem finding a date, especially after he changed his name to James Wilder and studied acting. He gained momentum rapidly, starring in several small films and a couple of TV series, most notably playing a young lawyer in *Equal Justice* and one of the leads in the remake of *Route 66*.

James was excited to hear from me, and we set a date to meet at Jerry's Deli the next morning, where I quizzed him about the female who answered his phone. I was surprised when he told me he had a new girlfriend, an actress, and they had been living together for ten months. Her name was Kirstie Alley.

After listening to him rave about what a talented lady she was and how lucky he was, it was obvious James was undeniably in love with her, even though she was eighteen years his senior. He spoke of her beauty, but her mind and intellect were what really impressed him.

A few days later, James invited me to lunch because he wanted to introduce me to Kirstie. When I told him I was with Gita and our two daughters, he said, "Bring them, Kirstie loves kids. She has a couple of her own." Kirstie couldn't have been nicer, especially with the kids, joking and at one point styling their hair. After meeting Kirstie, Myah would always refer to her as the lady with the "big" hair. It was also evident Kirstie was madly in love with James, with their hands clasped as she spoke incessantly about what a wonderful guy he was. At one point, Kirstie told me she thought I looked familiar and I replied that she might have seen me in the film *Stitches* with her ex-husband Parker Stevenson in which I played a gay florist.

Though James was not quite thirty, he was a very smart guy who knew how to make money in a short time. In fact, Kirstie moved into his stunning hilltop estate resembling a miniature version of the Hearst Castle. James, with the help of his dad, built two identical four-story homes adjacent to each other. His original plan was to sell one of the houses for the cost of building both of them, resulting in his owning one of them free and clear.

But, when James hooked up with Kirstie, he connected the two houses with a tunnel bridge, allowing them to have his and her homes. His place was immaculate, adorned with large antique pieces. Each home was equipped with an antique elevator which took you up and down the four floors and each had its own swimming pool, one for swimming and one for their pet koi fish.

One humorous incident occurred when I was visiting them with Myah, then nine years old. James showed us his master bedroom, which was being cleaned by their maid, and lying on the bed was a package of condoms. Myah instantly noticed them and asked, "What are those?" The maid, without blinking an eye, quickly responded in her Spanish accent, "Oh, little senorita, those are mints that I place on their bed every night. You know... like in a hotel?" "Oh yeah, I've had those," replied my daughter, as I quickly changed the subject and we moved to another room. I hoped James gave his maid an extra tip for her super quick thinking.

Talk about coincidences, less than a week later, I was sitting with friends at Jerry's Deli, when actor Dirk Benedict of *A-Team* fame joined us. I had appeared with him years before on a Canadian talk show, and he was relating to us a tale of woe about how he had fallen in love with a woman and moved away from Hollywood only to have recently been dumped by her.

I asked where he was living, and he told me his friend Parker Stevenson was letting him stay at his place. He continued chatting about how they both had so much in common, since Kirstie had left Parker for some younger stud actor, breaking his heart. I knew that this was not the time to mention that I had just had lunch with Kirstie and that same young studly actor. All I could think of was what a small world this place Hollywood truly was.

Dirk and Parker had nothing on me when, once again, my relationship with Gita came to another end when we had an argument over Myah. I was almost relieved, and this time positive, that we would never get back together again, and to ensure its finality, I began seeing other women. I had been out of the dating loop for years, and my first dalliance was with someone I'd known since she was ten and I was in my twenties, but now she was in her thirties and I was in my fifties.

Her name was Kathy, and Freeman reintroduced me to her after becoming acquainted with her on the Internet—the new dating service taking over the country. Kathy was as cute as a button and we began a sporadic relationship because she lived and worked in Colorado.

Call me stupid, call me idiotic, call me other names associated with those words, and you'd be correct. I was again sucked into Gita's spell when she persuaded me to join her and her sons for a weekend of skiing but only as friends. It was against my better judgment, but my better judgment was never any good and I tagged along. What a fool. What a chump.

It was supposed to be a four-day event, and I had no intention of becoming intimate with Gita, especially since I was now seeing Kathy, but on the first night those intentions were overpowered. I was furious at myself for my lack of willpower and immediately left the next morning. At last, I was firmly convinced that my relationship with Gita was finally finished forever, for good, and for all time.

But Gita was not. When she heard about Kathy, she became angry, and through mutual friends managed to locate her on the Internet. She then emailed Kathy, claiming that I was a serial dater who had constantly cheated on her, adding that I was infested with various forms of venereal disease. Kathy was left crushed and confused as to whether I was the diseased, deceitful, good for nothing, phony, perverted hypocrite who Gita had described. The fact that Kathy initially believed anything Gita told her, brought my evolving feelings for her to a slow crawl, which eventually ended our relationship.

Some weeks later, I was shocked beyond belief when I heard that Gita was pregnant. I was stunned, wondering if that one night with Gita on that ski weekend could have possibly caused her pregnancy. In my mind, since we had both been seeing others, someone else could just as easily have impregnated her. I had heard through her sister that she was dating others, so the possibility certainly existed that Gita didn't know who the father was. Upon hearing about my presumptions, Gita became furious, and our relationship went from being ended to being upended. And when I requested DNA proof, she went from furious to ferocious—and not in a pleasant way.

Gita refused to participate in a DNA test, promising that I would never see the baby. I couldn't understand her refusal and told her that if the baby was mine, I would accept all responsibility. She didn't want to hear anything I had to say, and I knew this was going to be an emotional roller coaster ride, and I hated roller coasters. At this point, all dialogue between us came to a complete halt, and all I could do was wait until she delivered the baby in November and attempt to force a DNA test.

Myah still wanted to stay in the Palisades with her mom because of the many friends she had in the area, and though I saw her most weekends and holidays, I felt we needed to spend more time together. One of the producers of the film *Insanity*, owned a quaint apartment building in Santa Monica only minutes from where Myah lived with her mom, so I rented one of the smaller units. My sole purpose was to have closer proximity to Myah because in my mind, she was still my number one priority and responsibility. Along with weekends, I was now able to also spend school days with her, which benefitted Myah, having both her mom and dad nearby.

After years of success on *Coach*, Jerry Van Dyke and his wife Shirley were able to purchase Bing Crosby's old house in Toluca Lake. They gave me a tour of the legendary crooner's home where he had raised his family, and I wondered how many times he sang "White Christmas" by the fireplace. Jerry also related how he met Bing's son Phillip who, while showing the home to them, pointed to various parts of the house saying, "This is where my dad beat me with a whip," "This is the staircase my dad threw me down," etc. I sensed uneasiness in the air mixed in with the mustiness.

Ironically, only months later, I met Phillip Crosby when we were both interviewed at a television station in Las Vegas. We had lunch and chatted about his life, and there was little doubt he disliked how he and his brothers were treated by his loveless dad. At this time, Philip's three brothers were already dead, Gary from lung cancer and Lindsey and Dennis from suicide. Phillip died six years later of a heart attack, probably provoked by the broken heart provided by his dad. Bing Crosby was the complete opposite of what the public thought he was. A sad Hollywood story of a rotten father and that certainly wasn't going to be me.

And I was right about Bing's house being eerie because shortly after Jerry and Shirley moved in, an earthquake shook the house to its foundation, causing considerable damage. Thankfully, though they were shaken up a bit, they were not hurt.

I attended Jerry's birthday party, where I met his brother Dick Van Dyke, and I was thrilled to be in the same room chatting with him. Though Jerry had told me Dick was a loner, I thought he seemed quite gregarious and very likeable. Another highlight was joking with another show biz legend, Donald O'Connor. It was a fun birthday party where, in the end, we all got to roast Jerry, and the person who garnered the most laughs was Harvey Korman.

At this year's Comedy Awards, Jerry Lewis was honored and so was I when he spotted me and gave me a huge hug. I still found it unbelievable that Jerry Lewis would remember me and we immediately began doing shtick together. I really appreciated that he treated me like a friend and felt fortunate that he didn't treat me like family.

Words can't describe how I felt when I heard that Gita gave birth a month prior to her due date on October 16. Her initial intention was to have the baby in her home using a midwife to assist with the delivery. Instead, she was sent into early labor after receiving an electrical shock in the meat section of Costco when she touched a metal railing. She was rushed by ambulance to a hospital where she gave birth to a baby girl she named Mary. Not surprising, with her religious beliefs.

My shock upon hearing the news of Mary's birth was amplified a hundredfold when I heard she was born with the chromosomal disorder known as Down syndrome. I did not know how to fully react, but I instinctively knew that if this new baby girl was indeed mine, I was prepared to give it all the love I could muster. I also knew I wasn't going to wait until Gita got a DNA test before taking responsibility. Though Gita and I were still not talking, she nevertheless welcomed my visit to see Mary when she arrived home from the hospital.

As soon as I laid eyes on this petite newborn baby, my eyes welled up with tears, and as I held her in my arms, an immediate bond was formed. There was no doubt, with her unmistakable, distinct features that she was afflicted with Down syndrome, but I couldn't stop cradling her in my arms, even when it was time for me to leave. This was repeated daily, sitting in a rocking chair at Gita's, whispering to this special child over and over that I loved her and there was no mistaking that I really did.

As days and weeks passed, Gita reluctantly agreed to a DNA test, and now I worried that I might not be the father of this little angel Mary. Now I hoped she was my daughter, and knew I'd be very upset if I found out she wasn't. And when the tests were complete, I couldn't have been happier to discover Mary was undeniably my little girl. Once again, I knew this new treasure entering my life was going to produce an entire new series of changes in my life. Once again, my philosophy that Change is Growth was going to flourish. I was ready and willing to adapt to major changes in my life and prepared for both of us to grow from it. Having Mary might have been a lowlight for some people but for me it was a major highlight. She was an unexpected gift, and one that I would cherish for the rest of my life. My only fear was how this new baby would affect my relationship with Gita. Initially it brought us together, but the romance was gone, now my only wish was that we could act like grown-ups for Mary's sake.

Since I was no longer under pressure, performing nightly or involved with Gita, I hoped that my breathing problem would have disappeared, but it didn't. In fact, it grew worse. Just sitting having coffee with my buddies, I would suddenly find myself gasping for enough air to finish a sentence. Everyone noticed, commenting on the possible seriousness of what might be wrong with me.

More doctors ensued, but with no results or a confirmed diagnosis of what was ailing me. Finally, one of the doctors suggested I had larger than normal skin growths in my nasal passages and recommended that they should be cauterized. In other words, they would burn the flesh inside my nose, allowing the area to have more space for me to breathe through. Sounded logical to me. Desperate, after dealing with this problem for more than a couple of years, I agreed. The end of the year was fast approaching, and an appointment was set for the week between Christmas and New Year's.

At the doctor's office, they strapped me to a chair while a nurse prepared me for cauterization. The doctor then proceeded to jab a large needle inside my nose to numb the area. I couldn't help but feel that this was not going to be pleasant, and I tried keeping my eyes tightly closed while reciting the alphabet backwards.

After a couple of minutes lying there with tears in my eyes, not from pain but from the fear of pain, he again jabbed some sort of probing device in and around the inside of my nose asking if I could feel anything. I admitted that I could feel him jabbing some sort of probing device in and around the inside of my nose, but there was no pain associated with it.

Convinced the area was sufficiently numb, he continued by gingerly inserting another foreign instrument inside one of my nostrils. I knew it was the tool to be used to burn the flesh on the interior of my nose because he told me he was about to burn the flesh on the interior of my nose. He asked, "Are you ready?"

"No," I nervously replied, "But go ahead anyway." I closed my eyes tighter and was not about to open them again when one of my nostrils got a whiff of the horrid smell of burning flesh in the other. It was nauseating, especially since it was my own burning flesh. I couldn't help but open one of my eyes ever so slowly only to see the nurse, standing alongside the doctor, with a look of revulsion on her face, grimacing at what she was witnessing. I shut my eyes tightly again.

It was only minutes, but seemed like hours, before the operation was completed. Afterward, I was given a prescription for painkillers, which he assured me I would need when the numbness subsided, and on that point he told the truth. He further informed me that it would take about a week for the scab that would result to decompose, crumble, and fall from my nostrils. And then, hopefully, I would be able to breathe normally again. I couldn't wait.

The poster for the film *Insanity*, which unfortunately never sold.

Me and Kathy.

Myah at the age of eight.

1999

Finally, for once, the doctor was right, as the scabs fell out of my nose. And lo and behold, I was breathing normally without gasping for air. I was so elated that I had finally met a doctor who was able to figure out why I was having a breathing problem. Life was great again.

My relationship with James and Kirstie Alley continued when Myah and I were invited to go bowling with Kirstie and her kids. We were also invited to Kirstie's birthday party, which was held at the main Church of Scientology in Hollywood. It comprised of a group of less than twenty who gathered in the restaurant located at the top of the Scientology Center.

I knew Kirstie was a Scientologist but was still surprised that James had become a member, because in our previous conversations, he wasn't much of a believer in anything. He told me he really wasn't committed to Scientology or its doctrine, but because of his feelings for Kirstie, he wanted her to know he was willing to try to understand it. I certainly didn't. If Scientology was about the health of mind and body, it was confusing to observe Kirstie and one of its leaders chain-smoke cigarettes.

The more I was around Kirstie, the more I noticed that she didn't seem very happy. Of course, the fact that she smoked cigarettes was a big indicator that something was lacking in her relationship with herself. Call me self-righteous but I can't help but believe that if you really enjoy your life, with all the knowledge about the horrific effects of smoking, you would not take a chance on ending it prematurely.

I also observed that Kirstie rarely smiled, joked, or laughed when she was away from the camera or crowds. During the limited time I spent with her, she seemed rather sullen and sad. But I have to say on the few occasions I saw her in front of a camera, she would light up a room with her beauty, sense of humor, and fiery energy, and you could see why she became a star.

My sense of humor vanished when, after about two months, my breathing problem returned. I couldn't believe it and tried again to self-analyze this absurd nasal nuisance, determined there had to be a logical answer. After much intense thought, it suddenly hit me like a ton of bricks and I became convinced I stumbled upon the answer.

I recalled a joke comics often use about hair loss: "Have you noticed that as you get older, you lose hair where you want it... and grow hair where you don't want it..." That line of thought exploded in my brain, "... like hair in your ears or nose?" In my twenties, I was almost hairless over my entire body, but in my fifties, the hair on my body flourished, almost to epidemic proportions. Hair was everywhere, including and especially inside my nose. I concluded that had to be it.

It had been roughly two months since the interior of my nose had been cauterized, and during that procedure, not only was the flesh burnt away, but also any hair would also have been eradicated. It takes approximately two months for an inch of hair growth and an inch of hair inside my nose would certainly impede the air going through my nasal passages.

I called my friend Jimmy, and when I told him of my self-diagnosis, he suggested I buy a nose-hair trimmer, which sold for around ten bucks. You just inserted it in your nostrils and it trimmed away most of the excess hair. I had never heard of them, but without hesitation, I hastily ran to the store and bought one.

In the parking lot, I ripped off the packaging, inserted it in my nose, and allowed the trimmer to do its job. Seconds later, I felt sudden exhilaration when I noticed my breathing was almost immediately back to normal. It was just the fucking hairs in my nose all this time! I couldn't help but think how all those fucking doctors I had seen with all their fucking knowledge and book learning couldn't figure out something so fucking simple. Excuse my language, but my distrust in doctors once again shot through the fucking roof.

Finally I had good news, but bad news for my talented buddy Rod Hull when, at the age of sixty-three, he died from a fall off the roof of his house in England while trying to adjust his television antenna to watch a soccer match. He and his family had made plans to come visit me in Los Angeles, but now that wasn't going to happen. At least I had wonderful memories of our times together, especially at his quaint English estate outside of London.

Fortunately, my good friend Freeman was alive and well, dating several women thanks to his success with the Internet. At his urging, I decided to give it a try, and with his help I e-mailed a few humorous letters to some women whose pictures I found appealing. One of the first to respond was an attractive blonde whose name was Adele. We online chatted for some time, joking and flirting, when she asked my first name and I typed in "Murray".

She responded with, "I used to know someone with that name years ago. What's your last name?" Not for a second did I think this was someone I knew because surely I would have recognized her picture on the computer screen. But when I typed in my last name, within seconds the words, "Oh my God!" flashed across the screen. She quickly responded with, "I was at your house about fifteen years ago. You had a pool table in your living room, right?" I replied, "I did."

"OMG!" flashed through my brain. Was this someone I had an affair with years ago? How embarrassing that would be if I didn't remember her. I continued to type, joking, "Were we intimate?" She typed in her phone number and told me to call her for the answer. I was now very curious. Who was this attractive woman who had been to my house years ago that I had forgotten?

I called, and when she answered, I didn't recognize her voice, though it sounded sexy. I reiterated, half teasing and half curious, "So, were we intimate?" "No, we were not," she quickly replied, adding, "I came to your house with Jay Leno." She continued, "We played pool. Don't you remember?" Slowly, my memory began to focus on who she was. She was a singer who had been Jay's live-in girlfriend for many years. "Yes, now I remember," I replied, and recalled that it was shortly after Jay's relationship with Adele ended that he met and later married his current wife Mavis. This chance internet meeting with Jay's ex-lover was out of the ordinary, but the real coincidence was that at the same time that Adele was living with Jay, I was dating his current wife Mavis.

Another bizarre coincidence was that Adele's last name is *Blue*, and the current singing sensation Adele's full name is Adele Laurie *Blue* Adkins. And they're both singers. Weird.

Adele and I subsequently went on several dates, spending many nights together, and joked about what a coincidence it would be if we ran into Jay and Mavis. After about a month, I understood why her relationship with Jay didn't last, which was probably for the same reason that ours didn't, but we don't need to go there.

Besides, my daughter Myah was becoming very picky about the women I began seeing and she was not fond of Adele. There's no doubt a kid's decision on whether they like someone is largely based on how they're treated by them.

Someone I wanted to treat better was my old friend Ted Zeigler, who had been placed in an assisted living facility. Ted was only seventy-four but suffered from sleep apnea, a condition which affects your breathing and can lead to more serious disorders. It was Ted who made the decision to put himself there, worried because he was living by himself and had no one to care for him if anything serious took place while he slept.

I didn't realize how serious his condition was until I took him to Tehachapi for a weekend, hoping we would have a good time. Unfortunately, Ted had aged considerably because of his illness and couldn't wait to return to his new residence where professionals cared for him. Personally, I was overcome with emotion and sadness, thinking back to the raucous times we shared, clowning around with abandonment on *The Sonny and Cher Show*. Getting old really sucks.

But having an eight month old baby keeps you young, and I thought it was time for my little Mary to meet my family in Canada. I was taken aback when Gita asked if she could join us, and for some unknown reason I agreed. So once again, Murray, Myah, Mary, and Margit (Gita) returned to the beach house.

At this point, our relationship was purely platonic, but as usual, after a few nights at the beach house, we somehow gravitated toward the same bed. I had suspicions that Gita wanted to get back together, but I was not about to go down that unpredictable, incompatible, and inconsistent road again. If I was ever to become involved with another woman, I wanted consistency to be a dominant factor; however, I did want to remain friends with Gita for Mary's sake.

When we returned to Tehachapi, the tense nature of our relationship was aggravated by my continuing to see other women, and because Gita was not getting her way, she began reducing my visitations with Mary—and being separated from my little girl hurt deeply. My bond with Mary had multiplied daily, where she became my number one priority above anything else, except of course for Myah.

Unable to reason with Gita, I saw going to court as the only option to at least guarantee regular visitations with Mary. I was not trying to get custody; I simply no longer wanted Gita to have control over the times I could see Mary.

In court, the proceedings turned ugly with lies spewing forth from her family members who lied mercilessly, attempting to paint me as an unfit father. Fortunately, in the end I was granted regular visitation, with Gita no longer making decisions depending on how angry she was with me.

And then the heavens somehow shined down upon me when Gita met a guy she was interested in and began a new relationship. With her new love dominating much of her time, her priorities suddenly shifted significantly and the court order, which ruled when, where, and for how long I was to see Mary, flew out the window.

Gita's attitude toward me suddenly changed, and her new, positive disposition gave me pretty much free reign on when Mary would and could spend time with me. I couldn't have been happier. Mary had become my life and my sole goal was to ensure she would be as healthy and as happy as was in my power.

My other major concern was also making sure Myah was happy, and renting an apartment only a few miles from her mom had made our time together more plentiful and gratifying. Myah also loved Mary like a sister, okay, more than a sister, and she treasured our annual visits to the beach house in Canada, often taking one of her friends with us. I attended most of Myah's school and sporting activities, especially basketball, which was her favorite until she learned about boys. Thankfully her interest in boys wouldn't peak for several more years.

Because Myah lived with her mom in an affluent neighborhood, celebrities were ubiquitous. When I attended one of Myah's basketball events, as I sat on the sidelines, director Steven Spielberg entered and stood behind me. On another occasion, as I accompanied Myah to the gym, I found myself standing alongside *Titanic* director James Cameron as he watched our daughters work out. Myah had grown used to seeing celebrities, and one time after seeing Leonardo DiCaprio at a gas station, she quipped, "Eww, he has zits."

However, the one celebrity Myah wanted desperately to meet was teen singing sensation Britney Spears. She idolized her, following her every publicized movement and searching her out on the Internet. Myah would sing Britney's songs nonstop, and it didn't take long before she sounded almost exactly like her. I found it fascinating that Myah possessed that same passion for Britney Spears that I had when I was a kid about Jerry Lewis.

I had intended on surprising Myah with tickets to a Britney Spears concert at Universal Studios, but within hours, it was sold out. However, luck was with Myah when unexpectedly, Linda Blair invited me as her date to the Blockbuster Entertainment Awards show. It was a fabulous musical event and we attended the party afterwards where I finally got to meet John Travolta.

For years I had wanted to know whether Freeman was telling the truth when he said that Travolta lived in the apartment next door to us during his Kotter years. When I asked Travolta, he readily confirmed Freeman's claim. I then proceeded to tell Travolta what a coincidence it was that he lived there at the same time that I was dating Debra Winger, who later costarred with him in the film, *Urban Cowboy*.

Travolta followed with yet another coincidence by telling me that the person who moved into that same small apartment after he moved out was director Quentin Tarantino, who years later gave him a starring role in the outrageously violent film *Pulp Fiction*. Yep, Hollywood is a small world.

At that same party, I met one of the members of the teen group 'N Sync, named Chris. When we were introduced, he told me how he and his dad used to watch The Unknown Comic on *The Gong*

Show all the time. I told him I thought he appeared too young to know who I was, but he revealed that though he looked young, he was older than all those young girls who worshipped him thought.

He was actually almost thirty, and as we chatted, he introduced me to his manager Johnny Wright, who I discovered also managed Britney Spears. When I mentioned that my daughter was a huge fan and how I tried to buy tickets for Britney's sold-out concert, he handed me his business card, telling me he would be glad to help me and to call him the following week. I told Myah about meeting Britney's manager and that there might be a chance that she would get to see Britney after all. She was excited beyond belief.

Now, I had been in these situations in the past, and it's rare when people in show business follow up on what they promise. So, a few days later when I called, I wasn't really surprised when Johnny Wright's secretary told me that he wasn't in and she would tell him that I called. After more than a week had passed and I hadn't heard a thing, I soon became discouraged, and then pissed off that I allowed myself to believe Britney's manager's bullshit.

But, to my astonishment, three days before the concert, I received a call from Johnny Wright, apologizing for not getting back to me sooner because he had been on vacation. He proceeded to inform me that four tickets would be left at will call, along with backstage passes for my daughter to meet Jerry Lewis... I mean, Britney Spears. I was truly astounded, confounded, not to mention dumbfounded, that this great guy Johnny Wright was a man of his word. On the night of Britney's concert, the tickets were front row and Myah was thrilled meeting and taking pictures with Britney backstage.

Unfortunately, the end of the year brought forth the unfortunate news of the breakup of James Wilder and Kirstie Alley. Also one of my breakfast buddies, actor and singer Robert Guillaume, suffered a stroke. For several years, he joined us at Jerry's Deli, spending hours talking about everything from show business to politics.

Mild symptoms of a stroke occurred one day as he was leaving Jerry's Deli, and Johnny Dark did his best to try to talk him into going to the hospital. However, Robert decided it was not that serious, instead he wanted to get to work on his new series, *Sports Night*. That decision turned out to be a mistake, when at the studio, his stroke resurfaced, resulting in more serious damage. A sad example of the power show business has over actors placing their work above their health for fear of losing a job.

I received even worse news when my dear friend Ted Zeigler succumbed to his illnesses and died. I had so many fond memories of a warm and caring man who could go from being steadfastly serious to hysterically funny at a moment's notice. He was an eccentric personality but a man I loved.

Ted Zeigler and Pat Paulsen were two of my best friends, and now they were both gone. But I still had three best guy friends left: Jimmy Delissi in Vegas, Kent Perkins, and of course Freeman King, who along with the others, I talked to almost every day. I didn't want to lose any more friends.

Little Myah

Myah with Britney Spears.

My beautiful Mary at six months.

Myah playing with Mary on the beach.

Me with Linda Blair attending the Billboard Awards Show.

2000

Though David Letterman was not a close friend, he had been a past comedy acquaintance, so I was concerned when I heard that he underwent quintuple-bypass surgery. What was surprising to me was that besides Letterman who had performed at my club Show-biz, several other comics from my place also had open heart surgery. Namely: Michael Rapport, Vic Dunlap, Gallagher, Charlie Hill, Kip Addotta and Roger Behr, which made me wonder if it was something in the food. Including Letterman that would be seven cases that I knew of, so I called his office suggesting it might be a good theme on a future show to have all the aforementioned on one show to discuss their mutual surgical procedure and compare. But this time, I never heard back.

I was fifty-six, semi-retired, and getting bored, so I decided I wanted to put on the play *Run for your Wife* once again, with the hopes of selling it to Las Vegas. My plan was to cast as many celebrities as possible in each role as a selling point.

Since I would only direct, I asked my pal Greg Evigan of *B.J. and the Bear* fame to take over my part, and he agreed. In Pat Paulsen's role I was able to get another TV actor, Eddie Mekka, known for his role on *Laverne & Shirley.* Luckily, I once again secured my friend Linda Blair to play one wife, with Charlene Tilton, one of the stars of *Dallas* to play the other. In two detective parts, I cast Johnny Whitaker, a child actor from the series *Family Affair*, and Robert Walden, one of the stars of the TV show *Lou Grant.*

I rented a small theater above Jerry's Deli but, unfortunately before rehearsals began, Greg Evigan landed a film in Europe and had to pull out of the project. Having already played the lead and with no time to find someone else, I again cast myself in the part. The fact that I was sleeping with myself had no bearing on it.

The play ran successfully for two weeks with lots of fun and laughs, but sadly I was not able to attract any interest from any of the hotels in Vegas. The economy in Vegas was in a downward spiral, and the hotels were not ready to invest in any new shows. Among my many friends who showed up to support me was James Wilder, with a new girlfriend, Nicollette Sheridan. I wondered if Kirstie Alley had a new boyfriend. I was available.

One night, I was at the Improv where Drew Carey was working out with fellow improv comedians for his new improvisational TV show *Whose Line is it Anyway.* On a break, Drew joined me for a drink, and I felt complimented when he told everyone how when he first decided to become a comic, he used to stand outside the lounge at the Sahara Hotel in Las Vegas and watch me perform.

As we continued to chat, one of the costars from his TV series, Ryan Styles, approached our table. Drew asked me if I had ever met Ryan and I replied, "No, but I'd love to. I think he's really talented." So I was pleasantly surprised when Ryan saw me and yelled out, "Hey, Murray. How you been?"

I was also taken aback, which is not a bad place to be taken if you have a good back, but I was a bit embarrassed when Ryan reminded me that he worked as my opening act years before on a comedy tour we did together in Canada. It was hard to believe I had forgotten this super clever and remarkable guy, who is also one of the nicest people in the comedy biz, extremely unaffected by its celebrity trappings.

I felt flattered that these two big stars of television used to open for me, but felt less than equal knowing that they were making a fortune, living the high life in Hollywood, while I was stuck barely surviving in Tehachapi. I'm kidding, of course. As far as I was concerned, the only thing I was stuck with was a fabulous life with people I loved and people who loved me. I never did then and neither do I now have any complaints about my journey through the Unknown. It's been beyond wonderful.

And an integral part of my fabulous journey was my daughter Myah, who we placed in a private school called Archer on the famed Sunset Boulevard in Brentwood—an affluent area bordering Beverly

Hills. It was not my preference, but Myah's mom convinced me that our investment into this overpriced educational system would be highly beneficial to Myah in the long run, though detrimental to my wallet in the short run.

Oddly enough, another series of coincidences ensued when I discovered that attending this same school were the children of two other people from the cable series *The Sex and Violence Family Hour*, which I performed in along with Jim Carrey back in 1983.

Jim Carrey's daughter Jane Carrey, along with the daughter of Harvey Frost, our show's director, were also students at the same school. Neither Jim nor Harvey nor I knew of each other's daughters attending Archer together. You have to admit the odds of our three daughters attending the same school at the same time almost twenty years later were astronomical, or at least three to one.

And the odds of my life getting better with age were still excellent. I was a single guy with two daughters: a one-year-old and an eleven-year-old, and I was happy as a lark. Whoda' thunk this confirmed bachelor would have wound up this way? By the way, are larks really all that happy?

Me with the lovely Charlene Tilton and her gorgeous daughter.

2001

I received a call from the Game Show Network asking if I would host the twenty-fifth anniversary celebration of the *Gong Show*. After some astute negotiations, again resulting in getting paid hundreds of dollars, I agreed. They also asked if I would appear on the Howard Stern Show to help promote the event. At first I declined, but when they offered to fly me to New York, put me up in a deluxe hotel, and pay me an additional fifty bucks, a date was set. Over the years, I had heard my name mentioned on Howard Stern's show by Linda Blair, Andrew Dice Clay, and Richard Belzar, to mention a few. To mention more would make me sound conceited.

So off to New York I went, where I met a new buddy of mine, Michael Christaldi, who I was first introduced to by Johnny Dark. Michael worked as a train conductor between Philadelphia and New York, and he was a huge fan of comedy but also longed to be in show business, studying acting on the side. I wondered if it was his good side, but once you knew Michael, you soon learned he was willing to have sex with anyone who could help him or couldn't help him. Thankfully, at this stage of my life, I could do neither.

Howard Stern's show was not only heard on radio but also seen on late-night cable, so Howard's producer asked if I would first appear with the bag on my head, which was fine with me. Apparently, Howard was made aware of an interview I did with a magazine called "The Onion," which was the source for many of his questions. I began with an assortment of one liners and visual jokes then we shifted toward more salacious dialogue, the mainstay of his show.

When I mentioned I wasn't particularly fond of Sonny Bono or Billy Crystal, Stern smiled and was in full agreement. We also talked about my two failed marriages, which led Howard to ask about my relationships with some well-known ladies. Besides bringing up Lucie Arnaz, Debra Winger, and a few others, the always controversial Stern then asked about my relationship with Jay Leno's wife Mavis, prior to their marriage. I was hesitant to travel that road but he was persistent and kept asking, "Was she a good lay?"

I really didn't want to engage in any banter that was negative or offensive related to Mavis or any other woman with whom I'd shared intimacy, and tried my best to ignore his "kiss and tell" questions. Like it or not, Howard was relentless, pressing me for more information, but I maintained respect and my repeated response was, "Mavis is a terrific lady."

At the same time, I kept trying to change the subject by replying to his repeated sexual questioning with innocuous questions, "So what's the weather like outside?" or "What'd you have for breakfast?" The end result was quirky and somewhat funny.

I recall first preparing for my interview with Howard with much trepidation, knowing of Stern's ability to make a fool out of guests he didn't like. But when the interview was over, Howard and I chatted briefly about our kids, and I found him to be a very warm, sincere, and an almost shy kind of guy, nothing like the wild personality he projected on the air. I liked him... and I think he liked me too.

When I returned to Los Angeles, my interview with Stern resulted in another break-up of my relationship with Johnny Dark. Over the years, Johnny had remained friendly with Jay Leno, who had been using him regularly on the *Tonight Show* to perform in some of their sketches. When Johnny hadn't been called to work on Leno's show in several weeks, paranoia set in, and he assumed that Jay wasn't using him because of Johnny's friendship with me. He had somehow convinced himself that Leno was furious with me over the comments made about Mavis on the Stern show and blamed me for losing his job.

When I spotted Johnny at Jerry's Deli, I told him he was full of crap, and that I didn't appreciate his ridiculous accusation. In my view, there was nothing wrong with mentioning dating someone as long as you don't make it sound scandalous or, even worse, uninteresting.

Still, I wasn't positive I hadn't offended Jay and decided to call his house to get to the truth. I've had Jay's home phone number for more than thirty years, and, as far as I know, to this day it remains the same. Anyway, when I called, Mavis answered the phone and was her usual charming self but surprised to hear my voice. After some lightweight chatter, I blurted out, "Is Jay pissed at me for mentioning you on the *Howard Stern Show*?" She quickly answered, "No, not that I know of." She then continued, "I've got Jay on the other line now. Why don't I have him call you?"

I thanked her, said bye, and within minutes my phone rang and it was Jay. I reiterated what I had said to Mavis and what Johnny had told me, prompting Jay to reply, "Johnny must be crazy. I'm not mad at you. In fact I heard your interview with Stern and thought you were funny. Believe me with all the gossip about me in the rag magazines, nothing you said was even remotely distasteful." He then told me that the next time he saw Johnny he would tell him so.

I never did receive an apology from Johnny or expected one; it just wasn't his nature or in his ability to apologize. But it wasn't my problem, it was his. Though I had long considered Johnny a buddy, I never considered him a best friend, even though I had known him just as long, if not longer, than others in my life. My problem with Johnny was that he was difficult to communicate with on any topic outside of comedy. Conversations related to politics, religion, or even sex would lead to horrific arguments. In my view, friends should be able to debate on any topic without it turning into name calling or loud arguing.

Since I was now capable of telling those I loved that I loved them, I also developed a criteria before I could say those three most important words. Before I could tell someone I loved them, five things needed to exist, whether male or female, lover or friend: First, I had to feel that they also loved me; second, I had to feel that I could trust them to be honest with me; third, I had to respect the kind of person they were; fourth, I had to consider them a best friend; and fifth, I had to be able to communicate with them, intellectually, spiritually, and emotionally without resorting to arguing or name-calling.

My long distance friendship with train conductor/actor/likeable guy Michael continued, when he visited Los Angeles and we met at the famed Improv. We spotted John Mendoza sitting with Drew

Carrey, Ryan Styles, and a few other comics, and we joined them. In the middle of our gab fest, in walked Chris Rock, who strolled over, pulled up a chair, and joined the comedy crowd.

Though I had never met Chris Rock, I certainly admired his talent, and when we were introduced, I was flattered when he told everyone that he and his dad used to impersonate me. Well, not me, but The Unknown Comic.

In spite of his compliment, within minutes, my impression of Chris was that he wasn't very friendly, and he seemed rather self-absorbed and distant in comparison with the other comics. But I thought perhaps he just had a lot of shit on his mind. I also observed that my buddy Michael was reveling in the comedy banter being thrown about, with everyone joking, laughing, and having fun.

As the evening progressed, Chris Rock excused himself and wandered outside to join some other people. Meanwhile, Michael and I also meandered outside, checked out the ladies, and took in some fresh air. Upon seeing Chris leaning against a wall chatting with his buddies, Michael asked if I thought Chris would take a picture with him. I said, "Of course. I'm sure he'd be okay with it. We were all just sitting at the same table. Why wouldn't he?"

Well he wouldn't. When Michael quietly asked about taking a picture, Chris flatly refused with no explanation, period. Why would you refuse to take a picture with a fan? I thought Chris was just plain rude. I guess my first impression of him was correct.

A similar story occurred when I was sitting in Jerry's Deli with Freeman and several friends. I couldn't help but notice a familiar looking face at the cashier, paying his check and staring at our table. When he caught my eye, I smiled and he smiled back. He then approached our table, pointed to Freeman and I, and said, "Hey, I just want to thank you for all the laughs over the years. I loved you guys on *The Sonny and Cher Show*. It was Academy Award winner, Cuba Gooding Jr., and I thought what a gracious thing for a star of his stature to do. And I would have bet a thousand dollars that he would have gladly taken a picture with my buddy Michael.

A few months later, my phone rang and it was a voice calling from my home town of Montreal. However, it wasn't someone I knew. It was an actor who told me he managed to get my home phone number through some extensive research on the Internet. I was confused when he asked if I could give him advice on how to play The Unknown Comic in a movie. Bewildered, I asked what movie, and he informed me that he had auditioned for and got the part of The Unknown Comic in the film *Confessions of a Dangerous Mind*, written by the host of the *Gong Show*, Chuck Barris. I had heard about the possibility of a film being produced from Chuck's book, but I had no idea it was already in production and was being directed by George Clooney.

Baffled and perplexed, I gave the guy legitimate advice on how to play me, but at the same time, I wondered why they hadn't asked the original Unknown Comic to play himself, which was me, myself, and I. I couldn't help but think that since I wore a bag over my head, which rendered my character ageless, that I should be the one to play the part. What made it even more upsetting was that the movie was being filmed in Montreal, the city where I was raised.

Through my own investigation, also using the Internet, I located the production company and the name of the producer. When I called and asked why they cast someone to play me when I was available, I was told that the characters from the *Gong Show* were being played by others because of age. When I reiterated that a bag over the head sort of eliminated that kind of reasoning, I was informed that I was too late anyway because the part of The Unknown Comic had been filmed that afternoon. Upon further investigation, I discovered that the real reason they hired someone local was because in Montreal they could get an actor for only $300 a day, instead of paying out several thousand dollars, plus hotel, and airfare for me, myself, and I.

At first, I thought there was nothing I could do about this transgression, because I had heard that public figures were subject to this kind of treatment, but I decided to call an attorney anyway. I was more than thrilled when I was informed that The Unknown Comic character, like Batman, Superman, or Mickey Mouse, was a copyrighted character I created, and, therefore, could NOT be used without my permission. They could use an actor to play Murray Langston without getting permission because I'm considered a public figure but not my copyrighted character. Yippee!

Once again I called the producer, this time letting him know emphatically that I didn't want my character to be used, and I enlightened him about the fact that they were infringing on my rights. I sensed an alarm go off in his voice when he said he'd get right back to me. And get back he did, only with a pitiful offer of $1,000 for all rights. I responded that I was not interested, though I might have accepted their offer had they been up front with me in the first place. But at this juncture, they could keep their $1,000.

That night, I responded to a knock at my door and was handed an envelope labeled "urgent delivery." Inside was a handwritten letter from George Clooney, expressing he was a fan of mine, and apologizing for any misunderstanding that may have occurred in the casting of The Unknown Comic.

In addition, the following day I received a phone call from George Clooney, who again offered his disapproval and disappointment with the way I was treated. He further told me he wanted to make up for it, and though the scene of The Unknown Comic had already been filmed, he wanted to add more footage with me playing myself, being interviewed without the bag. In addition to that, he offered me many times more than the $1,000 offered by his producer, plus first class air fare and hotel accommodation for a week. Without a doubt, Clooney sounded just as likeable and as charming as I had heard he was, and gladly accepted his offer.

A few days later, I saw George Clooney on the David Letterman show, bragging about the caliber of stars he had signed to appear in the movie such as Julia Roberts and Drew Barrymore. David got a big laugh from the audience when he said to Clooney, "I hope The Unknown Comic is in it."

When I arrived in Montreal, George Clooney was a complete gentleman, chatting with me on the set between breaks and even inviting me to sit with him at lunch.

To top it all, he made sure I was paid twice what our original agreement called for. No doubt, I will always be a huge fan of Clooney's, not just for his intellect and talent but for his overt generosity of spirit.

Months later, as I slept in my small apartment in Santa Monica, I was suddenly awakened with the shrill sound of the phone. I answered it and, through my grogginess, heard Gita's voice ordering me to turn the television on. I said, "What channel?" She said, "Any

Channel." I did, and for the next twenty-four hours I was glued to the set, watching the devastating tragedy of the fall of the Twin Towers. It was 9/11.

A month later, there's more tragic news for me on a personal level when I learned that my mom had been diagnosed with cancer of the blood, Leukemia. My mother was absolutely convinced she would be gone in a year because only a few years earlier her sister was diagnosed with Leukemia and died a few months later. Not a good way to end a year.

Letter from George Clooney.

My little Mary at age two.

Me with Chuck Barris on the set of *Confessions of a Dangerous Mind*.

Me and George Clooney.

Me with my two buddies Johnny Dark and Michael Christaldi.

2002

The phone rang and it was Kent. His voice sounded shaky, which was rare, and as I attempted to joke with him, which was not rare, he suddenly cut me off and said, "Freeman is dead." "WHAT?" I responded, "You're full of shit. I just talked to him this morning." I listened for Kent to tell me he was kidding. I wanted him to be kidding. He wasn't kidding. Freeman was dead. Another one of my best friends who I talked to almost daily was gone?

The next few days, I walked around in a dazed state, shocked to the core at the sudden loss of another of my best friends, who died on his birthday at only fifty-nine years old. Freeman and his girlfriend had left a clothing store where she had bought him a new suit for his birthday, and now he was going to wear it for his funeral.

Apparently, shortly after buying the suit, they were cruising along the freeway when Freeman suddenly grasped his chest and muttered, "Oh Shit." Those were his last words, as he fell forward, his head landing on the steering wheel. He had suffered a massive heart attack and died immediately. As the car swerved, his girlfriend reached down, pulling his foot off the gas pedal, then steered the car to the side of the road bringing it to a stop, screaming the entire time.

My daughter Myah joined me at the funeral service, where she experienced death for the first time, seeing Freeman laid out in an open coffin. He looked exactly the same, as I leaned in and cursed him under my breath for dying so early and at the same time telling him I loved him.

When I got up to speak, I felt confident that I could say what I had planned without crying, but that didn't happen. I talked about how we first met and played a cut from our comedy album where I interviewed him as a Martian from outer space. The lines were funny, and everyone laughed in all the right places.

I talked about how often I told my daughter that she could never be racist because she wouldn't exist if it weren't for a black man. It was Freeman who introduced me to her mother, and as I continued to speak of our friendship, I tried to fight back the tears, but it was useless. I began to sob, struggling to get through the rest of what I wanted to say, describing how much Freeman meant to me, and when I looked up, the entire crowd was also in tears.

Of my five best guy friends, I now only had two remaining: Jimmy and Kent. Though I felt another piece of me was gone, and I would be alone a little bit more, I was also determined to enjoy every day a lot more. The death of your friends reinforces the fact that life is so fucking short.

I called our old friend Debra Winger, now living in New York state, to let her know about Freeman's passing, and though she hadn't seen him in years, she expressed her sadness. We chatted about how she was much happier away from Hollywood and was very content living on the east coast in a country setting far from the film executives she now found repugnant. We also joked about how promiscuous we both used to be and how times had changed, with her being the mom of two boys and me, the dad of two girls. I ended our conversation, voicing my opinion that if she never did another movie, her roles in films like *Officer and a Gentleman* and *Terms of Endearment*, would guarantee her a place as one of the top actresses of our time.

Next, I worked on a pilot for a TV series called *The Rich Generation*, with Rance Howard, father of Ronnie Howard, but it never sold. So what else was new? It didn't really matter because my primary concern was still raising my two girls. My little Mary, who was now four, was getting cuter every day, and I relished every moment spent with her. I was touched when Myah told me how one of her friends, whose dad was a wealthy executive at Disney, told Myah she was jealous of her because she had a dad who was always there for her. She told Myah she would rather be poor and have an attentive dad than be rich and rarely see him. That made me feel special.

Still, Myah, who was thirteen, was at times getting more difficult to handle. She had moved into those troubled teen years I had been warned about. I always heard that raising teens could be tough but thought I could handle anything that came my way. However, when Myah reached the "I know it all and you're too old and out of touch to know anything worthwhile concerning my life" stage, I could get very angry at her.

Could her random outbursts have had something to do with the fact I spoiled her? Probably a little. Could it have had something to do with the many television shows that showed kids acting disrespectful toward their parents? Could have. Could it be because Myah was the product of a divorce, which can lead to a myriad of internal conflicts? Absolutely. But my guess was that most of Myah's occasional rants were a consequence of witnessing her mom regularly scream at her own mother, which led to Myah yelling at her mom, which resulted in Myah thinking it was okay to raise her voice to me. Without question, I respected my parents and never did or ever would talk back to them, so I would become incensed when Myah showed disrespect or talked down to me in any way.

Having given this topic much afterthought, I arrived at the conclusion that you can't spoil a child enough... until they reach the age of reason, then you have to pull way back. When they reach that age of six or seven and are able to figure out how to manipulate parents, that's when, in my view, spoiling kids should come to an end. Unfortunately, Myah was my first child, and it was too late to go back, so I had to learn how to figure out other ways to make our occasionally troubled relationship work for the both of us.

For the most part, Myah was a great daughter, but I guess as a first time dad I just expected more. For the most part, I was a great dad, but I guess as a first-time daughter, Myah just expected more. I began to wonder what would have been different if I had boys. For one thing, having a boy you only have to worry about one penis. Having a girl, you have to worry about millions of penises. My only conversation with Myah regarding sex was informing her that, in my opinion, the more you connect upstairs, the more you'll connect downstairs, which for me still holds true today.

I was grateful and proud of the fact that Myah never succumbed to peer pressure to drink, smoke, or experiment with drugs. Sure, she had eleven abortions, but every kid has to have a hobby. Okay, that wasn't true. In fact, having reached her teen years, Myah still hadn't shown any appetite for the opposite sex. Her obsession with Britney Spears was still number one in her world.

This year, our time spent at the beach house in Canada was even more special because of my mom's battle with cancer. But I was happy to see that she was doing exceptionally well, and I expected her to be with us for several more worthwhile years.

My other best friend Freeman King has died. Our first publicity picture.

My sweet Mary at age three.

My ex-girlfriend Shannon with Myah at a concert.

Me and Myah at the same concert.

2003

There was more sad news when I found out that I was about to lose another of my two remaining best friends: Kent. Thankfully, not due to any illness, but because he and Ruth decided they wanted to make a permanent move from Los Angeles to Kent's home town of Dallas, Texas.

I never thought Ruth Buzzi would ever want to stop working in show business, but I was wrong. Ruth was well off financially because of her fiscally conservative style of living, and Kent's investigative business had succeeded beyond what he had imagined. Along with some shrewd investments in the stock market, plus twenty dollars that I gave him, he had amassed a few million dollars on his own, enabling them both to retire in style. When they put their houses in Los Angeles and Tehachapi up for sale I knew they meant business, and I was sure going to miss them when they deserted me.

My two beautiful girls Myah and Mary provided me with a full plate of love, and between the two of them, I was kept quite busy, so loneliness was rarely an issue. Though Mary was living with Gita, I was with her almost fifty percent of the time, taking her to the beach, the mall, Chuckie Cheese, and in the summers to our beach house.

However, one small problem with Mary began to surface. When she was with me she would get more and more upset when it was time to turn her over to her mother. Not that Gita wasn't a great mom, she was terrific, but it didn't take much logic to figure out why Mary would get upset. When Mary was with me it was just her and I, laughing and having fun, with me spoiling her as much as possible and showering her with love. I can't recall a single instance where I raised my voice in any kind of anger at her, near her, or around her, except in jest. To this day, if she hears my voice reach an upper register, she immediately assumes a joke is about to take place and begins laughing. However, when she was with her mom, she had to compete for attention with her brother, her mom's husband, and her mom's work, resulting in her one-on-one time with her mother being limited.

Also limited was the time I was spending with Myah, since her girlfriends had become the dominate factor in her life. Because she was less interested in hanging out with her dad, it gave me more time to spend with Mary. And, in all honestly, I was thrilled that I no longer had to accompany Myah to countless movies targeted toward kids anymore, especially the films starring Freddy Prinze Jr.—Myah was growing up fast.

Romantically, I was still prolific in my prowess with women I either met on the Internet or through friend connections. Since my focus was on my daughters, my search for a long-term relationship was not at the top of my list, and though I would have welcomed someone who would knock my socks off, it was not a priority. It should also be noted that I rarely wore socks anymore.

Also, at this period in my life, I hoped I had learned from my numerous previous affairs that the most important elements in a relationship were having similar beliefs on the major issues that create a bond between two people. They would include politics, religion, health, child rearing, finances, and sex. They say opposites attract but, from my experiences, they seldom last, and I wasn't about to travel that bumpy road again. If a woman I dated displayed a lack of commonality, the relationship wasn't going to get much deeper. It made my playing field rather limited, but I was thoroughly enjoying my life and was not looking for someone to make me happy, because I was already happy. But if someone came along who could add to my happiness that would be fine with me.

I was spending less time in Tehachapi and more time at my small apartment in Santa Monica, which offered more fun with my girls because it was walking distance to the beach, the pier, and the mall. I found it surprising that, for the most part, I preferred my petite one room apartment to my expansive 3,000 square foot gorgeous home in Tehachapi. With Myah continuing to live in the Palisades with her mom and spending less time with me, my larger home was slowly becoming an unnecessary burden.

And since Ruth and Kent were moving and putting their house in Tehachapi up for sale, I decided it was time for me to also unload mine. When I first built my house, my initial intent was to keep it for the rest of my life, but even though my Spanish-styled home was still beautiful and impressive, with both my girls living with their respective moms I no longer enjoyed it. My place had turned into a house and was no longer a home. It was also too remote and getting too run down from the lack of time I was spending there.

Even though the real estate market was doing fine, I knew I would suffer an extensive loss due to the location, but I didn't care. I'd rather lose $100,000 and be happy than stay put and be unhappy. And $100,000 was exactly how much I lost on the sale of my home; a fourth of my investment in it.

Because my daughter Mary would remain living in Tehachapi with her mother, there was no doubt I would have to eventually find another home nearby, but until then, I temporarily rented a small apartment close to them.

My little Mary is simply gorgeous.

Me with Michael and my other gorgeous daughter Myah.

2004

Within months after selling my house, California property values began to plummet. Luckily, I had the cash from the sale of my place and figured it was time to seek out a property I could steal. I drove past a piece of undeveloped land on three acres only one mile from the center of Tehachapi. I knew I had to buy it and paid less than what you would pay for a car, only $23,000.

It had a magnificent view of the city, and since I was living by myself, my plan was to build a smaller, less ostentatious house. Once construction had begun, I hired a tractor operator to level the land and lay out driveways. I was fascinated watching him work and maneuver a backhoe and eventually learned how to operate it myself.

I subsequently rented a back hoe, and while digging around, I uncovered an above ground spring on my land, which was like discovering a gold mine. I was even more fortunate when an artesian well was also uncovered, which shot water out of the ground like an oil well. I couldn't believe it. I had my own fresh, clean spring water without paying a penny for any of it. When my home was completed, I moved in, loving the peaceful serenity of my new place, which was only a mile from the center of everything in the city.

As part of a school project, Myah asked for my help in writing a song. Songwriting had always been a hobby of mine from the time I was a kid until today. In fact, I wrote more than a dozen songs for the two films I made, composing both the words and music. I had that uncanny ability to create melodies in my head even though I had no musical training, or the ability to play an instrument, except for the drums. Myah had somehow developed that same ability.

Together, Myah and I came up with a rap riff which went:

When someone treats you bad, makes you mad, makes you sad.
Don't let them get under your skin, just grin and walk away.
Don't give in to the games they play.
It's useless to be toothless at the end of a fight,
trying to determine who is wrong and who's right...
'cause everyone knows that the winner in a race...
is the one who walks away with a smile on their face.

We later composed another pop song entitled, "Does he love me or does he not?" We never wrote another song together after that.

As the year came to an end, Kent and Ruth officially moved to Texas, leaving me destitute. Though we talked on the phone and communicated through the Internet, it just wasn't going to be the same, but we did promise to visit with each other.

At least I still had my other best friend, Jimmy, who unfortunately lived three hundred miles from me, in Las Vegas. Nevertheless, we made sure that we visited with each other often, with Jimmy making occasional trips to Tehachapi and me making regular visits to Vegas. Jimmy had become more than a friend; he was my confidante and there was nothing we wouldn't share with each other. It was Jimmy who taught me that all you have to do if you want to be loved... is love.

2005

I was offered a job to perform on a cruise ship going to Europe, which I readily accepted, because besides being paid a nice chunk of money for two shows in ten days, I could also bring a guest. Since I wasn't dating anyone, I invited Jimmy who jumped at the opportunity, having never been to Europe. He wasn't great to cuddle with, but we had a fabulous time, feasting on food and wine as we travelled from Madrid, Spain, along the coast of Italy, to France and Monaco. At each stop, we would visit all the tourist attractions, engaging in nonstop laughter as I joked with anyone and everyone we came in contact with.

In France, Jimmy was surprised when we took a cab and I began talking to the driver in French. Actually, I was just as surprised finding out that I still had a limited command of the language. "Parlez vous Francais?" We followed up that cruise with two more that year, one through other parts of Europe and another along the coast of Mexico. Again, Jimmy joined me and we loved every minute of it.

What I didn't particularly love was giving up my apartment in Santa Monica because I no longer needed it to stay close to Myah. Through a series of bad real estate decisions, Myah's mother was forced to move from the beach community of the Palisades to the more affordable Thousand Oaks where she rented a house.

Coincidentally, about this same time, I heard from my old girl-friend Connie, who I hadn't seen in years. She really was my old girlfriend because she was now in her fifties, which made her old enough to be my wife. Seeing her, it was hard to believe we had been engaged some twenty-five years earlier, and I was surprised at how she held on to her good looks, considering the drug and alcohol route she had travelled. She also maintained her vivacious and outgoing personality, and I still found myself attracted to her, though I knew I should probably keep my distance. She told me she was regularly attending Alcoholics Anonymous, though she was at times a shaky member, but she hadn't indulged in substance abuse in years. I was also surprised to learn that we both had daughters who looked very similar and were close to the same age.

Connie further informed me that she had recently ended an abusive marriage and was struggling to get back on her feet as a single mom. I was also happy to hear that her apartment was only a few miles from where Myah and her mother lived. After a few weeks of seeing each other, I suggested that it might benefit both of us if I paid a portion of her rent and became a part-time roommate.

This would enable me to have a place close to Myah, and in the back of my mind, evaluate whether Connie had changed significantly in a positive way where we might at some point rekindle our relationship. But that was not to happen. Though we began living together, which led to sporadic intimacy and sex, there was an emotional wall maintained between us, and after a few months, I began to notice cracks in that wall.

Most notably, I observed three characteristics that appeared constant. Number one, she seemed self-absorbed, which you'd have to be when you place your own desires ahead of those you love and those who love you, especially your kids. Unfortunately, this selfishness was one of the reasons her ex-husband had legal custody of their daughter. Secondly, she thrived on negativity because, in my view, the more negative one feels their life is, the more reason they have to use alcohol or drugs. And thirdly, from my conversations with her, I noticed that she refused to accept responsibility for her actions, instead blaming her ex-husband and/or parents for her troubled circumstances.

Another commonality she shared with many converted substance abusers was a newly acquired addiction to religion. Connie would frequently try to talk me into going to church with her, and we know that was not going to happen. This was a major issue with me becoming involved with anyone, and so after about six months, I moved out. After much consideration, I knew I wasn't capable of changing her and neither was she capable of changing me.

Myah's relationship with her mother and stepdad was also changing, and for the worst. At least that was her side of the story. I wondered if the problems were related to the fact Myah was approaching sixteen. Regardless, Myah moved back with me in Tehachapi, where she began attending her third year of high school. Though her disrespectful attitude would occasionally rear its ugly head, for the most part everything was hunky dory, though I'm not really sure of the exact definition of hunky dory or even how it's spelled.

My younger daughter Mary also started school, which she enjoyed, and everyone loved her because she was so darn lovable. Sort of like her dad. I frequently heard that kids with Down syndrome were very loving, but that's not really true. One little girl in Mary's class who also had "Down's" was violent and prone to fits of anger, resulting in her being removed permanently.

From my observations of children with "Down's," they're no different than other children when it comes to love, except that they magnify their feelings and emotions. In other words, if you shower a child with love, usually they respond by showing love to others, but if a child is deprived of love, most likely they will respond with anger. In children with "Down's" those responses are magnified so that they will appear to love excessively when they're loved, but likewise they will display disproportionate anger when they're not loved.

Because problems with speech are a primary concern with Mary's disorder, we enlisted the aid of a therapist, with the hopes that sooner rather than later she'll be able to communicate her likes and dislikes to us. The one and only frustration I have ever felt with Mary was when she would try to tell me something and I was unable to figure out what she was attempting to say. Nevertheless, Mary was still the one constant in my life who never failed to bring a smile to my face and add joy to my days.

Not so joyful was receiving news that my mother was near death and would probably not last more than a few weeks. I immediately flew back to Canada, and, fortunately, the grim news became good news when she recovered after several blood transfusions. It was apparent this parent was not going to easily give up the life she so enjoyed.

Me with Connie, thirty years after we first met.

Me with my best friend Jimmy Dilisi on a cruise.

2006

I love my daughter Myah, but there were parts of her developing personality that I didn't like, and my patience and understanding were being stretched to the limit. Fortunately, Myah could be sent to her mother where she would attempt to be respectful and well-mannered for a least a few months before being sent back to me. Throughout this confusing and turbulent period, I hoped that Myah would sooner rather than later realize that she didn't have to engage in battles with me, because I loved her and would always be there for her.

I would also always be there for my mom, and when my sister called again informing me that the doctors believed she had less than a week to live, I immediately flew back to Canada to be by her side. Thankfully, my mom survived the week, and my belief was that it was because we told the doctors we couldn't pay the hospital bill, so they gave her a few more weeks until we could come up with the money. Okay, that's not true. Canada provides free medical care.

Actually, I was grateful to have had a week alone with my mother in which we shared good conversation. One topic I was curious about was religion, mindful of the fact that my mom never missed a Sunday mass. When I asked if she believed wholeheartedly in the teachings of the Catholic church, especially heaven and hell, her response took me by surprise. She said, "I don't know what happens after we die, nobody does, but I've always enjoyed the social part of the Catholic church, hanging out with my friends and playing bingo." Odd that a game based on gambling would play a part in someone's religious foundation.

When I asked my mom what she thought love was, her response was equally interesting replying, "I think love is friendship. If you have friends, you have love. So always be sure whoever you fall in love with is also your friend." Half the town of Bathurst considered my mom their friend. She was truly loved.

Unlike my dad, my mom still had difficulty saying the words "I love you," normally responding to that phrase with, "me too." However, on my last day before leaving, as I kissed her and said goodbye, she muttered weakly under her breath, "I love you"... and though those precious words were barely audible, what I heard came across Loud and Clear.

On the flight back, I thought about my career, or lack of one, and especially my little girl Mary, and I arrived at the conclusion that I no longer wanted to fly unless absolutely necessary. I wasn't afraid of dying, because I felt overly grateful for the life I've had, far surpassing anything I imagined, so at sixty-two, for me, everything in my future was icing on the cake.

It was because of the deep bond that existed between Mary and I. The thought of her never seeing me again made me shudder with fear and anxiety. In my mind, because of her inability to comprehend death, if something happened to me, for her it would be devastating beyond belief, and I no longer wanted to take that risk.

These feelings for Mary gave me a deeper understanding of religion and how it must have originated. My gut feeling is it's lights out after we die, and as much as I'd love to reunite with my family and friends in some Disneyland in the sky, I cannot convince myself that there's any logic to that scenario. However, if Mary ever reached a level where she could somewhat comprehend death, I would much rather that she believed in an afterlife and that we'll see each other again after I'm gone. But as for myself, as much as I'd love to believe in that pie in the sky, my logical side refuses to indulge.

Nonetheless, I decided I would retire completely from stand-up, and I hooked up with my old buddy Paul Block, who booked me on the *Tonight Show* so long ago. We began creating game shows, developing some distinctive and unique concepts, and though we came close to getting a deal, close was all we got. Suddenly, reality shows were the rage, so we changed our direction and developed several original ideas, and we met with my old *Candid Camera* buddy Rac Clark and his dad Dick Clark. Once a month we would pitch ideas to them and, once again, though there was interest, we couldn't seem to land a deal.

Paul was offered an Internet job, sending him to San Francisco, so I teamed with my actor friend, Greg Evigan, and together we created more reality shows, pitching them to anyone who would listen. Again we met with Dick Clark, and he wanted to produce a pilot on one of our ideas: an award show which gave money and trophies to small town heroes. Each small city or town would submit their favorite hero, and the eventual top ten would be selected by the viewing audience. Not a bad idea but no takers.

We pitched another reality show called *America makes a Movie*, in which the viewing audience selects the script, director, music, actors, and actresses in the making of a film. We thought we had a winner when we submitted it to Stephen J Cannell, the prolific producer of so many shows, including *The Rockford Files, Barretta,* and *The A-Team*. He loved it, but unfortunately, after getting turned down by one network, feeling rebuffed, he refused to take it any further.

Through Cannell, I learned that the networks, though willing to look at your ideas, were mostly reluctant to invest in a concept unless it had been tried before. Basically, the networks had grown chicken shit and were looking to other countries for their hit shows, Americanizing them and putting them on the air after they were a proven success elsewhere. They were not prepared to gamble millions on American ideas when so many other countries such as England, Japan, and Germany had proven hit reality shows that they could easily adapt to U.S. audiences. Once we realized we were spinning our wheels, Greg and I moved on our separate ways.

At age sixty-two, I could now collect social security early, and that's what I opted for. Along with my pensions from Aftra and Sag, I felt I could lead a comfortable life. When the SSI sent me my earnings statement I was slightly stunned, and I suspect you too will be amazed at my income over the past fifty years. Especially with the fact that the most money I ever earned in any year was in 1996, totaling $63,000. Most years, my earnings were in the $30,000-$40,000 range. And yet, financially I'm in fabulous shape and even richer in my personal life. I find it inexplicable that so many wealthy celebrities who earned millions filed bankruptcy: Ed McMahon, Mike Tyson, Larry King, Wayne Newton, and Willie Nelson to name a few.

Reading through my memoirs, and considering the almost 800 television appearances I made, the twenty films I appeared in, along with countless nightclub performances, you'd think that I would have earned ten times more than I had. However, though I earned $1,200 per show during my Sonny and Cher years, we did twenty-two shows annually, which amounted to a little more than $26,000.

At the height of The Unknown Comic's popularity, there were a few money-making years where the corporation formed by my accountant earned close to $200,000. But when the salaries of my band and dancers were deducted, along with percentages taken by my managers, agents, accountant, and lawyer; then add to that the cost of hotels, travel, props, etc., etc., my net earnings would usually amount to less than $50,000. My major security net was my investment in houses, and though I lost some money on a few misguided ventures, there's little doubt that real estate in the long term did not let me down.

The average annual income in the U.S. is around $45,000, which was about what my yearly earnings amounted to. And I'm happy to say that I have no problem comfortably taking care of myself and my family for the remainder of my life, which hopefully will be substantial.

My secret for success and happiness on a limited income was uncomplicated. Keep it simple and concentrate on your needs, not your wants. The reason becoming wealthy was never a dominant factor in my life was because I learned early that simplicity was one of the keys to being happy. It's just simple logic. If you have five cars, or five homes, or five of anything, you have five times more worries and five times more probability that problems will arise with those five things.

Throughout my adult life, my primary concern was to stay out of debt. I've never purchased a car on credit, always paying cash. In my early years, I preferred driving an older car rather than a new one with payments. I simply did not want the pressure of having to come up with a payment every single month.

In my view, buying a house as quickly as you're financially able is the most effective way to secure your future. I'm not talking about a quick turnover but with a plan to live in it for at least five to ten years. The odds of losing money on a home that you've owned for that length of time are almost zero.

And once in a home, concentrate on paying if off as soon as you can. If you are lucky enough where your home appreciates, doubling or tripling in value, sell it and buy another house with your profit and pay cash for your next place, which is exactly what I did. I own a beautiful home on several acres and have not had a mortgage payment in over thirty years. There is simply no better feeling than owning your car and home outright with zero payments due, especially if you're middle class, like I've been most of my life.

And lastly, never allow a credit card to take over your financial life. I had one credit card years ago, but when debit cards arrived, which only allow you to spend money that you have in your account, I immediately limited myself to that one card. So with no mortgage, no car payment, no credit cards, at this stage of my life, everything is wonderful.

I'm also one of the fortunate one percent. Not of this country but of the world, which is the case if you're worth more than $34,000. Think about that. If you're worth more than $34,000 you are in the top one percent of the world. Eighty-five percent of the world earns less than $200 a month so that's why I should be ashamed of myself if I ever feel deprived or unhappy with my lot in life. I consider myself a very lucky guy.

I'm also a part of another one percent of this country. Not the super-rich, but the one percent who served in the military, which allowed me to receive free medical through the Veterans Association. Unbelievably, because I lead a fairly healthy life style, I had never used their services, but that was about to change.

Me with Dick Clark, from my *Sonny and Cher Show* days.

2007

Myah was almost eighteen and her relationship with her mom and stepdad had become intolerable. She begged me to help her get an apartment, and found a job selling clothes in Santa Monica to help out with the rent. We both knew that with the little Myah would earn, I wasn't going to take money from her, and since I also missed living in the area, I rented a small one room apartment one block from the ocean. Myah was now officially on her own, but with a little help from her dad.

One day, Myah told me that she had developed a passion for songwriting, and her dream was to one day write a pop hit for her idol Britney Spears. She told me that she had her own MySpace page on the Internet and had garnered close to a million hits on several songs, which she wrote and recorded on her laptop computer.

I didn't give it much thought, until one day when I stopped to visit my cop buddy Dave at his house. Dave was well versed in computer technology, and though I had dabbled in computers in their infancy, my knowledge of current technology was limited to e-mails and Internet dating. I asked Dave if he would look up Myah's MySpace page and play one of the songs she wrote. He obliged, and the first song he played had the provocative title "Stiletto Sex."

As we listened, it sounded cute, until she began singing lyrics which included the words, "Fuck" and "Cunt." Needless to say I was shocked, while Dave was laughing hysterically at my stupefied reaction. However, when I paid closer attention to the words and music of other songs that she wrote, I understood why she was getting so many hits. Without a doubt, Myah possessed the basic skills and talent to potentially succeed as a singer/songwriter. That is, if she had the desire and dedication to work hard. I hoped her newly found passion would lead to some measure of success, though I was keenly aware of the odds against it.

The odds of writing a play are equally as farfetched, so when my agent George called and asked if I would be interested in such a venture, my first response was no. He then asked if I had heard of the play *Vagina Monologues*, and when I told him yes, he informed me that he had someone willing to pay me a substantial sum of money if I would write a funny male sequel.

Having plenty of time at my disposal I agreed, and within a week, I had completed a four-character play which I called *The Weenie Man-o-logs*. The investor, a sweet, older hippie gentleman named Rich Miano, loved the script and asked if I would produce and direct it at a theater they operated in Hawaii. Their goal was to break it in, then hopefully sell it to one of the hotels in Las Vegas.

Besides getting paid, I was also a fifty percent owner in the play, so again, I agreed. Next, I auditioned and hired three talented comic actors to perform in the play with me. They were: Thai Rivera, a very funny gay comic; Danielle Kasen, a talented lady who had been in Vagina Monologues; and Kato Kailin, who had managed to extend his fifteen minutes of O.J. fame, taking advantage of his gregarious personality and ample comic abilities.

We rehearsed in Los Angeles for weeks, and then flew off to Hawaii to perform in *Weenie Man-o-logs*, which ran for a month and was a success, but not for the producer. The actors were thrilled getting paid to have fun in Hawaii, and two weeks into the run, I flew my daughters Myah and Mary to join me, resulting in a fantastic vacation for us.

Unfortunately, because Las Vegas was in a serious downward slump with hotel revenues falling drastically, we were not able to get *Weenie Man-o-logs* into any of the Vegas venues unless the backers put up their own money. Because the entire country feared a recession, the producer felt the odds in Las Vegas would have been against him and bowed out.

April 13 was a gigantic lowlight in my life, when my sister Annette called and tearfully told me that my mom's light might be going out for good. She said the doctors told her they were sure Mom wouldn't survive her battle with cancer one more week. This time Annette was convinced they were right because Mom had recently lost weight at an enormous rate. I asked Annette if I could speak with her, but she said Mom was too weak to talk and her energy was depleting fast, which made me realize it was very serious.

So, once again, I hurriedly booked a flight to Canada, but this time it was too late. As I prepared to leave, I received a call from Annette, crying uncontrollably because our mom had passed on. I was really extra saddened to know that Annette was the only one of us five kids who was able to be with her to say a final goodbye for the rest of us.

Upon arriving in Canada, I showed up at the same funeral home that held my dad, and I solemnly strolled toward the same viewing room. When I saw my mom laid out in the coffin, I couldn't hold back the tears. Unlike my dad, she looked nothing like the mom I had known. Annette assured me that she looked much better than before she died because the makeup artist worked extra hard to make her look peaceful. Still, I was fixated on the fact that she didn't look like my mother. I bent over, kissed her, and felt pain in my heart knowing I wasn't with her at the end to let her know how much I loved her.

My mom rarely went a day without bread and molasses for breakfast so we decided to repeat the scenario that we engaged in prior to our dad being buried. But instead of sharing brandy we would share bread and molasses with our mother, before laying her to rest. My sister Sue suggested that, at the same time, we should sing a song my mother sang to us when we were kids, "Que sera sera," sung by Doris Day. The lyrics were "Whatever will be, will be. The future's not ours to see, Que Sera, Que Sera."

If anyone would have videotaped our rendition, it would surely have made YouTube. As we five kids gathered around our mother, I divided a slice of bread into six pieces, added a dab of molasses to each, then handed them out, placing the last piece on our mom's lips.

Slowly we began singing, "Que sera, sera. Whatever will be, will be," etc., etc., and within seconds of the first verse, all five of us burst into tears, blubbering and sobbing as we struggled through the remaining lyrics. It had to be one of the saddest scenes to witness, yet if anyone who didn't know us saw it, I'm sure they would have laughed hysterically at this highly emotional spectacle.

I was never one to believe in ghosts or the hereafter, but on my return trip I almost succumbed to that kind of thinking. I was seated in a private compartment on the train as it pulled into Montreal, reflecting on all that had transpired with my mom's passing. My pensive solitude was suddenly interrupted when a woman passed by my room, singing "Que sera, sera, whatever will be, will be...."

Momentarily stunned and confused, my immediate thought was that somebody was playing a practical joke on me. When I realized that wasn't a possibility, I wondered if somehow, someway my mother was trying to say a final goodbye to me. Within minutes, the same woman returned, passing my room again, still singing the same song. I leapt to my feet, quickly opened the door, and looked both ways but didn't see anyone. I walked briskly in the direction I thought I had heard the singing, hoping to find the woman and ask her why she was singing that song, but I never did.

Was it coincidence or was it something spiritual? That was a question I couldn't help but ask myself over and over. What were the odds that a woman would be singing such an obscure song, a song I hadn't heard in probably fifty years, so soon after I had just sung it to my mother? No matter what the odds, this was one of the most inexplicable things that ever happened to me. My mom passed away at the age of eighty-four. "I Love You, Mom."

2008

Back in Los Angeles, Myah wanted to move from the beach to an apartment closer to Los Angeles, where she could pursue her fledgling songwriting career. Because I was a supportive dad, and not wanting to bring an end to spoiling Myah, I told her I would continue paying rent for the new apartment. We discussed her attending college part time but Myah convinced me that she wasn't ready to go. In her mind, working daily on her songwriting and music was her college, and I figured that the thousands of dollars I'd be spending on rent, would rival the thousands to put her through college anyway. After all, she was my daughter and my responsibility until she was eighteen, and she was now nineteen. I need to work on my math.

I have to say that Myah did not shy away from working jobs in her pursuit of a career. She was hired by a wealthy couple as a personal assistant, and later as a receptionist at a hair salon. Because of her cute personality she had no problem getting work, which she needed for extra money and to make monthly payments for a used car I helped her purchase.

Because I wanted to help her establish her own credit, I secured a loan from the bank under her name for $5,000 for the purchase of her first used car. Unbeknownst to her, I worked it out with the bank so that I put $5,000 of my own money in an account for her, which secured the loan. But, as far as Myah knew, it was the bank's money and not mine. I figured if she thought that she was making payments to me rather than the bank, she would not feel as responsible for making those payments on time. And I was right. Within a year, her credit was established and she has been diligent in protecting it.

Even though I was now living on a fixed income, I knew I wasn't going to give up continuing to work at something. I'm a firm believer that life is about living and not merely existing, a lesson I learned from my dad.

Some thirty years ago, a movie was made called *Can I do it 'til I need glasses*. The film consisted of using comedians to act out the most popular dirty jokes of that day. Even Robin Williams performed in a couple of the jokes before he became famous. In my opinion it was a terrible movie because the majority of jokes they used were just not very funny, yet it was still a success, making a substantial amount of money for its producers.

Over the years, I had been filming jokes that had been shown on the Playboy channel and other cable outlets, and I began to think that it might be time to film an updated version of that premise. My agent George was able to convince a wealthy friend of his to invest $100,000 in my idea, and so I began shooting a low-budget film I called *Dirty Jokes... the Movie*.

I enlisted the help of my long time comic friend Vic Dunlop, who had an equal amount of experience producing low-budget films, and we became partners, with him producing and me directing. To protect the innocent, we changed our names to read, Produced by Joe Traylor and directed by Jeb Trasch, in a Traylor-Trasch Production.

I compiled the best jokes I could find, and using many of my comic actor friends we filmed over eighty jokes. Three months later, we completed our little movie and rented a theater at Warner Brothers studios where we screened it to a packed house, and the laughs from the audience were voluminous. We were confident that finding a distributor to release it was going to be speedy and effortless, at least as easy as it had been in the past with the other two films I produced.

But since my previous films were completed more than twenty five-years ago, times had changed, and no one was interested in low-budget movies anymore. The costs of placing films into theaters had escalated into the millions, with print costs, promotional costs, and kick back costs so that gambling on a movie made for $100,000 was simply no longer considered a worthwhile gamble, period. So on my shelf it sits.

Unlike my little movie, my eighteen-year-old daughter Myah's music career was gaining momentum, when one of the songs she wrote for Britney Spears and placed on the Internet was heard by a producer at Britney's production company. Myah received a call from them, and though they weren't interested in the song Myah wrote, they wanted to hire her to sing background on Britney Spears upcoming single called "Circus."

Once again, I couldn't help but think how her working with Britney Spears was similar to my experience with Jerry Lewis. As a kid watching my idol Jerry Lewis, I hoped to one day perform with him, and it came to fruition. Similarly, my daughter Myah, who as a kid idolized Britney Spears, was suddenly asked to sing alongside her. Her name Myah Marie was listed on the record "Circus" as a background singer, and she was paid the whopping sum of $500. Not much, under any circumstances, but it was hopefully the start of something big.

I received more sad news when I heard that Harvey Korman died. At our last lunch together he confided in me about his ongoing battle with depression, and remarked how he thought that amongst his friends I was the abnormal one, who seemed to completely enjoy my life. And he was right, though I was often curious about depression and whether it was a physiological or psychological aberration. Although I've had bouts with loneliness, heartbreak, and anxiety, I don't ever recall feeling depressed, and I often wondered where my cheerful and positive attitude originated. I've frequently considered taking a course and studying depression, but I was afraid it might cause me to become depressed.

2009

Another year had passed, and Myah befriended Chris, another aspiring songwriter, and they wanted to move into a more spacious two bedroom apartment together. For me it would be a tad less that I'd have to pay, so I helped them move. My two beautiful daughters continued to keep me busy, as did my home on three acres, most of it needing constant upkeep, especially during spring and summer.

At sixty-five, I still felt the same as I did in my twenties. Unfortunately, in my twenties I was a wreck. Actually, that's not true. I was then, and still continued to be, healthy and energetic. When I woke up in the morning, I still sprung out of bed, feeling happy and ready to enjoy another day, unlike many of my contemporaries who complained about various symptoms of the aging process, whether it was chronic illnesses or incessant aches and pains.

I was lucky enough to have remained free of colds or flu bugs of any significance for almost thirty years. I don't mean lucky in that I had good genes, but lucky because since my thirties, I dedicated myself to taking care of my health. My belief was that "life" simply couldn't be enjoyed very much if you were sick. And I loved enjoying my life.

Because I loved my girls and my life so much, I never wanted to jeopardize losing any precious time with them by not applying the tools required to stay healthy. In my view, the two necessary components for staying healthy are desire and discipline. Like depression, I really had no idea why desire and discipline came so easily to some people and was so difficult for others to achieve. But I was extremely grateful that I'd been able to apply desire and discipline to my daily activities, though it wasn't often easy.

My desire and dedication led me to making a concentrated effort to eat properly, with a diet consisting of non-processed foods at least seventy to eighty percent of the time. If I was sedentary for longer than a day or two, or not active on my property, I would always engage in some form of regimented exercise involving push-ups and sit-ups for about twenty minutes a day.

I don't want to appear preachy or self-righteous, and if you think so perhaps you might want to skip a few paragraphs, but my primary suggestion to anyone who seeks a more enjoyable and satisfying life, would be to eliminate five things from your thinking: Stress, Hatred, Guilt, Jealousy, and Worry. Each one of these emotional states creates a negative impact on your life, making it more difficult to be happy. I can honestly say that I am happy ninety-nine percent of the time. My belief is that as long as my kids and I are physically and mentally healthy, I have absolutely NO reason NOT to be happy.

But, as you get older, which according to my mirror has officially begun, you are prone to injuries because our bodies lose some of their muscle tone and strength. This year I inflicted upon myself a severe hernia caused by lifting several large rocks on my property, thinking I was still as strong as I was in my twenties. The end result was a visit to the veteran's hospital where I underwent a minor operation, and a few days later, I was fine.

This same year, another health issue occurred, which turned out to be extremely painful: kidney stones. Again, though I was doubled over in pain for a few of days, convinced I was about to give birth to a chainsaw through my penis, I made a speedy trip to the veteran's hospital. I was given medication for the pain and told I would have to wait for the ragged stones to work their way out. They did, and a few days later I was back in tip-top shape with the top of my tip still a little sore.

Even though in my mind I was still barely out of puberty, my life was beginning to feel like a slow moving funeral procession, especially when my long-time buddy Dom DeLuise died. The memorial service for Dom was incredibly moving, filled with raucous laughter and touching words mingled with tears, as family and friends from Mel Brooks to Ruth Buzzi expressed their love, not only with dialogue but with very funny comedy routines.

One of my favorite memories of Dom was his fifty-fifth birthday that I was invited to share along with many of his comic buddies: Don Knotts, Bob Newhart, Buddy Hackett, Sid Caesar, Harvey Korman, Peter Marshall, Louie Nye, Dick Martin, Shecky Greene, Steve Allen, Tom Poston, and the lone female Connie Stevens. Of those thirteen great personalities—yes, I'm including myself—only Connie Stevens, Peter Marshall, Bob Newhart, Sid Caesar, Shecky Greene, Pat Harrington Jr., and myself remain. I recently saw Connie and she also keeps this picture close to her heart.

With death flourishing all around me, I decided to mount a play about suicide. It was conceived by someone who I had never met, named Colin Mackintosh. Through a mutual friend, he e-mailed me a short story he wrote, thinking I might be able to do something with it. It was an intriguing tale about a man in his seventh-story office building who is about to commit suicide by jumping out his window, when suddenly a burglar enters to rob him. The guts of the story is about the relationship they develop, as the burglar tries to talk him out of ending his life.

I loved the script, which was highly informative and oddly entertaining with suicide as its premise, but it was only about thirty minutes in length. I asked Colin if I could rewrite it, adding more comedy and extending it to two hours, which would enable me to mount it as a play.

He agreed, and in a few months, I completed the script, which was only a two character play. I sought out and found a fellow actor to play the role of the suicidal businessman while I played the burglar. Next, I rented a small theater in Hollywood and ran it for a week hoping that it would be entertaining enough to eventually film as a small movie for cable television. I absolutely loved acting again, but after our run, other things began to take priority in my life and so the play was put on hold.

Likewise, nothing much happened with my daughter's music career since her stint as a background singer on Britney Spears's record until a music producer offered her a contract. However, he wanted her to move into one of the rooms in his house in Las Vegas where he was based and where he promised to produce several songs that Myah had written. After meeting with him, I was convinced he was legitimate, especially after he agreed to pay her a monthly salary.

He also lived with a woman, eliminating any worries his interest in Myah was elsewhere. So off to Vegas she went, and for the first time in years, I was no longer paying rent for an apartment for Myah.

Dom's birthday party.

2010

A song Myah wrote, sang, and recorded called "Everything I Can," was getting airplay on certain dance radio stations around the world. Because it wasn't a pop hit it didn't get any crossover play, so it wasn't going to make her rich, but it was still pretty damn cool. There was a dance music station on my direct TV playlist, which I kept tuned in to, and several times a day, I'd hear Myah's name mentioned when her song was played. I was very proud of her progress considering the enormous competition in the music business.

The song getting airplay had nothing to do with her producer in Las Vegas, and Myah had become disenchanted with him, expressing her desire to move back to Los Angeles. I told her whenever she felt a need to return, I would drive to Vegas and pick her up.

I drove to Vegas anyway when I heard horrible news that another of my best friends, Jimmy, had been diagnosed with lung cancer. Jimmy had been a heavy smoker, and at my urging he had quit twenty-five years earlier, but he knew that those years indulging in cigarettes, among other drugs, most likely contributed to his cancer. The doctors convinced him to take the chemotherapy route, a road I'm not sure I would have taken. I say not sure because there is no way that you can know what you would do until confronted with that situation.

The result was painfully shocking to Jimmy's system and horribly destructive to his body. He lost his bountiful locks of exquisite grey hair and was subjected to months of a miserable existence, while his immune system was slowly being destroyed in an effort to rid his body of the cancer.

In the beginning, with his strength and appearance deteriorating, Jimmy, who always kept himself perfectly groomed, did not want anyone, including myself, to visit with him. His normally confident, self-assured personality was not prepared to accept the pity of anyone seeing him less than the way he wanted them to see him.

Thankfully, as months passed, Jimmy slowly gave in and began to welcome those close to him to get even closer. Jimmy had always been one of my best friends, if not the best, and I was determined to spend as much time with him as I could. After all, he and Kent were the only two best friends out of five that I had left. My major concern during my time spent with Jimmy was to joke and make him laugh, and at the same time, convince him he could beat this cancer and go on another cruise with me. It was comforting to know that his wife Judy, who loved him so much she would willingly trade places with him, would be there to care for him with every ounce of her being.

With so many close friends and acquaintances getting cancer, I decided at the age of sixty-six, it might be time for me to get a colonoscopy because I'd never had one. I felt healthy and wasn't worried in the least that something dreadful was going to be discovered. As the doctor prepared me, my comment that I hoped he'd take me to dinner and a movie afterward didn't so much as evoke a smile. He probably heard it before.

When I awoke, I was told the results were not great, and they recommended I return for another colonoscopy in three years rather than the normal five. They removed three polyps, which in their words had the potential to turn into cancer. I asked if they also had the potential to NOT turn into cancer, and when they replied yes, I felt confident all was well. I was not about to worry about potential. There was also the potential that as I left the hospital, I'd get trapped in the elevator with two good-looking nurses who wanted to have a threesome with me.

As the year came to a close, Myah's producer friend was no longer her friend, and she moved back to Los Angeles. We found another apartment, and I was back to spoiling my little Myah by paying her rent again.

Mary at thirteen and me.

2011

The year began productively for Myah, who received a call from Britney Spears's record producer asking her to sing backup on Britney's upcoming album called "Femme Fatale." This time, instead of the measly $500 she received on the previous single "Circus," she would sing background on seven tracks on the album and receive $1,500 per song. She is proud of the fact that her name Myah Marie is listed on each of the records which she of course hopes will help her in the future keeping in mind that Sheryl Crow sang background for Michael Jackson before she sprung to fame on her own.

Myah had also developed a relationship with a record-producing friend named Bennett, who was two weeks younger than her, making Myah a "Cougarette." I liked Bennett a lot, and I felt confident it might last because they'd been friends for several years before becoming involved, something I'd never experienced: friendship before a relationship. What a concept. Bennett was also half black, and I joked that their relationship might not last because Myah found out it was the "Top" half.

As I've mentioned, I've always felt just as healthy as I did when I was in my thirties, but that doesn't necessarily prevent you from being injured in an accident, especially if you have a tendency to show off. I was invited by my friend Michael to go bicycling along the Santa Monica coast. I hadn't been on a bike since my teens but felt confident I'd have no trouble picking it up again. The end result was that I would need to be picked up... off the ground.

I was thoroughly enjoying cruising on a winding beach path, checking out the bikini-clad ladies, and chatting with Michael, who was riding a few feet in front of me. As we laughed and joked, I suddenly lost control of my bike and my front tire connected with his back tire. I wiggled and waggled before falling off the bike. In my attempt to regain control, I twisted my ankle and suffered a severe groin injury when I tumbled to the ground. At the time, I didn't realize the severity of my injuries, until that night when the pain was so intense, I had to literally crawl from my bed to the bathroom.

By the following day, the pain was so excruciating I rushed to the V.A. Hospital to be checked out. They confirmed a sprained ankle and a pulled groin muscle. Yes, there's a joke there somewhere. I was given pain pills, and though I was determined not to take them, within seconds of leaving the hospital I took several. For weeks, I had to limp rather than walk, and as time passed, my injuries seemed to get worse rather than better. On another visit to the doctor, he explained that the outcome from falling off a bike at age sixty-six was usually more severe than if you're in your thirties. Duh!

It wasn't a good time to take my little girl Mary on a weekend cruise aboard a ship to Mexico but it had been planned for months prior to my bike mishap, and even if I could change my plans I wouldn't, knowing how much she was looking forward to it. I managed as best I could under the circumstances, and though it was mostly painful, limping from above deck to below deck or from stem to stern, it was worth the experience, enjoying it through Mary's eyes. I did bring along a cane, which made it easier hobbling to the various shows, miniature golf, the pool, and the plentiful eating places serving copious amounts of food.

Months later, my ankle seemed to be improving, but my groin injury was getting worse. I made additional visits to the V.A., taking an assortment of tests from X-rays to an MRI, wondering if I was destined to be disabled for the rest of my life. The constant lingering pain in my groin was interfering with not only my physical abilities, but also putting a damper on my sex life.

Ultimately, my injuries unexpectedly vanished one morning when I jumped out of bed and noticed that I had jumped out of bed. After more than six months, the pain was finally gone, and I was, at long last, injury free. Life was greater than great again.

I hadn't been in a serious relationship in over a dozen years, since my little Mary was born, and I was very happy trekking through my days as a single guy. I sort of liked the fact that I was void of the responsibility to please anyone other than my two daughters and myself. I will admit that for years I was looking for the perfect woman and, believe it or not, I actually found her about two years ago. But unfortunately it didn't work out because she was looking for the perfect guy. Go figure.

Actually, I really wasn't searching for another relationship, until my friend Kent engaged in some Twitter chat with an attractive woman named Debi, who was in her fifties. At some point, I was mentioned in their tweets and Kent, playing cupid, set us up as Twitter friends. Debi and I chatted for a while, and then set a date to meet one night, and our one night turned into one night after another, and those nights led to many more nights, which was a good thing for my thing and her thing and things only got better.

After about a month, I envisioned the possibility of opening the door to a new relationship; a door, which after too many personal failures, I knew could easily be shut.

Though pessimism before going into a relationship was not my nature, my inner voice was determined that having major issues in common would be a major factor in any future liaisons. My previous two wives were truly opposites on most major issues.

As Debi and I spent more time together, I learned that our views on two very important topics—politics and religion—were almost identical, which in my mind was essential. However, our philosophies on health and managing one's life differed somewhat, but I hoped that perhaps we could meet somewhere in the middle. Debi also exhibited an extraordinary amount of stress in her daily activities. That was the antithesis to my way of life, and I was concerned that kind of nervous tension might be the one thing that could get in the way of a serious relationship. But, if I couldn't be in a serious relationship, I was always amenable to a silly relationship. In fact, in many ways, especially at this stage of my life, silly might be my preference. Previously, I had been seeing two other women sporadically, however, Debi kept me so contented that I brought those relationships to an end.

I'm aware that I have issues that many women may find unappealing.

I can be overly opinionated and sometimes too critical of others, causing me to appear somewhat less compassionate than I really am. However, I believe that in a personal relationship, if I was going to work diligently at taking care of myself, I'd want the person I'm involved with to think the same way. I understand people who want to live their lives smoking, drinking, and/or living off junk food, and I accept that as their way of life, and they'll usually find someone who lives a comparable lifestyle. However, I could never personally be totally involved with someone who doesn't respect themselves enough to want to share with me a healthy way of living.

Another major concern with dating anyone was how she would treat my daughters. I know it's difficult to be involved with someone who's as dedicated as I am to my children, but that's not going to change, especially with Mary who will always be a part of my life. I wondered if Debi was up to the task, and because she seemed dedicated to working on our relationship, I was eager to see where it would lead.

I hadn't been on stage in almost four years—because I had made the decision to retire years before—when my agent George called and asked if I would perform with comic Paul Rodriguez at the Riviera Hotel in Las Vegas. I gladly accepted because I could easily bring my daughters with me, plus I was running out of money to buy food. Besides, even though I retired from show business, I was pretty sure hardly anyone was aware that I retired, so perhaps I should try it again.

Myah and her boyfriend showed up the first week, and Mary joined me for the remainder of my gig. One night at the end of my performance, I brought Mary on stage with a bag over her head and the audience loved it. So did she. I had forgotten how good I was, and it was a blast revisiting my stand-up roots, then it was back to retirement.

While working in Vegas, I visited with Jimmy every day, and I was ecstatic when he shared with me the news that, after months of suffering from the aftermath of chemo, the traces of cancer were gone. Jimmy's hair was back, his spirits were lifted, and I was thrilled that it looked as if he was going to be with us several more years.

As I looked back on my life, which had been so much fun, so fantastic, so fabulous, so fascinating, so fanciful, so foolish, so flexible, so functional, so feisty, so full of life, love, and laughter, I wanted to share some of it with my daughters, and so in my spare time, I began to write my memoirs. My initial intention was to let my girls know what a tremendous life I've enjoyed, hoping they would learn a little from my past to create a sunnier future for themselves.

When I informed Debi and some of my family and friends about penning my previous sixty-eight years, they strongly suggested that I should try to get it published and let others partake of the sumptuous yet simplistic life I've led. Gotta say, I've been one lucky guy.

Mary with bag over her head.

Mary and I at Beni Hana's.

My sister Annette and I having breakfast with Myah and Bennett.

2012

Most of this year was dominated by slaving over a hot laptop writing these memoirs a few hours a day, a few days a week, and looking forward to more positive events and/or changes in my life. One big change was my citizenship. I arrived in the U.S. from Canada in 1962, and in 2012, I finally decided to apply to become a U.S. citizen. Since my daughters were born in the U.S. and because I served four years in the military, and would probably be buried in a veterans cemetery, I figured the time had arrived. Thankfully, because I was a veteran, I was rushed through the process, and now, fifty years later, I am a citizen of the United States... but still remain Canadian, giving me dual citizenship. Oddly, I don't feel any different.

My good friend Kent was feeling different when he was diagnosed with skin cancer around his eye and had to submit to surgery. This relentless, ubiquitous disease has now poisoned the last of my two remaining best friends.

And worse news when, after a few months, Jimmy is told malignant tumors have returned, not only in his lungs but they have also spread to his brain and back. Once again, though detesting the thought of more chemotherapy, Jimmy surrendered and allowed another round of treatment, with the hope it might rid the cancer from his now very weakened body.

Still, through all these insufferable and agonizing days, weeks, and months, Jimmy maintained an unbelievable spirit, never once complaining, blaming, or bemoaning his situation, refusing to accept pity. During this time, I tried to make trips to spend time with him at least every other week, and I was grateful that I could still make him laugh. I was determined to see Jimmy as often as possible, hoping he would win his battle with cancer, but knowing that at his age, the likelihood of living even one more year was now very unlikely.

In my spare time, I continued writing about the years of my life, supported by Debi, who believed in me wholeheartedly. I noticed we were developing more things in common. For instance, we both liked to take naps during sex.

Debi also joined me on most of the trips to Las Vegas, and though I had previously been a happy guy, she managed to add more happiness to many facets of my life. I don't recall having been involved with such a generous person who was willing to give of herself unremittingly. In all my previous relationships it was mostly the other way around, and a guy could get used to this reversal of fortunes.

In April, the doctors informed Jimmy that there was no longer anything they could do. Jimmy was officially dying and the end was positively within sight. Jimmy's attitude did not waver, his ever-present smile enduring, wanting everyone to know he was okay with the dire news. He was one remarkable man, and as another friend remarked, he was showing everyone the proper and classy way to die. Jimmy was put on home hospice care, requiring a nurse to stop by once a week to ensure he received the meds needed to ease his pain, which was more frequent and more severe. Judy heard about the positive effects of marijuana on cancer victims, so Jimmy was supplied with as much as he wanted. He told me that the pot decreased his pain far more than the medication or pills.

Jimmy and Judy's timeless love for each other was apparent to everyone, as she remained by his side constantly to cater to any of his many needs. Judy took a leave of absence from her work, and it was obvious that she could care less if she ever returned, because her life was not her work, her life was Jimmy. Their love was resolute, and I couldn't help but think that there really was no such thing as true love having a happy ending, unless of course you both die at the same time.

Knowing that Jimmy had only months, or even weeks, to live, I now visited with him as often as possible. His seventy-eighth birthday was nearing, so a party was planned. Jimmy had everything and needed nothing, so getting him something special took some thinking. In the end, Debi and I purchased a very classy and unique bottle of champagne to celebrate his final birthday in style. Jimmy had already told me that the only pain he wanted to feel was "Cham-pain." On the weekend of his birthday, family and friends gathered while Jimmy sat smiling in his wheelchair as each person tried to spend a measurable amount of time chatting with him.

Jimmy was more than a brother to me. He was a buddy, comrade, partner, companion, and confidant who, over the past forty years, had spoiled me with his friendship and love. When we presented Jimmy with the champagne, he said that he'd rather wait until my birthday, which was a few weeks later so that we could share it together. I liked that a lot because it meant he was determined to hang on until I turned sixty-eight.

When Debi and I returned to Vegas to celebrate my birthday with Jimmy and Judy, I could see that he had grown much weaker, barely able to move from his bed to the wheelchair. And still, as we served the champagne, assisting Jimmy to drink through a straw, we were able to laugh and joke. But it was no joke that the end was very near. So near that while Jimmy slept, Judy asked me to write out his obituary for the newspaper.

I hated writing the words extolling what Jimmy meant to me and the many others who loved him, especially with him lying in the next room, but I did.

When it was time to leave, Judy told me that Jimmy wanted to see me—even though I had hugged and kissed him goodbye only moments before, telling him I would return the following weekend.

In his room, I grabbed his hand as he looked up at me, smiled, and said, "I just wanted to tell you I really love you, buddy." When I left the room I was internally shaken, feeling he knew he wouldn't see me again... but I hoped he was wrong. He wasn't. A few days later, Judy called me moments after he passed. She said the end was very peaceful, and when I hung up, I sobbed, until my grief was satisfied. I will miss the man who taught me so much about love.

Still, my days are overflowing with the love of the girls in my life. Unfortunately, a little bit of bad news for Mary, who has developed a thyroid problem and has to be put on medication.

I continued to perform on rare occasions; the most recent was a weekend of comedy at the Eldorado Hotel in Laughlin, Nevada—with Weird Al Yakovich on Friday and The Unknown Comic performing on Saturday. I'm pleased that so many folks still show up to see my foolish yet entertaining antics.

I slowly returned to having fun with continued practical jokes, this next one with Debi. As we sat alone in a Jacuzzi, enjoying its warmth, an older couple joined us. As they entered the hot water, they introduced themselves, and a spark of foolishness entered my brain.

I greeted them, then introduced Debi as my sister from Canada who was visiting for a few days. After some time had passed, and we've chatted a little more, I suddenly pulled Debi close to me and begin kissing her hard on the mouth as the couple looked on with their mouths dropping wide open. Of course, Debi, who is not all that comfortable with my prank, begged me to tell them that we were not brother and sister, so I said, "If you incest," and told them the truth.

As the year came to a close, I had a couple of health issues that popped up, which I had to take care of. At the age of sixty-eight, I still felt extremely energetic and physically capable of doing anything. But I guess time does take its toll. I developed another hernia on the opposite side of my groin only, unlike my previous hernia a few years earlier, this one was painful. Not horribly painful, more aggravatingly painful. I returned to the V.A. where my previous visits had been wonderful. This one was not so wonderful. I was told that they were backed up and that it would be at least three months before they could schedule me for surgery. I explained that it didn't seem right that I should have to be in continuous pain for three months. The best they could do was prescribe pain medication and inform me that if the pain became unbearable, to return to the emergency room.

A few weeks later, it became an emergency situation, but I would not return to the V.A. I was staying in Los Angeles, when I developed searing pain in my lower groin, much worse than the kidney stones I had previously passed. It was midnight, and I was literally incapacitated with horrendous stabbing pains, bent over in a fetal position, and virtually unable to move. Debi suggested calling an ambulance, but I refused, preferring to slowly crawl to her car where she took me to a nearby hospital. After an examination, it was determined that my colon was trapped in my hernia, which was causing the agonizing pain, and I was rushed into surgery. Thankfully, after two days in the hospital, I returned home to recuperate. But when shit happens, it can really happen, and two days after I was home, as I slowly and methodically tried to get out of bed, I suddenly felt a sharp pain in my left knee. Within minutes, the pain became excruciating whenever I tried to move, and my knee began to swell to twice its normal size. Again, I had Debi take me to the hospital, and after X-rays and an MRI, it was discovered I had a torn meniscus, along with a tiny deteriorated piece of bone that had broken off and lodged in a sensitive area inside my knee. Once again, I was told I would require surgery, which they scheduled for that Friday, only days before Christmas. I knew there was a reason I never cared much for Christmas.

Twice in one week I was given anesthesia and knocked out for surgery, and afterward, I was told that it would take four or five months before achieving a complete recovery. For me that really sucked because I like to be on the go rather than on crutches and a cane, which was what I had to do for the first several weeks. So I was forced to literally limp into the next year. But I would still prefer injuries over a disease, so when all was considered, I was still one lucky guy.

Except for the fact that my relationship with Debi was not doing very well. Though we agreed on most major issues, a multitude of smaller issues had gained a strangulation hold on our togetherness, and we began to see each other less and less. What I hadn't known until recently was that Debi suffered occasional bouts of extreme depression, where she would hole up in her house alone and sob, especially after an argument. Though I tried to express how I thought that communication was the most important ingredient in a relationship, she steadfastly refused to discuss or accept any help from me, which only led to more problems. Her view was that it was a chemical imbalance and that I could do nothing to help her because I had no medical training, and that she was not going to take medication which would put her in a zombie state.

Other issues we disagreed on were my dedication to staying healthy and her lack of any real interest in a commitment to her own health. I believe she began to resent the fact that I didn't have a cold in over thirty years while she had several during our time together. Other differences included my relishing a neat home, while Debi bordered on hoarding—having a home overly packed with stuff. It made me suspect living together might prove intolerable. These and other small issues would sometimes lead to larger skirmishes, which would result in neither one of us being happy, and it became obvious that it was just a matter of time before we were no longer to be. I was once again single. When it finally ended, I experienced emotional pain like every break-up I've endured, and I wondered how much I was to blame, or was I simply destined to be unlucky in love? Well, the one good thing about being single again is that I can go back to getting out of bed from either side.

My little Mary on a Harley.

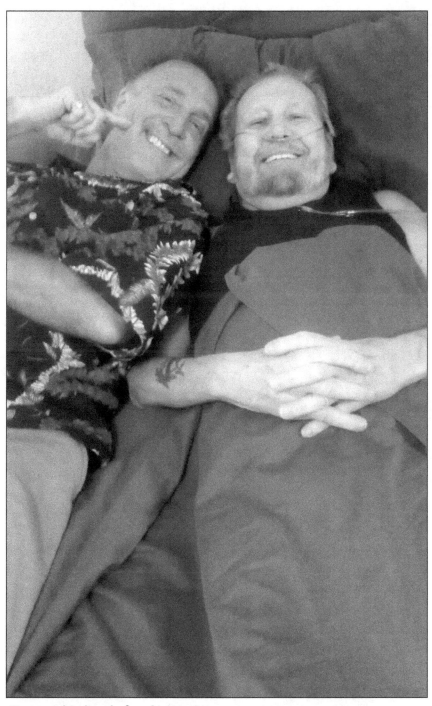

Jimmy and I, days before his passing.

My show in Laughlin on a billboard.

2013

Like almost every year of my life, the first six months of 2013 contained many ups and downs. I heard a saying once that life is like a roller coaster. You can either scream at every bump or simply throw your hands in the air and enjoy the ride. I'm really enjoying the ride. Even with my recent surgeries, I looked at them as adventures to learn from, not as the beginning of the end of my physical health.

I even joked with the doctor who performed my knee surgery. In the operating room, he had two male nurses assisting him, and I told him that I suspected one of them molested me while I was sedated. His response was, "Yes, one of my male nurses did molest you, but there would be no extra charge." You gotta love a doctor with a sense of humor.

My daughter Myah and her boyfriend, Bennett, along with his twin brother Justin and his girlfriend Cosmo decided to form a singing group, which they called "My Crazy Girlfriend." Their initial songs are infectious, and they lined up a couple of gigs performing at the Whiskey and the Viper room in Hollywood. I went to see them at both venues, and they are really good. I hope great things are in store for them because they are not doing very well financially. Everyone knows how difficult it is to make it in the music business. Getting a record deal is akin to winning the lottery.

Myah and her boyfriend had been living in an apartment in Hollywood overlooking the Capitol Records building, which they could see from their window and dreamed of one day being signed to them. Unfortunately, unable to afford it any longer, they had to move into a less expensive place, which I helped them to do financially.

Myah was anxiously waiting to hear from the Britney Spears camp about working again on her third album, which would give them some extra income to help out.

With time on my hands, feet, and ass, I decided to put together a joke book on two very highly overpublicized personalities: Donald Trump and the Kardashians. The first half of the book is called, "The Joke Book for People Who Think Donald Trump is a Joke." The book is then flipped over and the second half of the book is called, "The Joke Book for People Who Think the Kardashians are a Joke." It didn't take long to find a publisher, and the book should be out long before these memoirs.

What is nothing to joke about is when my daughter Myah called and informed me that the Britney Spears camp finally called her asking about her schedule, which meant they were about to go into production on Britney's upcoming album. Myah was excited and grateful that a small payday would be soon forthcoming.

My other daughter Mary was moved to another school in a special needs class, and twice I invited the entire group to my home, where I cooked and let them wander around my property with ponds, hiking trails, and plenty of trees to pick fruit from. My time with Mary was at least fifty percent including three out of four weekends, and I cherished every moment we spent together. To me, Mary is without a doubt liquid love. Mary still cannot talk in full sentences and both of us find it extremely frustrating when she wants to tell me something, but her words come out difficult to comprehend. I cannot wait for the days, which are only a few years away, when she'll be able to articulate and communicate in full sentences. I love taking her to school, speech class, and dance class, and though her words do not yet come easy, it's obvious that she loves to sing and dance. Whenever Myah and her boyfriend Bennett are around, Mary will perform for them, pretending she has a microphone and belting out unrecognizable songs in her own inimitable style.

I taught her a Knock, Knock joke which always gets chuckles from new people we meet.

MARY: Knock, knock.

OTHER: Who's there?

MARY: Dishes.

OTHER: Dishes who?

MARY: Dishes the way I talk.

It's almost May, almost four months since my knee surgery, and I finally discovered I was once again back in tip-top shape with only a few weeks until my sixty-ninth birthday. There's a joke there, but let's face it, that would be too easy. However, once again I was physically feeling no different than I did when I was in my thirties. Life is back to normal, or at least as close to normal as my life ever really gets.

I talked to my buddy Rich in Hawaii, who told me that he might be willing to invest in filming the play *7th Story Man* and would like to see it in person before committing to it. I called my friend Michael and asked if he would like to be in the play with me and he jumped at the opportunity, so we decided to begin rehearsals and shoot for an August opening at a dinner theater a friend of mine owns.

Now, between the books, the play, and my daughter Mary, things couldn't look much brighter... until I get a phone call from Myah and her boyfriend. They are both on the line, talking at the same time with some news, and I can't tell if they are upset, angry, or excited. Bennett asks me if I'm sitting, and I reply, "I'm lying down, is that good enough?" They are both trying to talk over each other, laughing along the way, so I thought to myself, *Okay, they're excited.* Then Myah jumped in saying, "We are about to sign a record deal with Capitol Records." This is such exciting and welcoming news.

This was the same label that they could see from their previous apartment and has among its artists Katy Perry and Coldplay, and not only still lists, Rod Steward, the Beach Boys and the Eagles but also signed the Beatles in the beginning of their career. Though Myah is only twenty-four, she has been working diligently since the age of fifteen and now, nine years later, her overnight success may be close to happening. Though they may have a record deal, they will still need a hit record to catapult them to the success they deserve. After having heard their original songs and seeing them perform live, I feel very confident that fame and fortune for them is just around the corner. If they do achieve major success, I want nothing from them... except perhaps a new car... and a house on the beach... and a hundred dollars in cash. I'm just kidding. They can keep the hundred dollars in cash.

It's June 27, and I am now officially sixty-nine years old. As usual, I spend it at Beni Hana's with my two girls, and though I am back to being single, the love of my girls remains constant and satisfying.

At sixty-nine, I'm proud of the fact that I am still in pretty darn good shape for an old guy, and so I decide to take another naked picture as The Unknown Comic, which I first took almost forty years ago. I was actually surprised that, except for a few more pounds, I actually looked in almost identical shape to the picture from forty years ago.

My old girlfriend Connie came to visit, and we decided to stop by the Improv, a comedy club I hadn't been to in years. To my surprise, the Improv had new owners and was having an official opening night party. I was also surprised to discover that they had commissioned my old artist buddy Wyland to paint caricatures of famous comics all over the newly remodeled building. And I was shocked and honored to see my "Unknown Comic" character almost dominating the expansive wall painting. The biggest coincidence was that Wyland was there for the opening. After we hugged, he told me that when they asked him to paint the wall, he made sure that I was a major part of it.

Besides occasionally hanging with old buddies like Jerry, Dave, Michael, and Bob, along with a host of other newly acquired pals, my beautiful life continues to be healthy, in mind, body, and spirit. Though I'm not rich or famous, I cherish and enjoy every minute of every day. I did spend time on the fringes of wealth and fame and wasn't that impressed. The significant things that continue to make me feel beyond wealthy are my two daughters, my health, my siblings, my friends Ruth and Kent, my buddies and acquaintances, my desire to stay busy, my property, my memories, and my love of life. I can sit in front of my home with a glass of wine, a smile on my face, and sincerely revel in the intangibles that are the real essence of happiness.

My religious beliefs are constant, and I have no fear or worry about what will happen to me after I'm gone. I think, for the most part, I've conducted my life in a fulfilling and satisfying manner. If by some remote chance there is an afterlife, I'm confident I'll be fine. If not... then I fucked up. But I do believe that peace in the world will not be achieved in my lifetime and will only succeed when religion and the love of God are replaced with education and the love of each other.

Though I'm semi-retired, I have no plans on merely existing, and I make sure that every day I accomplish something, whether it's as mundane as watering plants or painting a room, or writing a joke book, play, or script, or simply posting humor on Facebook or Twitter. My philosophy that "Change is growth" continues to be a challenge I look forward to every day. My advice to anyone is to always move forward, push ahead, and never quit. Because if you quit, you'll never know how close to success you might have been. Think about the guy who invented Preparation G.

Having written these memoirs, I realize I've not just led one life but a multitude of them. I've been a kid, a student, a paperboy, a delivery boy, a thief, a soldier, a sailor, a radar man, a disc jockey, a drummer, a painter, a computer operator, a shoe salesman, an actor, a comedian, a husband, a director, a producer, a writer, a landowner, a gardener, a back hoe operator, and an author. Though I continue looking forward to leading many more lives, being a father has been the most important and satisfying for me

Throughout my writings, I've repeated how lucky I've been. Some people prefer the word blessed but that would mean that a God liked me better than others who weren't so blessed. I've been truly lucky.

My life today can be best described by a Steven Wright quote... "I plan on living forever... so far, so good." Sure, I've been told no one lives forever but that's not going to keep me from trying.

So, as I've already mentioned, once you learn to not only enjoy each day, but to enjoy each and every minute... life at every stage will be great.

To be continued....

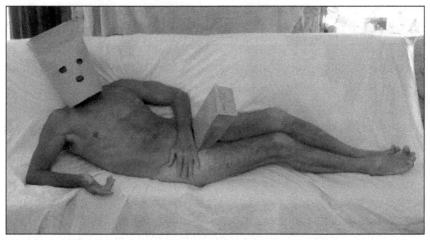

Naked pic of me taken on my sixty-ninth birthday.

Wyland and I at the opening of the New Improv with my caricature on the wall.

Kent and Ruth with Mary.

Me with the two unconditional loves of my life, Mary and Myah.

INDEX

CPSIA information can be obtained
at www.ICGtesting.com
Printed in the USA
BVHW060258220620
581996BV00005B/273